Basic Research Methods
in the
Social Sciences

George S. Howard

University of Notre Dame

With an appendix by
Paul R. Solomon, Williams College

Scott, Foresman and Company
Glenview, Illinois

London, England

Acknowledgments

Fig. 5.2   Aronson, E., Willerman, B., & Floyd, J. The effect of a pratfall on increasing interpersonal attractiveness. *Psychonomic Science*, 1966, 4, 227-228.

Fig. 8.3   Donald T. Campbell and H. Laurence Ross, "The Connecticut Crackdown on Speeding: Time-Series Data in Quasi-Experimental Analysis," Vol. 3, LAW & SOCIETY REVIEW, (1968) p. 44.

Fig. 8.5   Eron, L. D., & Huesmann, L. R. Adolescent aggression and television *Annals of the New York Academy of Sciences*, 1980, 347, 319-331. Copyright (1980) by the American Psychological Association. Adapted by permission

Boxes 14-1; 14-2   Reprinted with permission of The Free Press, A Division of Macmillan, Inc. from *Qualitative Sociology: A Method to the Madness* by Howard Schwartz and Jerry Jacobs. Copyright © 1979 by The Free Press, pages 39-40.

Box 15-1   Copyright 1973 by the American Psychological Association. Adapted by permission

Fig. 16.1   Hyde, J. S., & Rosenberg, B. G. Half the human experience: The psychology of women. Lexington, Mass.: D. C. Heath, 1980.

App. C Probs.   Problems 1, 4, 8, 11, and 23 and their solutions from RIVAL HYPOTHESES: ALTERNATIVE INTERPRETATIONS OF DATA BASED CONCLUSIONS by Schuyler W. Huck and Howard M. Sandler. Copyright © 1979 by Schuyler W. Huck and Howard M. Sandler. Reprinted by permission of Harper & Row, Publishers, Inc.

App. E, Table E-1   Reprinted from pages 1 and 2 of *A Million Random Digits with 100,000 Normal Deviates* by The Rand Corporation (New York: The Free Press, 1955). Copyright 1955 and 1983 by The Rand Corporation. Used by permission.

Library of Congress Cataloging in Publication Data
Howard, George S.
   Basic research methods in the social sciences.

   Bibliography: p.
   Includes index.
   1. Social sciences—Methodology. 2. Social sciences—
Research. I. Title.
H61.H76 1984   300'.72   84-1320
ISBN 0-673-15546-3

Dedicated to my first and finest teachers,
John and Margaret Howard

———————————————————————

Preface

This book grew out of my experiences teaching a required course called "Research Methodology in Psychology" to undergraduates at a large state university. My students in this class were extremely heterogeneous on almost every relevant dimension. For many of the students, this course would be the only contact with the social sciences, and most had no experience with statistics. With the deck thus stacked, I attempted to develop a course that would be comprehensible. I tried to make the course interesting enough to involve the undermotivated and broad enough to show research in psychology as close kin to efforts in several related disciplines in the social sciences. This book represents my attempt to make those ambitions concrete.

Research methodology represents the application of disciplined logic in the service of obtaining empirical evidence relevant to theoretical or practical interests. I believe this definition applies equally well for all the social sciences; thus, knowing about research methods in one discipline should enhance our understanding of methods in the other disciplines. What I have attempted to do in this book is to sketch the logic of scientific inquiry broadly enough so that applications to each of the disciplines can be easily made. Obviously, because of important differences in the various disciplines, some topics are more important for one discipline than another.

Because of the manner in which I have defined my domain of interest, I have included some chapters that are rarely found in basic methods texts in psychology (for example, the chapters on single-subject research and evaluation research) and some that, to my knowledge, have never been presented (such as the chapters on qualitative methodology and on studying humans). Obviously, some chapters typical of texts in experimental psychology are not found in research methods books for disciplines outside of psychology. I believe the book surveys methods broadly enough to be truly a text of research methods for the social sciences.

Examples and illustrations are an important part of any basic methodology textbook. Since I am a psychologist, it is not surprising that the majority of my examples deal with psychological research. Still, I have tried to offer sufficient examples from anthropology, sociology, business, and so on to suggest to the reader that the application of the logic of inquiry extends well beyond the traditional content boundaries of psychology.

Has our approach to education become so specialized that our understanding is needlessly compartmentalized and fragmented? This book is an effort toward reintegration, toward taking a more holistic view of research efforts in the social sciences. It focuses on the ways in which the research efforts of the various social sciences are similar, while still acknowledging the important differences that distinguish various modes of inquiry in these disciplines (Appendix D describes differences among the social sciences).

The book presupposes no expertise on the part of the reader. Therefore, students with any background should be able to grasp the contents. The presentation of statistics is conceptual and intuitive. A computational statistics chapter is also provided to show students exactly how to go from raw data to summary statistics to conclusions. Appendices on conducting an experiment and writing a research report provide step-by-step blueprints of these important research skills.

Maintaining students' interest and enhancing their motivation to learn still more is an important function of any textbook. The examples chosen, both real and hypothetical, were designed to be as interesting and involving as possible. Examples that illustrate the pursuit of theoretical knowledge as well as of practical goals are interspersed to emphasize the diversity of motivations that can stimulate scientists to seek empirical evidence. The book strives to present research as an exciting, challenging endeavor.

As they read this book, I hope students will be struck with the dynamic, evolving nature of methodology in the social sciences. I have tried not only to characterize how research is currently conducted but also to stimulate the reader to consider how our current praxis might be further improved. Finally, I would be remiss if I had not stated explicitly the role of research methodology in the task of evolving and improving our current supply of research methods (see the section of chapter 16 entitled "On Improving Methodology via Research on Research Methods).

I am greatly indebted to many people for their contributions to this book. I would like to thank Professors Nancy J. Harkey, Ralph W. Hood, Steven Kerr, R. R. Schmeck, Paul R. Solomon, Thomas K. Srull, Eric Sunstrom, and George E. Weaver for their insightful comments. Scott Maxwell, Nancy Gulanick, and a large number of my former and present students also offered cogent advice. Beverly Peavler, Bruce Borland, Trig Thoreson, Pauline Wright, Edna Noble and Jackie Haslett were most helpful in preparing the manuscript. Finally, I am especially indebted to Katie Steele for her herculean efforts in the development and shaping of the project.

Contents

Contents

Contents

What Is Science?

Chapter Preview

Chapter 1 begins by describing two approaches to knowing, the
rational and the empirical. Out of these ways of knowing grew our
scientific approach. The scientific approach, while empirical in
nature, is a combination of the best of both the empirical and the
rational. The basic characteristics of the scientific approach, and
how researchers choose topics for research, are detailed. Finally, the
researcher is considered as an individual who attempts to
recognize meaningful patterns or relationships in the world of
behavior and who demonstrates these relationships through
experiments.

Every research methods course is, at heart, an exercise in epistemology—the study of how we come to know things. Humans can obtain knowledge in several ways. It has been suggested since the time of the early philosophers that the various ways of knowing can be grouped into at least two broad categories: the rational approach and the empirical approach. This chapter begins by briefly describing these two approaches. The remainder of the book will focus on a thorough elaboration and delineation of empirical methods of research as they have come to be used in the behavioral and social sciences.

What do we know? At the crux of this question lies the problem of determining what knowledge is and how we can determine when we possess it. Some might think this a trivial question. To them, it is obvious that we know many things. Is it not our knowledge of the operations of the world that allows us to proceed through life in an orderly fashion? For example, I came to work in my automobile this morning. In order to do that, I had to know quite a bit about how to start and operate an automobile and about the rules of the road (such as which lanes I am allowed to drive in, what the various colors of traffic lights mean, and so on). Obviously, we do possess tremendous knowledge of the people and objects in the world. The critical questions, then, become: How did we secure this knowledge of the world? How do we know this supposed knowledge is correct? Are there ways in which we can come to know more about the world and all in it?

The Rational Approach

The rational approach to knowledge presumes that the world is orderly and that underlying laws govern the operation of people and things. The essential point to understanding the rational approach is that it assumes there are certain preferred ways to come to know the world. These ways are through reasoning, intuition, and authority (such as religion, the great philosophers of antiquity, and so on). Humans can come to understand some of the laws of nature; and as soon as they appreciate the wisdom of nature, they can begin to recognize the basic principles that underlie many of the operations of the world. This knowledge of basic principles allows people to then predict and understand many events.

4

Similarly, events that do not fit these basic principles become causes for wonderment and puzzlement. Often, a search may begin for a more complete understanding of such an event. Since rationalists believe that all knowledge can be derived from the already known laws of nature, they search for this new understanding by rearranging basic truths. Mees (1934, p. 17) gives an example from the philosopher and scientist Sir Francis Bacon, who describes an extreme example of the rationalist approach meant to parody that position.

In the year of our Lord 1432, there arose a grievous quarrel among the brethren over the number of teeth in the mouth of a horse. For thirteen days the disputation raged without ceasing. All the ancient books and chronicles were fetched out, and wonderful and ponderous erudition, such as was never before heard of in this region, was made manifest. At the beginning of the fourteenth day, a youthful friar of goodly bearing asked his learned superiors for permission to add a word, and straightway, to the wonderment of the disputants, whose deep wisdom he sore vexed, he beseeched them to unbend in a manner coarse and unheard-of, and to look in the open mouth of a horse and find answer to their questionings. At this, their dignity being grievously hurt, they waxed exceedingly wroth; and joining in a mighty uproar, they flew upon him and smote his hip and thigh, and cast him out forthwith. For, said they, surely Satan hath tempted this bold neophyte to declare unholy and unheard-of ways of finding truth contrary to all the teachings of the fathers. After many days of grievous strife the dove of peace sat on the assembly, and they as one man, declaring the problem to be an everlasting mystery because of the grievous dearth of historical and theological evidence thereof, so ordered the same writ down.

Today, although the rational approach still underlies a number of our attempts to reason about what should and should not occur, belief in the efficacy of pure rationalism is not nearly as strong as it was back in the fifteenth century. Consequently, this anecdote seems rather foolish to us; we have become much more accustomed to the youthful friar's method—the empirical approach to securing knowledge.

The Empirical Approach

The empirical approach consists largely of stating questions, hypothesizing relationships, and postulating laws we believe might be true. We then begin a process whereby we contend that if our belief is

5

correct, then we would expect certain events to occur. When using this approach, individuals judge a belief according to its ability to predict observable events.

Human beings are empirical in many ways. The essence of the empirical approach lies in making sense of the world through observation. For example, suppose you wonder what day it is. An empirical approach to answering the question is to go outside, pick up the newspaper on the front porch, and see what day of the week is printed on the front page. In other words, you can simply observe something you believe will provide valid knowledge regarding the question. It should be obvious to you that this technique for securing knowledge is not 100-percent accurate. For example, you might have picked up yesterday's paper, not realizing it was a day old. Another empirical approach to answering that same question is to ask a friend what day it is. Similarly, this empirical approach is not universally correct. The person you ask might not know what day it is, might be misinformed regarding what day it is, or might even be trying to deceive you regarding what day it is. Consequently, you must exercise caution in the way you obtain empirical answers to questions.

Let's consider another simple example to emphasize the difference between the empirical and rational approaches. Suppose I see a magic trick wherein a magician seems to make a person hover in mid-air. My understanding of the law of gravity dictates that the attraction of the mass of the earth should cause this person to fall unless prevented by some force operating counter to that of gravity. However, as I observe this magic trick, I cannot discern the operation of any such force. This becomes a source of puzzlement for me, and I initiate a search wherein I will either learn what force might be maintaining the subject in mid-air (for example, a hidden wire that suspends the subject) or, at some level, revise my belief in the law of gravity. (Of course, this latter possibility is extremely unlikely and would only occur in the face of terribly overwhelming evidence.) By systematically studying the magician to learn how he performs his trick, I have taken an empirical approach to discovering why this event seems to contradict my accepted beliefs in nature. The rationalist approach, on the other hand, would involve attempting to solve the problem by reasoning from basic truths instead of investigating the situation.

6

The Scientific Approach

The scientific approach is a subset of the empirical approach. In fact, one can think of the scientific approach as a standardized or formalized method for obtaining empirical answers to questions. In many respects, current scientific methods wed the best aspects of the logic of the rational approach with the observational aspects of the empirical orientation into a coherent, systematic perspective. The box entitled "Methods of Knowing" provides an overview of methods used in the rational, empirical, and scientific approaches. The material also represents the general form of many of the specific research methods considered throughout the book.

Christensen (1980) points out that a distinction should be made between the scientific method and scientific techniques. The scientific method refers to a systematic approach to inquiry that employs the basic logic of justification and its acceptance or rejection of hypotheses and theories. The scientific method does not rest simply on the use of specific scientific techniques or instruments. For example, to use a microscope is not necessarily to employ the scientific method. A microscope is an instrument for gaining empirical knowledge. One could use such a scientific instrument in a nonscientific fashion; for example, hammering a nail with a microscope has nothing to do with science! Conversely, one could conduct a totally scientific investigation wherein only the crudest nonscientific instruments were employed. Therefore, we must note that the instruments or techniques a person employs do not determine whether the person is engaged in science. Rather, the logic used in approaching and obtaining solutions to problems determines whether an individual is engaged in a scientific study as opposed to some other casual form of empiricism. What, then, are the characteristics of the scientific method?

The Scientific Method: Basic Tenets

Certain characteristics seem to be common to most scientific endeavors. The following discussion lists characteristics typically associated with scientific approaches to gaining knowledge. Because of the atypical nature of some scientific questions, certain of these requirements can be dismissed in particular instances. However,

Methods of Knowing

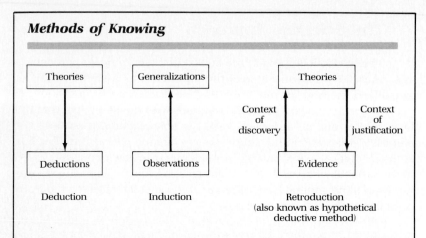

Deductive reasoning begins with basic beliefs, theories, assumptions, propositions, and so on, the validity of which is assumed and untested. With logic, one can arrive at conclusions, corollaries, deductions, and implications that logically follow from the initial beliefs. Deductive logic was the essential method of the rationalist approach.

Inductive reasoning begins with observations and evidence of empirical regularities or empirical relationships (that is, things that tend to go together, such as taller basketball players' getting more rebounds than shorter players). By using inductive logic, a scientist works from the observed evidence to create laws. Induction is an important component of all sciences.

Retroductive reasoning becomes progressively more important as science matures. In retroduction, the observed evidence (the evidence agreed upon by the scientific community) is taken as a given (agreed upon as being true for the time being). In the context of discovery, an idea is hit upon as an explanation for the observed evidence. But here retroduction goes beyond induction: The scientist asserts that if the idea (the hypothesis or theory) is correct, then it might also imply other empirical relationships that have not yet been observed. If these predicted empirical relationships turn out to actually exist, the hypothesis

(continued)

or theory has received some confirmation. That is, the new predictions, when confirmed, lend support to the theory.

Theory testing and theory development are very important for some behavioral sciences (such as psychology) and less important for others (such as economics). However, within each discipline there are great differences in the degree to which individual researchers use induction versus retroduction as their dominant tool. When you read about patterns recognized by scientists in the last section of chapter 1, it may occur to you that recognizing patterns involves forming theories and hypotheses. The experimental demonstrations scientists use to test their theories are the "predicted empirical relationships" of the retroductive approach.

consistency with as many of the requirements as possible enhances the adequacy of the scientific approach employed.

The first characteristic of the scientific approach involves *control*. By control, we typically mean the ability to rule out competing explanations for the phenomenon under investigation. That is, if we are able to demonstrate that the phenomenon is influenced by only one of many possible causes, then we have obtained knowledge we can deem scientific. To the extent that we are unable to rule out the possibility that the results may be due to causes other than the cause specified, our study is uncontrolled and we are less likely to accept its conclusions. More will be said about control in later chapters (for example, chapters 3, 4, 7, and 10).

The second characteristic of scientific approaches is that they are based on *observables*. This is typically accomplished in the social sciences through the use of operational definitions. Operationalism requires scientists to speak in a language other scientists understand. That is, scientists must clearly define terms, procedures, and operations rather than loosely using terms that can have different meanings to different scientists. For example, *hunger* can have many different meanings. However, when a particular scientist specifies that in a particular experiment *hunger* means the state of animals kept at a certain percentage of their normal body weight, then all scientists will know what definition has been employed when they seek to interpret the scientist's results. Obviously, this does not mean all scientists will agree that this is the best operational definition; all it means is that some basis of communication among these scientists has been established.

Operational definitions allow for the possibility of *replication*, the third requirement of science. Scientists are interested in events that are repeatable; they typically are not interested in events they have reason to believe will occur only once. Most scientists study events because they believe these events represent the operation of certain mechanisms that will reoccur. Therefore, when a scientist reports that a given set of operations led to a particular outcome, we believe that if other scientists perform those operations at another point in time or in another place, they will obtain similar results. This repeatability is important, because we are interested in obtaining a knowledge of the world that has some enduring quality. That is, we are seeking knowledge that will help us predict or understand future events.

Goals of the Scientific Approach

The philosopher of science Stephen Toulmin (1961) asserts that the most appropriate goal of science has always been, and always will be, to give us an understanding of the mechanisms involved in the operation of the world and all in it. However, we need ways to determine whether our understanding of the world is correct. The most obvious way is to make predictions based on our understanding of some particular phenomenon. We can then assess whether our predictions were better than they would have been without that understanding. This is not to say that all events are predictable. Our understanding can help us not only to make predictions but also to know why we should not expect some events to be predictable.

Prediction also gives us a powerful tool. Theoretically, if we can predict the behavior of people and things, we can exert some control over these events and the ways in which we are influenced by them. Predicting and controlling behavior, then, are potential results of understanding. Toulmin states that once an individual has moved into the realm of prediction and control, he or she is involved in forecasting, which is a technology. However, we certainly employ the understandings garnered by science in developing and improv-

10

ing our methods of forecasting and modifying the events of the world.

In summary, science is concerned with gaining understanding of the world. The technologies of prediction and control are often the spin-offs of this scientific knowledge.

What Shall We Study?

The world provides us with virtually limitless opportunities to study phenomena. Confronted with this dazzling array of possible topics of investigation, how does the scientist go about deciding what to study? Several major areas seem to provide the fodder for most scientific investigations. The first is curiosity—the natural human tendency to try to understand why things are as they are. Many scientists become involved in their disciplines because of a fundamental curiosity about the operations involved in those domains.

A second fertile source of ideas is the necessity to solve certain pressing problems. For example, clinical psychologists who work with hyperactive children might be interested in knowing if certain drugs can calm their patients enough to allow the clinicians to have more successful therapy sessions with them. This problem-solving approach to science is defended by individuals who view science as a tool to be used for the advancement of human enterprises. However, some thinkers wonder if this approach can ever lead to a coherent view of science that provides anything other than solutions to very limited problems.

Research ideas are also obtained by scientists as they read journals, books, grant proposal announcements, and proposals for contracts by various government and private industry sources. Journals and books provide researchers with the thoughts and findings of other scientists. These ideas often spur scientists to ask related questions and even to doubt the findings of other investigators.

Finally, a breakthrough in any area of science can constitute a source of ideas for study in many related and unrelated areas. Such a breakthrough can occur at virtually any level—it may be a theoretical breakthrough, a new technique for collecting or analyzing data, a new research instrument (such as the electron microscope), or simply an unusual and interesting finding. Any breakthrough can spur related research in many diverse and unrelated fields.

11

Science as Pattern Recognition

The popular view of what scientists look for in their research is heavily influenced by breakthroughs in the medical sciences. For example, it may be suspected that germs or viruses are responsible for an observed disease. The medical researcher's task, then, is to find the culprit and to develop some mechanism for killing it or preventing its spreading in patients. Similarly, medical researchers develop techniques that allow them to perform progressively more delicate operations. Research in these cases might lead to the development of new techniques or the elaboration and refinement of existing techniques. However, research in the behavioral sciences typically possesses a different character.

The psychologist Carl Rogers (1973) tells us that conducting research with humans often involves making sense of the bewildering array of phenomena we experience in the world. The task of the behavioral scientist, then, is to identify meaningful patterns within the phenomena being investigated. Figure 1−1 shows a complex, confusing pattern. The pattern contains a message, which we can think of as a meaningful pattern a scientist might wish to understand. Can you pick out the message? While the message in Figure 1−1 is a word, in science the message usually involves important relationships. For example, scientists might ask questions like these: Does stress lead to heart disease? Does advertising lead to increased sales? Does overcrowding lead to increased violence?

In Figure 1−1, the additional irrelevant information in the picture makes the message difficult to understand. A similar problem exists in scientific studies: meaningful relationships can be difficult to detect in the world about us. The experimental techniques described later in this book (in chapter 3) allow researchers to remove more and more of the irrelevant information from their experiments in order to

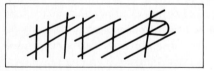

Figure 1−1   Confusing Pattern

12

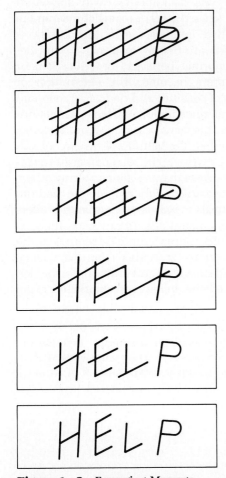

Figure 1-2 Emerging Message

better appreciate the meaningful patterns in the world. By simply removing more and more irrelevant information through control procedures, we can highlight meaningful patterns that operate in our daily lives, but that are difficult to ascertain without the disciplined observational techniques of research methodology. Figure 1—2 gradually removes more and more of the irrelevant information that obscured the meaningful pattern in Figure 1—1. As irrelevant information is removed, the pattern begins to clearly emerge.

13

Rogers (1973) asserts that a good deal of subjectivity and intuition are still necessary in science, since the first sensing of meaningful patterns comes from very subjective hunches, beliefs, and intuitions of scientists and practitioners who are deeply involved in the phenomena of interest (such as abnormal behavior, or education, or industrial relations). Research, then, becomes the elaboration or refinement of the subjective ideas of sensitive and dedicated men and women attempting to understand meaningful patterns of relationships in their areas of interest. In this view, research is not a sterile, uninteresting model of activity. Rather, the behavioral researcher has much in common with the artist or writer, who also perceives meaning in the world and attempts to express that meaning in a way others can understand and appreciate. The artist might employ the medium of paint or clay, while the writer deals in words; the researcher offers insights through experimental demonstrations. In any case, the goal of furthering our understanding and appreciation of meanings in the world is similar in all three vocations. It is this common goal of increased understanding, which the scientist and artist share, that led Jacob Bronowski (1973, p. 330) to the following remarkable claim about modern physics:

The picture has shifted ... to atomic structure. That is the intellectual breakthrough with which modern physics begins. Here the great age opens. Physics becomes in those years the greatest collective work of science—no, more than that, the great collective work of art of the twentieth century.

14

Additional Readings

Toulmin, S. *Foresight and understanding: An inquiry into the aims of science.* New York: Harper & Row, 1961.

McCain, G., & Segal, E. M. *The game of science.* Monterey, Calif.: Brooks-Cole, 1969.

Goldstein, M., & Goldstein, I. F. *How we know: An exploration of the scientific process.* New York: Plenum Press, 1978.

Variables, Observations, and Measurement

Chapter Preview

At the beginning of chapter 2, a distinction is made between how scientific results are expressed (as relationships between theoretical variables) and how research is conducted (through use of operational definitions). Several measurement procedures are then described. The issues of the reliability, or repeatability, and the validity, or accuracy, of measures are then considered. Finally, ways are described for expressing two characteristics of groups of scores—central tendency and variability.

Chapter 1 claimed that science looks for patterns in the world. The goal of science is to express these patterns as laws showing relationships among variables. This chapter considers issues involved in making connections between the theoretical concepts used in scientific laws. It also describes how these concepts are specified in research projects.

Variables and Operational Definitions

Research investigations seek to determine the relationships among variables. For example, a researcher who wishes to determine if there is a relationship between frustration and aggression may look at subjects who have been frustrated and subjects who have not been frustrated to see if these groups differ in the amount of aggression they exhibit. Similarly, a researcher might wonder about the question, "Is it true blonds have more fun?" The variables to be studied are "blondness" and "fun." Or the researcher might wonder, "Could critical, stressful life events be implicated in the development of cardiovascular diseases?"

Remember chapter 1 said that science deals in observables. Most people think of research in the social sciences as showing relationships between variables such as "frustration" and "fun." And indeed, the results of studies are presented in such terms (for example, we might read: "Research shows that prolonged exposure to stressful life events can lead to greater risk of heart disease."). But have you ever seen "frustration," or "fun," or "stressful life events"? So far we have dealt only with variables considered on the theoretical level. We use the terms *theoretical variables* and *conceptual variables* to speak of variables at this level of abstraction. However, researchers can determine relationships among variables only after finding ways of quantifying or operationalizing each theoretical variable in a study. To do this, they employ *operational definitions*.

To operationally define a variable, researchers must clearly specify the steps or operations used to measure it. A researcher interested in "strength" as a theoretical variable might decide to measure it according to the amount of weight on a barbell that subjects can pick up. This is an example of quantifying a variable with an operational definition. Similarly, an operational definition could separate or categorize individuals according to hair color. The variable "hair color" could be operationalized by having judges look at the hair of every subject in an experiment and simply categorize it as either blond or nonblond.

A final point to be made about operational definitions is that many, many possible operational definitions exist for any one variable. For example, in addressing the question of whether blonds have more fun, we might do any of the following to operationally define the variable "fun":

1. Have a rater count the number of times the person smiles each day.
2. Count the number of dates or social engagements the person attends in a week.
3. Ask the person, "How much fun do you typically have, on a scale from zero (no fun at all) to five (my whole life is fun)."
4. Ask two individuals who know the subject well to rate how much fun the person has according to the scale in item 3.

Obviously, there are many more potential operational definitions than the ones given here. However, there is no one correct or best operational definition for a variable. Some operational definitions may be good, some may not be good; but all are fair game for scientific investigation. We will see later how researchers choose operational definitions for the variables in their studies, and we will look at some criteria by which they can later determine the wisdom of the choices they made.

Methods of Measurement

Several types of operational definitions have been frequently chosen by social science researchers. This section deals with a few of the more frequently employed measurement techniques to demonstrate how researchers translate theoretical variables into operational definitions.

Self-Reports

Many of the measures employed in several areas of the social sciences are self-report measures. Any time an investigator asks a research subject to provide information about himself or herself verbally or in writing (perhaps in response to questions or to items on a questionnaire), the researcher is gathering self-report data. Researchers might ask subjects to respond to items by using a particular scale. For example, subjects are often asked to respond to questions such as "How would you rate your social life?" by choosing an answer from a scale ranging from "very dissatisfied" to "very satisfied," or similar responses. Typically, numbers are associated with various points on the scale, as will be seen below.

Many famous surveys in various areas of the social sciences have employed self-reports. For example, in the Kinsey sex behávior survey, subjects were asked in long interviews to report on their sexual behavior. Similarly, the familiar political polls, wherein individuals are asked for whom they intend to vote, are self-reports. Political scientists have developed extremely accurate techniques for forecasting the results of political elections on the basis of such polls.

There are demonstrable limitations to the use of self-reports. The problems associated with these measures are often referred to as response-style effects (Millham & Jacobson, 1978). Response-style effects include several influences known to contaminate self-report ratings, such as memory distortions (where individuals systematically recall some qualities or events about themselves and forget other qualities or events) and social desirability distortions (where one type of answer is commonly viewed as better than another, as in "Are you an honest or a dishonest person?" "Are you a sensitive or an insensitive person?"). A substantial amount of research has documented the existence of response-style effects; so a researcher can never be totally uncritical of the data he or she obtains from subjects' self-reports.

There are also certain times and circumstances in which one might expect that a self-report would be contaminated. For example, suppose prisoners were asked if they felt they had been rehabilitated during their time in prison. It would not be surprising if they said yes, no matter what they thought, since they might believe a positive response could get them an early parole. Similarly, if I asked students to rate this course on a student evaluation form and then sign the form, I might expect that some students would respond positively to the questions about the quality of the instructor because they feared I would lower their grades or think poorly of them if they did other-

20

wise. In situations like those just described, asking self-report questions will probably yield less-than-perfect data. Thus, the use of self-reports should be discouraged in such situations, or the situations should be altered to reduce the problem of contamination (for example, I could make the student evaluations anonymous).

On the other hand, recent research has demonstrated that self-reports can be extremely accurate in some instances—far more accurate than many researchers had suspected (Howard, Maxwell, Weiner, Boynton, & Rooney, 1980). This tremendous accuracy exists in spite of the possibility that subjects may either consciously or unconsciously distort their responses. The accuracy may be due, in part, to subjects' ability to base their responses on a tremendous amount of familiarity with their own behavior. For example, suppose I were to ask you how assertive you are. It appears that your ability to review substantial amounts of personal history can enable you to provide more representative responses, based on the many situations in your life that have called for assertiveness, than could other alternative operational definitions of assertiveness. Again, remember that a self-report requires that subjects be honest in responding to questions. Researchers should strive always to arrange the conditions in such a way that the likelihood of subjects' providing truthful data is maximized.

Another positive note about self-reports is that obtaining them is extremely cost efficient. Very little effort is required on the part of the experimenter or the subject. Finally, it should be added that certain psychological phenomena are accessible only through self-reports. An obvious example is human intentions. My intentions are only knowable to you if I choose to tell you about them. You can observe my behavior and attempt to infer my intentions from that behavior, but you can never really know precisely what my thinking is unless I tell you. It is also obvious that a researcher can never check the validity of a self-report of my intentions. However, if we are to study phenomena such as intentions, plans, goals, irrational thoughts, and purposes, as many social scientists do, it is necessary to use and to assess the accuracy of self-reports of these phenomena.

Measures of Behavior

Behavioral measures are collected with the aid of a person other than the research subject. This person either rates, counts, or reports the subject's behavior. An alternative procedure is the use of some mechanical recording device (such as a response counter in a Skinner box—a machine that automatically counts the number of times a lever is pressed by an animal). A simple example of a behavioral measure would involve a rater sitting in a class and counting the number of teacher-student interactions in a class period. The number of teacher-student interactions can then be estimated by this rater, whose sole function is to keep track of the number of interactions. This sort of operational definition might be preferable to one obtained from a student in the class (whose main task is to learn the material) or from a self-report by the teacher (whose main task is to make the course interesting).

A second example of a behavioral measure is obtained from the bathroom scale you use to keep track of your weight. If we wondered about the adequacy of a program to control weight, we might monitor subjects' weight by weighing them periodically to determine whether taking part in the program was associated with weight loss. This behavioral approach can be contrasted with the self-report approach, which might simply ask the individual if he or she had lost weight. In this instance, the behavioral method is the more appropriate.

One of the strengths of behavioral measures is that they are relatively free from response-style effects. Behavioral measures are especially strong in this regard when they are collected unobtrusively—when subjects do not know they are being observed.

The weaknesses of behavioral measures are less obvious. If a researcher is interested in measuring a theoretical variable that is likely to be situation specific (likely to occur in certain situations but not in others), obtaining adequate behavioral measures of the variable might be difficult. For example, suppose a researcher is interested in your level of assertiveness. The researcher might call you on the telephone and identify himself as a student in this research methods class. He then might ask to borrow your class notes. As the conversation proceeded, the researcher might make progressively more unreasonable requests (Would you xerox your notes and give him the xerox copy? Would you deliver these xerox notes to his house?). The point at which you made an assertive refusal to the caller's requests would determine the researcher's assessment of your level of assertiveness. This is the technique used by McFall and Twentyman (1973), and it is a frequently employed behavioral measure of assertiveness. However, suppose you had recently been sick and had borrowed someone else's notes, which had enabled you to get a good grade on a test. Your recent positive experience with another student's generosity might prompt you to bend over backward to try to help out this fellow student (who is, in reality, a researcher). Consequently, you might not refuse to go along with these rather unreasonable requests. You would be graded as unassertive, although you might be a very assertive person in virtually all other situations (for example, in returning a well-done steak when you had ordered medium rare, in asking a boss for a raise, and so on). In this regard, the behavioral measure gives a poor representation of your typical level of assertive behavior and, consequently, is inaccurate and misleading.

It is recommended that researchers use data obtained from behavioral measures in conjunction with self-report measures, in order to gain a clearer and more thorough picture of the phenomenon under investigation. These two methods can be employed to check each other's accuracy and to suggest when one or both might be less than adequate for a variety of reasons.

Physiological Measures

Physiological measures result from the recording of some bodily response, typically by a recording instrument. Examples of such measures include blood pressure, heart rate, EEG (electroencephalogram), EKG (electrocardiogram), GSR (galvanic skin response), and body temperature. Measures such as these have long been employed in research in, for example, medicine and physiological psychology. GSR is an index of general emotional arousal and has been used often in studies of situations in which emotional arousal might be an important component. Many lie-detector tests are based on GSR responses in combination with other physiological indices (such as heartbeat and breathing rate).

Physiological measures are often important when the hypotheses under investigation are clearly physical or physiological in nature. An advantage of physiological measures is that it is difficult for most subjects to control them. However, these measures also involve limitations; for example, they are extremely difficult and expensive to obtain and are subject to many extraneous physical and physiological influ-

23

ences. In addition, there are often problems in interpreting precisely what the physiological responses mean.

Archival Data

Archival data generally refers to any data collected at some point in the past, typically not for the purposes of the investigation at hand. The income tax records of the Internal Revenue Service are potential archival sources. The national census surveys, which are conducted in the United States every ten years, are sources of data for many researchers interested in demographic and sociological questions. A third example is former president Nixon's audio tapes of White House conversations. These recordings served as archival data for the Watergate prosecutor's office in its attempts to determine if justice had been obstructed in the Watergate case.

One strength of archival data is that since the data have already been gathered, the expense involved in collecting and preparing them is usually minimal. A second strength involves the fact that the data were collected for some purpose other than the study; they are not likely contaminated by the unintended data distortions that can result from the knowledge that an experiment is taking place. One of the limitations of archival data is that the data might not have been collected in precisely the manner experimenters would have liked. That is, questions might have been phrased slightly differently than would be optimal for the researchers' purposes. Also, some critical questions might not have been asked of subjects. When this has occurred, there is very little chance for the experimenter to go back and obtain the missing, vital information. Yet another problem involves the potential lack of quality control in the collection of the data. The researcher is never sure how carefully the data were gathered and recorded. Finally, archival data reflect a set of responses that occurred at another time. The researcher has no way of knowing if the passage of time has changed some of the relationships among variables. What might have been a strong relationship at the time the data were collected may have weakened over time. For example, studies conducted on sexual attitudes in Victorian England would present a picture different from the one similar studies would show today.

24

Issues in Measurement

Reliability

Reliability refers to a scientific observation's repeatability, or replicability. If an observation or rating is not repeatable, its usefulness as evidence in scientific endeavors is limited. To begin to understand the concept of reliability, we might consider a situation in which we wish to test the reliability of a scale on which the subject of an experiment will be weighed. Suppose we know the subject weighs 180 pounds. This is the person's true score, and we could obtain this true score by measuring the individual many times on many different scales. Remember, the reliability of a scale simply refers to the repeatability of a measurement by that instrument. Suppose our subject gets on our scale, and it reads 180 pounds. Now, he gets off the scale and gets back on; again, it reads 180 pounds. Suppose the person does this ten times and receives a score of 180 each time. We can then say the scale is reliable, because the same score was obtained every time.

There are several types of reliability, including test-retest reliability, interrater reliability, and split-half reliability.

Test-Retest Reliability

Test-retest reliability refers to the ability of a measuring instrument to be reliable over a period of time. The example of the scale is an example of test-retest reliability. In that instance, the time between test and retest was only a few seconds. In the social sciences, most studies of test-retest reliability involve much longer periods. For example, one would expect that an individual's intelligence would not change dramatically during a fairly short period of time. That is, a person should not become noticeably more or less intelligent over a period of several weeks. Therefore, if I administered a standard IQ test to a group of subjects and then had them take the test again two weeks later, I could estimate the reliability of that IQ test by comparing the scores from the original testing time with the later scores.

A test's reliability is expressed by a correlation coefficient (this topic will be discussed more fully in chapter 11). A reliability coefficient of +1.0 would imply perfect reliability between the two sets of

IQ scores, whereas a reliability of .00 would imply no relationship between them. Most psychological tests given at two-week intervals could be expected to have test-retest reliabilities that range between +.7 and +1.0.

You might wonder why the test-retest reliability of IQ scores was obtained over a two-week period whereas in the scale example the interval between weighings was only a few seconds. One reason is that one measurement should not influence the next measurement. If subjects had taken a timed IQ test and then taken it again a few seconds later, they might have remembered the answers they gave the first time and quickly answered those items the second time. This would have given them extra time to answer additional items, leading to a higher IQ score. The two-week interval between testings allows the memory effects to be diminished somewhat. On the other hand, if the IQ test was boring or taxing, taking it twice with only a few seconds between tests might lead to lower scores the second time. The two-week interval helps diminish boredom or fatigue effects.

A second reason for the difference in intervals between weighings and IQ tests is related to the assumption that the subject's level on the theoretical construct of interest (the subject's true score) will not change from one testing to the next. While a person's weight will not change in the few seconds it takes to step off the scale and step back on, if the interval between measurements has been several weeks, the person's weight might well have changed. Such changes would look like unreliability in the scale if one assumed the person's weight had not changed over the two-week period. You can see why the most appropriate interval for obtaining test-retest reliabilities varies from one theoretical variable to another.

Interrater Reliability
A second form of reliability involves the degree of similarity between the results of two judges rating the same thing at the same time. For example, two judges might rate a group of pictures for attractiveness. By comparing the scores of one judge with the scores of the other, we could obtain a correlation coefficient to reflect the degree to which the judges agree in their ratings of attractiveness. If one judge saw some pictures as attractive while the other judge saw them as unattractive, a low interrater reliability would result.

Split-Half Reliability

A third form of reliability is interitem, odd-even, or split-half reliability. These three terms refer to a variety of techniques that provide estimates of the internal consistency within measurement scales. They are typically employed when a researcher is examining a theoretical variable (such as assertiveness or self-esteem) by looking at multiple assessments of that variable (such as multiple items on a questionnaire). For example, if I were assessing your assertiveness, I might want to base my estimate on your answers to a large number of questions related to assertiveness. I might test the reliability of this group of questions by correlating scores of two or more subsets of items. That is, I might compute your average assertiveness based on your responses to the odd-numbered questions (questions 1,3,5, and so on) and also on the even-numbered questions. The relationship between these two estimates of your assertiveness would help me to calculate the odd-even reliability of the measure.

Validity

A discussion of validity must include an explanation of two constructs. The first, which was mentioned earlier, is the *true score*—a hypothetical value that represents a totally accurate score or rating. Of course, only if a researcher were omniscient would he or she know precisely the true value of the variable of interest for every subject. The second concept is *measurement error*—the degree to which scores are different from the true score because of unreliability or systematic confounding. (Systematic confounding is a form of bias that influences successive measurements in the same way. If you weighed 230 pounds and I asked you your weight several times, you might say you weighed 180 pounds each time. Your embarrassment might have led you to systematically confound your replies to make them more socially acceptable—but less accurate.) To the extent that the score observed is influenced by chance or irrelevant or contaminating influences, the true score is obscured. The validity of a measure refers to the degree to which the scores obtained in using the instrument successfully approximate the true scores.

In the example of weighing a subject discussed earlier, when we obtained a score of 180 each of ten times, we concluded that the scale was reliable. If we were omniscient—if we knew that the person's true weight was 180, we could conclude that this scale was also valid. Now, let us consider a related example. Suppose our scale is broken. Each time a person who weighs more than 170 pounds steps on the scale, the dial moves to 170 and stops there. If a 140-pound person stepped on the scale, it would read 140. But if a 190-pound person stepped on the scale, it would read 170. If our 180-pound subject weighed himself ten times on this scale, the score would be 170 each time. The scale is perfectly *reliable*! Remember, reliability does not imply accuracy—it simply refers to repeatability.

We refer to problems associated with obtaining accurate ratings as problems of validity. The scale in this latter example is thus said to be reliable, but invalid. We recognized the invalidity because the average of all observations was 170 pounds, while we knew the true score to be 180 pounds. We will say much more about the concept of validity in subsequent chapters.

Scaling

Once a researcher has determined the theoretical variable with which he or she wishes to work, the next step is to determine an operational definition for that construct. As mentioned earlier, the possible operational definitions of most theoretical constructs are virtually limitless. Any operational definition, however, can be categorized by its measurement properties.

Once measurements have been obtained, they must be summarized and their meanings for the study interpreted. This is accomplished by use of statistics. Certain measurement properties determine what types of statistics can be used. This section considers scaling issues for various types of operational definitions to set the stage for the statistical issues described in chapters 11 and 12.

The crudest type of scale involves an operational definition that assigns observations to categories without ranking these categories. For example, the construct "academic major in college" can be used to categorize students into various groups—psychology major, political science major, engineering major, and so on. However, one cannot assign a rank order to the various disciplines in any nonarbitrary way. That is, one cannot say that engineering should be ranked higher or lower than political science, which in turn cannot be ranked higher or lower than psychology. This *nominal* scale, then, simply notes differences but makes no assumptions regarding the meaning of those differences.

A second type of scale, slightly more sophisticated than the nominal scale, is the *ordinal scale*. An ordinal scale rank-orders the observations in some nonarbitrary fashion. An example of an ordinal rating system is the classification of the minor leagues in baseball. The lowest minor league in this rating system is Class A; the next, Class AA; and the third, Class AAA. One can reasonably assume that the quality of baseball played in the AAA league is higher than the quality of baseball played in AA. However, one cannot say that the jump from Class A baseball to Class AA baseball is of the same magnitude as the jump from Class AA baseball to Class AAA baseball. This last assumption (that the intervals between points on the scale are equal) is the distinguishing characteristic between the ordinal scale and the *interval scale.*

An *interval scale* has the rank-order properties of an ordinal scale; but in addition, the units of measurement are of equal distance from one another. An example of this type of measurement is the Fahrenheit temperature scale. On the Fahrenheit scale, a rise in temperature from five degrees to ten degrees (a five-degree jump) involves the same magnitude of increase as a rise from ten degrees to fifteen degrees.

The final and most sophisticated type of scale is the *ratio scale.* The ratio scale has all the characteristics of ordinal and interval scales; and in addition, a ratio scale possesses an absolute zero point. (If you will remember, zero degrees Fahrenheit is a relative point—it does not imply an absence of temperature. Therefore, there is no true absolute zero value for the Fahrenheit scale.) Weight provides an example of a ratio scale. The absence of weight (or no weight at all) corresponds to a zero value on the scale. Thus, there is a true absolute zero value meaning to the scale value of zero. In addition, the equal interval assumption is satisfied: If you add five pounds of weight to a given quantity, regardless of where that quantity is on the scale, the same type of increase will result.

While researchers long for the sophistication and precision of the ratio scale in their research endeavors, most social science investigations employ ordinal and interval scales. This is due, in part, to the fact that most phenomena of interest to social scientists are not amenable to ratio measurement scales. However, as a general rule, in any instance in which researchers have the choice between an ordinal scale and an interval scale, we would hope they would choose the interval scale. Where the choice is between the interval and the ratio scale, we would opt for the ratio scale.

For reasons that will be described more fully in later chapters, social scientists need to gather many scores on numerous people in their investigations. Researchers can then accurately describe these data by using descriptive statistics. The next section discusses the major descriptive statistics employed in social science research.

Distributions of Scores

Once the researcher has selected an appropriate operational definition for the variable of interest in a research endeavor, this operational definition is used to characterize or assess subjects. After each subject has been characterized as having some score on the variable, the researcher has a *distribution* of scores. An example of such a distribution of scores is the distribution of intelligence scores of the students in this class. If we were to note the IQ score of every individual in the class, those scores would constitute a distribution.

Any distribution can be described according to two characteristics. The first is the central tendency of the distribution; the second is its variability.

Central Tendency

Central tendency is an index of the most representative score in a distribution. There are several different measures of central tendency. The first, and probably the most familiar, is the average, or *mean*. We find the mean by summing all the scores in the distribution and then dividing that total by the number of scores.

The second index of central tendency is the *mode*, the most frequently occurring score in a distribution. To compute the mode, we count the number of times each score occurs in the distribution; and the score that occurs most becomes the modal value. If there is a tie—if two different scores occur most frequently—then we call the distribution *bimodal*, or having two modes.

The last index of central tendency is the *median*. When the scores have been arranged in hierarchical order, the median is the score that precisely divides the distribution in half. Therefore, computing the median consists of rank-ordering all scores from lowest to highest and then identifying the score at the fiftieth percentile. For example, if I had a distribution of eleven IQ scores and I ranked them from lowest to highest, the sixth score would be my median value. If I had ten scores in a distribution, the median value would be halfway between the fifth and the sixth scores.

Variability

The second major characteristic of a distribution is the *variability*, or the amount of spread among scores. The indices of variability to be considered here are the range and the standard deviation. The *range* is the difference between the highest and lowest scores. To compute the range, we rank the scores from highest to lowest and subtract the lowest score from the highest score. Therefore, if my distribution of IQ scores went from 70 to 120, I would subtract 70 from 120, obtaining a value of 50. The range, then, would be 50.

The *standard deviation* can be thought of as roughly analogous to the average distance from the mean to each score in a distribution. That is, if I had a distribution of scores that were all 1s and 9s, the average (the mean) would be 5 and the average distance of each score from the mean would be 4 (the difference between 1 and 5 and between 9 and 5).

Standard deviation is obtained by use of the following formula:

$$\text{s.d.} = \sqrt{\frac{\Sigma \, (X - \overline{X})^2}{N}}$$

In this formula, X is each score in the distribution; $\overline{X}$ is the mean of the distribution; N is the number of scores in the distribution; and Σ means to add up the squared deviations. For example, consider the following distribution of scores: 1, 1, 3, 5, 5. In order to calculate the standard deviation, I must compute the mean of the distribution by summing the scores and dividing the total by the number of scores:

$1 + 1 + 3 + 5 + 5 = 15 \div 5 = 3$

31

The result, 3, is expressed as $\overline{X}$. Now I am ready to compute the standard deviation:

$$\Sigma\,(X - \overline{X})^2 = (1 - 3)^2 + (1 - 3)^2 + (3 - 3)^2 + (5 - 3)^2 + (5 - 3)^2$$

$$\Sigma\,(X - \overline{X})^2 = (-2)^2 + (-2)^2 + (0)^2 + (2)^2 + (2)^2$$

$$\Sigma\,(X - \overline{X})^2 = 4 + 4 + 0 + 4 + 4 = 16$$

$$\frac{\Sigma\,(X - \overline{X})^2}{N} = \frac{16}{5} = 3.2$$

$$\sqrt{\frac{\Sigma\,(X - \overline{X})^2}{N}} = \overline{3.2} = 1.77$$

The standard deviation of the above distribution of scores is 1.84.

Table 2−1 presents a distribution of twelve scores and computes five types of descriptive statistics (three measures of central tendency and two of variability) for that distribution.

Table 2−1   Descriptive Statistics for a Single Distribution of Scores

Scores	$(X - \overline{X})$	$(X - \overline{X})^2$	
1	−3.5	12.25	Mean $(\overline{X}) = \dfrac{\Sigma X}{N} = \dfrac{54}{12} = 4.5$
2	−2.5	6.25	
2	−2.5	6.25	
2	−2.5	6.25	
2	−2.5	6.25	Mode (most frequent score) = 2 (this score
4	−0.5	0.25	occurs four times)
5	0.5	0.25	Median (midpoint) = 4.5 (midway between the
6	1.5	2.25	sixth and seventh highest scores)
6	1.5	2.25	Range (highest to lowest) = 10 − 1 = 9
6	1.5	2.25	Standard deviation (s.d.) =
8	3.5	12.25	
10	5.5	30.25	$\sqrt{\dfrac{\Sigma\,(X - \overline{X})^2}{N}} = \sqrt{\dfrac{87}{12}} = 2.69$
$\Sigma X = 54$		$\Sigma(X - \overline{X})^2 = 87.00$	

Note: N (number of scores) = 12
    Σ = summation of
    X = each score
    $\overline{X}$ = mean

Additional Readings

Webb, E. J., Campbell, D. T., Schwartz, R. D., Sechrest, L., & Grove, J. B. *Nonreactive measures in the social sciences.* Boston: Houghton Mifflin, 1981.

Anastasi, A. *Psychological testing.* New York: Macmillan Co., 1982.

Cronback, L. J. *Essentials of psychological testing.* New York: Harper & Row, 1960.

Correlational Research and True Experimental Research

Chapter Preview

Chapter 3 considers two general approaches to obtaining empirical evidence bearing on research questions—observational methods and experimental methods. The basic difference is that observational procedures do not actively attempt to intervene in the behavior of the phenomenon under consideration, while experimental approaches do. The definition of experimental research offered here involves the use of techniques designed to eliminate hypotheses that compete with the experimental hypothesis. This goal is most easily met through the use of random assignment to form experimental groups that are equivalent on all dimensions except the variables under study.

When an investigator attempts to answer a research question, he or she may choose from a wide array of approaches for obtaining evidence. One type of approach involves the observation of the phenomenon as it presents itself to the scientist. Astronomy is an example of a science in which observation is a predominant tool for investigation. That is, astronomers attempt to understand the movement of the celestial bodies by observing them. By simply observing phenomena as they present themselves to us, we can sometimes note patterns and come to a more thorough understanding of the structure underlying their operation.

A second, very different approach to obtaining knowledge involves the active intervention in a system by the scientist. By noting the reactions of that system to the intervention, the scientist can obtain increased knowledge of the system's operation. An example of this approach comes from the science of selective breeding in genetics. Here, scientists will, for example, graft species of flowers together to form new hybrid species. Such intervention allows the scientist to judiciously test his or her hypothesis regarding the probable outcomes of these non—naturally occurring events.

Research in the social sciences employs both observational approaches and active intervention. The active intervention approaches are typically referred to as *experimental*, while the observational approaches are sometimes referred to as *correlational*. There is no strict break between observational and experimental approaches; the two types overlap a good deal and often are combined in research practice. In fact, one group of research methods, called *quasi-experimental* approaches, are thought to lie somewhere between observational and experimental approaches.

In order to understand the purposes of experimental designs, we must consider the logic of causation that underlies experimental approaches. This logic involves the researcher's attempt to construct an empirical demonstration in which all possible alternative causal influences can be logically eliminated so that the effect of one particular cause can be observed. The next section highlights some of the difficulties associated with logically eliminating the effect of all possible alternative causal influences.

Problem: How to Identify a Causal Influence

Most human behavior is multiply determined. That is, many

influences combine to lead us to act in a particular way. For example, you are now reading your research methods textbook. Why are you reading it? One influence might be your desire to get a good grade in the course. You may believe that by studying, you will increase the chances of obtaining a satisfactory mark. A second factor could be your wish to avoid the embarrassment of being called on in class and not knowing the answer to a particular question. A third factor might be your feelings toward the teacher. Perhaps you like the teacher and would be pleased to have him or her think more highly of you because you have learned the material. A fourth reason could be that your friends are all busy, you are bored, and studying is the best of a limited number of activities you have to choose from at the moment. It is quite possible that all these causes (and many other influences, of which you may or may not be aware) are working together to increase the likelihood of your studying. Can we say that all of them are *causing* you to study? Most scientists would agree that each of these reasons for your behavior might exert a moderate influence on you. These influences culminate in a tendency on your part to perform a particular activity.

At this point, let us suppose that another individual enters this conversation and suggests the possibility that the temperature in your room is a causal influence in your choice of whether to study. Have we any method of determining whether this potential new cause actually influences you? The essential problem is to separate out the influence of a suspected cause (for example, the temperature in the room) from the other causal influences operating on an individual. One simple step toward a solution to the problem is to observe the amount of time you spend studying when the room is at different temperatures. While this step might be helpful, it is fraught with potential errors that relate to our interpretation of the meaning of our observations. Thus, we refer to such observational approaches as weak designs. The reasons for considering observational methods weak will be elaborated on in a later section. The following section will consider somewhat stronger methods, the experimental methods.

A Simple Example

Before considering complex examples of observational and experimental research, let us focus on some of the differences between the two perspectives by looking at a simple example. What if you suspected that the number of students in a classroom was an important influence on the number of questions students asked in class? After stating your belief that class size influences the number of student questions, you would set about deciding how to empirically determine if your belief is correct.

An observational technique you could employ would be to attend a large number of classes at your school and count the number of questions students asked in each class. You would need to be sure that you attended a sufficient number of both large and small classes. If you noticed that substantially more questions were asked in small classes than in large classes, you would have achieved some degree of support for your belief as a result of your observational study. Some of the difficulties with this type of study will be elaborated on in the next section.

If, instead of observational techniques, you used experimental research techniques, you would intervene in the phenomenon under study. In this instance, you might first recruit some teachers of rather large classes to participate in your study. The teachers would agree to teach a small section of their classes as well as the larger sections. Then, at the beginning of the semester, you could randomly choose a few students from these teachers' class lists to attend the small sections of the classes. (Random assignment will be described later.) If you noted that students in the small class sections consistently asked more questions than students in the large class sections, you would have achieved some experimental support for your belief.

This simple example of observational and experimental techniques provides some perspective on the two approaches. However, the example is obviously incomplete and overly simplistic. The remainder of the chapter fleshes out some of the points outlined in this preliminary discussion.

Observational Approaches

Year after year, the total number of home runs hit in the Astrodome in Houston, Texas, is substantially less than the number of home runs hit in most other ballparks in the major leagues. That information can be obtained from an observational research project.

That is, we need only look at the number of home runs hit in the Astrodome and at other parks over a number of years to find out that the Astrodome total is far less than the average for other ballparks. Having noted this phenomenon, nonscientists often leap to the conclusion that it is difficult to hit home runs in the Astrodome. In fact, this conclusion might be true; but at this point in a scientific investigation, we could not be sure it was the Astrodome itself that caused the observed relationship.

If we had taken observations over a five-year period, we might have found that the character of the Houston Astros had remained largely unchanged over that period. Perhaps the Astros have had fewer home run hitters than most other teams in baseball. If this is the case, the Astros might, because of their weak hitting, be the sole cause of the low number of home runs in the Astrodome. (After all, two teams play in every game in the Astrodome, and one of them is always the Astros.) Our observation of the low number of home runs in the Astrodome does not allow us to eliminate the possibility that the Astros are a weak hitting team, which might be the real cause of the low number of home runs being hit. We call this alternative possibility a competing explanation of the phenomenon we are observing. The alternative possibility competes with the causal explanation (that the Astrodome is a poor park for home runs) that we suspect to be producing the phenomenon (fewer home runs than expected).

There are usually many competing explanations for any phenomenon. For example, another competing hypothesis might be that the Astro pitching staff is stronger than any other. Again, since the Astros are always one of the two teams playing in the Astrodome, the strength of their pitching staff should have a causal influence on the total number of home runs hit in the park. Even if these two competing hypotheses were ruled out, we still would not know if some unknown explanations were responsible for the paucity of home runs. This is the essential problem of observational techniques—their inability to rule out competing explanations.

Suppose we were able to eliminate all competing explanations and conclude that the low number of home runs was due to the Astrodome's being a difficult park in which to hit home runs. Obviously, the next question would be "Why?" Scientists would be interested in precisely what specific cause was responsible for the reduced number of home runs. Is it the dimensions of the ballpark?

Perhaps the Astrodome simply has a larger playing field than other ballparks; therefore, it is more difficult to hit home runs there. Perhaps it has something to do with the humidity or temperature in the Astrodome. These two factors are artificially controlled; and perhaps it is this intrusion of uniform playing conditions into the previously random domain of nature that somehow produces the lowered number of home runs. It might be that the noise level in an enclosed building, as opposed to an open ballpark, is making a difference. Or perhaps the lighting in the Astrodome is poorer than natural light.

As you can see, the number of potential causes can be staggeringly large. Before scientists would be willing to say they understood the phenomenon, they would need to verify or disconfirm each of these potential causal influences. At this point, observation allows us to note the trends in the phenomenon and to speculate about their probable causes; but it does not allow us to determine exactly what the causes are.

Experimental Approaches

As was noted earlier, the essence of experimental approaches is the researcher's intervening in the normal flow of events and observing the results. But what *types* of interventions are helpful to our understanding of phenomena in the world? Suppose we noted that the distances to the outfield fences in the Astrodome were longer than in most other ballparks. Further, suppose we suspected this was the only cause for the reduced number of home runs in the Astrodome. We could move the fences closer to home plate so that the distance from home plate to the fences in the Astrodome was equal to the average distance in other ballparks. What would performing this action accomplish?

If the Houston ball club had better hitters than average, we might see more home runs hit in the Astrodome than in most other ballparks. If the Houston hitters were substantially poorer hitters, we might still see fewer home runs hit than average. Moving in the fences would probably increase the number of home runs hit, but that would not allow us to conclude that the distance of the fences was the salient influence in the original phenomenon. Similarly, we cannot rule out the possibility that other influences (such as lighting, humidity, temperature, and so on) are responsible for the lower

40

number of home runs. Studies wherein we raise or lower the levels of these variables will suggest whether more or fewer home runs are hit at higher or lower temperatures, humidity levels, light intensities, and so on. But these findings still do not answer the original question of whether it is more difficult to hit home runs in the Astrodome because of these conditions. Again, the possibility that the Astro pitchers and hitters are better or worse than their counterparts on other teams always remains a stumbling block to our interpretation of the findings.

A somewhat different approach to experimental intervention produces far greater payoffs. The possibility that the Astro ball club contained better or worse athletes than other teams has remained a stumbling block in our interpretations thus far. If we had reason to believe that the Astros had ballplayers who, on the average, were no better or worse than those on other teams, the interpretation of the hypothetical studies suggested above would be more clear-cut. Can we intervene in a way that will give us confidence that the Astro ballplayers are "typical" or "representative" or "equal to" the players on other teams? It turns out that in order to do that, we would need to employ a procedure called random assignment. The box entitled "Random Assignment" explains what this procedure involves and describes an exercise that may give you some additional confidence that random assignment does produce the desired effects.

If we had it in our power to randomly assign players to ball clubs and could thus make the Astro ball team a random, representative subset of ball players in the major leagues, we could then more effectively test other potential causal influences. Obviously, though, major league baseball would never allow such a procedure. We can now begin to realize the strongest limitation of experimental approaches. The need to obtain strict control over various aspects of an experiment sometimes makes performing experiments impossible or at least difficult and costly. Later in the book, when more complex designs are discussed, you will see that one need not always have the power of random assignment to be able to draw causal inferences. At present, however, we will consider further the most frequently used approach in conducting experimental research: the random assignment approach.

When we wish to conduct an experimental investigation, the logic we follow involves establishing two or more groups, which we will compare with one another. These groups will be made as similar

Random Assignment

The chapter claims that random assignment will yield groups of subjects approximately equal on the average in every regard. It might be helpful to work through a real example to show how random assignment achieves the desired effects.

First, let us define what is necessary for assignment to be considered random. The essential requirement is that each subject have an equal chance of being assigned to each category.

How might this qualification be fulfilled in an actual procedure? A common practice is to randomly assign subjects to two groups by flipping a coin. If, for example, we are interested in ascertaining whether tutoring will improve students' performance in a research methods class, we might flip a coin one time for each member of the class. "Heads" means the student will receive tutoring; "tails" means the student will not be tutored. To find out if tutoring is helpful, we will compare the final examination grades of the tutored and untutored groups.

Why is it important that these groups be randomly assigned? The answer is that if the two groups are different from one another on some relevant variable (if, for example, the tutored group consists of better students than the other group), and if we find the tutored group achieves better final exam grades, we have a problem of interpretation. Namely, are the higher grades due to the fact that students in the tutored group are better students, or are their grades higher because the tutoring worked to increase their knowledge? In our example, we cannot tell which of these potential causes led to the observed effect (or whether both contributed).

I performed a random assignment of students in my research methods class using the coin-flipping procedure described above. My operational definition of the theoretical variable, better or worse students, was determined by asking each student his or her grade-point average. Student 1 received heads and had a grade-point average of 2.9. In shorthand form, that can be written S_1 H 2.9. The following results were obtained: S_1 H 2.9; S_2 T

3.7; S_3T 3.3; S_4T 2.9; S_5T 3.6; S_6H 3.3; S_7H 3.5; S_8H 2.7; S_9T 3.1; S_{10}H 3.8; S_{11}T 2.2; S_{12}H 3.0; S_{13}T 3.7; S_{14}T 3.7; S_{15}H 3.2; S_{16}H 3.6; S_{17}H 3.1; S_{18}T 3.4; S_{19}T 2.6; S_{20}H 2.7; ... S_{50}T 3.2. Note that if I had stopped randomly assigning after the second subject (S_2), I would have had two groups with one subject in each group. The average GPA of the H group would have been 2.9, whereas the average GPA of the T group would have been 3.7. In fact, the two groups would have been very different with regard to average GPA. Consider what the results would have been if I had stopped the random assignment procedure at various other points in the process:

	Stop After Subject 2	Stop After Subject 8	Stop After Subject 20	Stop After Subject 50
Mean GPA of:				
Heads group	2.90	3.10	3.18	3.14
Tails group	3.70	3.38	3.22	3.13

You will note that as more subjects are assigned to groups, the GPA means get closer to one another until they are essentially equal at the end of the process. As a general rule, one can be more confident that random assignment has achieved its desired purpose (to make the groups equivalent) as more subjects are assigned to groups. The general rule of thumb is that the researcher needs to have at least six subjects in each group in order to have *any* confidence that the groups are equivalent. At the opposite extreme, if I were to assign one hundred subjects to each group, most social scientists would be comfortable that the groups were probably equivalent on all relevant dimensions.

But remember that random assignment is thought to equate groups on *all* dimensions—that is, even on irrelevant dimensions. Therefore, I asked my students for information on two other dimensions—weight and age—that I believed would probably be irrelevant to the grades they would obtain on the final examination. Group mean weight and age at various stopping points are displayed on the following page: *(continued)*

43

	Stop After Subject 2	Stop After Subject 8	Stop After Subject 20	Stop After Subject 50
Mean weight of:				
Heads group	188	163.0	161.1	160.6
Tails group	160	155.3	159.5	161.3

	Stop After Subject 2	Stop After Subject 8	Stop After Subject 20	Stop After Subject 50
Mean age of:				
Heads group	20	20.0	19.8	19.9
Tails group	20	19.5	19.6	19.8

You can see that the groups become more equivalent in mean weight as greater numbers of subjects are included. However, the groups are reasonably equivalent on mean age at all points. In theory, with sufficient subjects, the groups should be equivalent on all dimensions.

as possible to each other with respect to almost all possible causal influences (for example, hitting skill, intelligence, and so on) on the phenomenon under study (such as the number of home runs hit). However, the groups are made dissimilar on one dimension—the potential cause the experimenter wishes to test. This potential influence is called the *independent variable*. The independent variable relates to the cause side of a cause-and-effect relationship. The effect side of the relationship is reflected in the *dependent variable*. If two randomly assigned groups are equal in every possible way, except for the independent variable, then any differences found between the two groups on the dependent variable can be attributed logically to the influence of the independent variable on the dependent variable.

To demonstrate, let us look at another example. Suppose we had two groups of students who were alike in every respect except one— one group of students was offered a cash incentive for getting good grades and the other group was not. If we noticed that the cash-incentive group obtained substantially higher marks on tests than did the other group, we might infer that the money incentive helped to produce an increase in the amount of material the students learned. The critical issue is obtaining two groups that are equal in every way.

As you know, this is typically done by the random assignment of subjects to groups.

Why is random assignment so popular with researchers? In the money-incentive example, a student's intelligence probably influences the amount of material that he or she learns. Is there some way we can control for intelligence without employing random assignment? One might recommend that we administer IQ tests to all the subjects and then assign subjects to the cash-incentive group and the non-cash-incentive group in such a way that the average IQ score for each group is equal. This might have the effect of equalizing the two groups on IQ; however, it would not help us control other factors known to influence student performance.

Can we be certain that the groups are equal with respect to these other possible causes? For example, suppose we equated the two groups on intelligence as described above but did not equate the groups on students' motivation for getting good grades. Now suppose that, in reality, cash incentives had *no* causal influence on student performance but student motivation had a great influence. If the cash-incentive group had (unknown to us) a higher average level of motivation than the other group, we would note that the cash-incentive group performed better than the non-cash-incentive group; but we likely would erroneously conclude that the cash incentive produced the effect of higher grades when, in reality, the effect resulted from differences between the two groups in students' motivation. You can see that *all* characteristics must be equated between groups if we are to have confidence that the effect observed in the dependent variable is, in fact, produced by the independent variable. Random assignment accomplishes this goal.

To summarize, the interpretation of an experimental study that employed random assignment of subjects would be something like this: when the influence of all other variables is equalized between the groups, the independent variable does (or does not) have a demonstrable impact on the dependent variable. You can see that the basic logic behind true experiments involves noting that particular variables (the independent variable and the dependent variable) appear to be in a cause-and-effect relationship with one another.

One of the major drawbacks of experimental approaches, as described thus far, is that many conditions potentially interesting as independent variables cannot be operationalized in a meaningful way. If, for example, we wished to look at intelligence as an independent variable, we would run into problems: There is no way for an experimenter to change subjects' intelligence so that randomly formed groups can be made systematically different on intelligence as an independent variable. Similar examples include individuals' biological sex, socioeconomic status, and personality traits, such as introversion-extroversion. In each of these examples, humans have become the way they are through biological and social development processes that are difficult (or impossible) to reverse. These variables, which are part of the human subject and are not amenable to specification as independent variables in studies that employ random assignment, are referred to as *subject variables*. Situations exist, then, in which true experimental studies simply cannot be conducted.

Further, in some instances a researcher may decide that a correlational approach is preferable to an experimental study for particular practical topics. To understand why, consider the basic question answered by each kind of study. In their simplest sense, experimental studies can be thought of as answering the question, *"Can* a particular variable have a causal influence on some other variable?" Even though a particular "can" relationship has been demonstrated to exist, one might never actually observe that relationship in practice. On the other hand, observational approaches address the question, *"Does* a particular relationship appear to happen in a particular setting?"

An excellent example of this difference has recently appeared in the research on student evaluations of teachers. A number of studies (for example, Holmes, 1972) have found a relationship between the grades students receive and their ratings of their teachers. The results of these studies might be summarized as follows: It appears that students' expected grades *can* have an effect on their ratings of an instructor. However, subsequent studies (Howard & Maxwell, 1980, 1982) have demonstrated that, although expected grade *can* have an influence on satisfaction rating, in actual practice this influence appears to be negligible. Stated somewhat differently, it appears that in actual practice grades do not influence students' evaluations of their teachers in any meaningful way.

This chapter highlighted the superiority of experimental studies in allowing researchers to eliminate explanations that compete with the explanation being investigated. It also noted that some potentially interesting variables (subject variables) do not lend themselves to experimental investigations. The next few chapters will describe some additional difficulties with experimental approaches relative to observational approaches.

Additional Readings

Keppel, G. *Design and analysis: A researcher's handbook* (2nd ed.). Englewood Cliffs, N.J.: Prentice-Hall, 1982.

Kirk, R. *Experimental design* (2nd ed.). Belmont, Calif.: Brooks-Cole, 1982.

Sampling and Assigning

Chapter Preview

Chapter 4 presents the logic behind drawing samples of subjects to represent particular populations. Difficulties resulting from biased samples are described, and issues related to the proper generalization of the results of studies are examined. The differences between independent groups and repeated measures designs are then explained. Finally, appropriate assignment techniques are considered.

Populations and Samples

One might state that a major aim of a social science is to provide knowledge about people in general or about certain subgroups of people, such as college students, minorities, children, people in organizations, schizophrenics, and so on. It would be impossible, however, for a scientist to study all the people who constitute the populations he or she wishes to understand. Therefore, scientists must study samples they believe represent those populations.

To do that, scientists must be able to assume that a sample is indeed a good representation of the people in the population he or she wishes to come to understand. That is, the results obtained from studying a sample of subjects should represent a good approximation of the results that would have been obtained from studying every subject in the population of interest. To repeat, scientists are interested in coming to understand aspects of particular *populations* of individuals. To approximate the results they would find if they were able to study every member of that population, they draw a *sample* of subjects small enough to be studied easily. Their findings will suggest the results they would have found had they studied every member of the population. Populations, then, represent groups of individuals with specified characteristics—for example, the current population of the United States, U.S. citizens currently attending high school, all people currently alive, or the members of this research methods class.

You can see that the groupings are often somewhat arbitrarily limited. For example, in the preceding paragraph, the population of high school students did not include students of other countries, grammar school children, or college students. These limiting conditions are often called the *rules of membership* in a population.

The rules of membership are established for two reasons. The first involves the area of interest. Here, the researcher must examine his or her conscience as to what is the real motivation for this particular study. If the researcher is primarily concerned with improving high school education in the United States, he or she might be well advised to consider only the population of U.S. high school students. If, however, the researcher is interested in making statements that apply to all areas of formal education across all age groups, then he or she might wish to use a broader sample. You can see that the definition of an appropriate sample of subjects is closely related to the

50

population about which the researcher wishes to draw conclusions. The leap of faith whereby a researcher assumes that the sample can be substituted for the population is referred to as drawing a generalization. That is, to draw a generalization is to infer that the relationships observed in a sample are similar to the relationships operating in the entire population of interest.

Sampling from a population that is extremely limited, such as the population of *this* class in research methodology, provides only for generalization to a very limited grouping of people. Therefore, it is important for researchers to understand clearly how generalizable they wish their results to be. If it is essential that they obtain a high degree of generalizability across a broad range of subjects, then they should define the population of interest quite broadly. If, on the other hand, their aims and goals are more modest, then it is appropriate to define the population of interest in as specific and limiting a manner as possible.

At this point, you might wonder why the researcher would not care to generalize to as large a population as possible in every instance. In one sense, the researcher would like to be able to generalize to a virtually limitless population, since the importance of a finding increases in relation to the number of people for whom it is appropriate. However, increasing the population of interest imposes tremendous additional demands on the sampling techniques employed in the study. In this sense, it might be in the researcher's best interest to limit the population of interest as far as is reasonable.

If I were to wonder about some characteristic of this class, my population of interest would be the students in this class, and the sampling techniques I could employ to obtain a sample of this population would be reasonably simple and straightforward. If, however, I were interested in obtaining information I could generalize to all students in the United States, the sampling procedures required to generalize appropriately would impose a staggering task. The amount of effort, funds, and time required to perform this enormous sampling task might make my research project unfeasible. If I really am only interested in improving the learning in this particular class, my interests are probably best served by conducting an intensive study with the members of the population of this class as subjects. This intensive procedure will probably yield results appropriate for my population of interest, while requiring minimal effort. Once again, we see that much research in the social sciences involves the balancing and negotiating of trade-offs.

51

Representative and Biased Samples

Having defined a population of interest, the next critical step is to obtain a sample that is *representative* of that population. Let us consider an example of the problem of representativeness. Suppose I were interested in whether the reading level of this book was appropriate for this particular class in research methods. I might ask the five people in the front row of my class how easy or difficult they thought the material in the textbook was to understand. Suppose they all said the book was extremely readable and understandable. Can I accurately infer from that response that the population of students in the class is in agreement with these statements? If this group of five students constitutes a representative sample of the class, then their responses should be typical of the responses I would obtain from the entire class.

Suppose, however, that the five people in the front were all psychology majors and members of the honors program. They had originally met at a reception held for National Merit scholars and had come upon one another again at the reception held for new members of Phi Beta Kappa. Seeing one another in class on the first day, they began to talk and decided to sit in the front of the room and exchange class notes. Further, they each read the book and then met in a study group wherein they helped one another with difficulties they had had in reading it. This is, of course, an extreme example of how a group might be formed that is, in all probability, not representative of the population of interest. Through my haphazard sampling technique (simply choosing the five people closest at hand), I have drawn a sample that is clearly not representative of all people in my class. While my sample subjects tell me that the book is very easy to read and understand, in reality they might be the only five members of the population who would give me that response. Perhaps the rest of the class would contend that the book is almost totally unintelligible.

In this case a *biased* sample of subjects led to an erroneous conclusion and an inappropriate generalization. A biased sample, then, is a sample of subjects that is not representative of the population to which the researcher wishes to generalize. A *representative* sample, on the other hand, tends to display characteristics among its members that are proportional to the characteristics of the members of the population of interest.

Sampling Techniques

Haphazard Sampling

Haphazard sampling can be understood as a procedure whereby the researcher obtains subjects in the manner most convenient to him or her. The example above was an example of haphazard sampling. If you were interested in the political attitudes of people in a particular city, and your sampling technique involved standing outside the Democratic Party headquarters and interviewing each individual who went in, it is not unreasonable to suspect that the sample of individuals with which you spoke might overrepresent Democrats and underrepresent other political groups such as Republicans, Independents, and so on.

Researchers can have very little confidence in the representativeness of samples gathered haphazardly. Consequently, the use in research studies of haphazard sampling techniques is minimal; and journal editors discourage the use of these techniques. The reason for this bias against haphazard sampling is obvious: The representativeness of the sample is always in doubt, which makes any generalization of the results to the population of interest very speculative and quite possibly inaccurate.

Quota Sampling

Quota sampling is one step better than haphazard sampling, because it looks at the numerical percentages of various subgroups in a population and reproduces these percentages in the sample. For example, suppose you were interested in obtaining the opinions of football players in the National Football League, and you suspected that attitudes would vary among offensive players, defensive players, and players primarily responsible for the special teams, such as punting and field goal kicking. You might begin by noting the percentages in the league of offensive players (perhaps 40 percent), defensive players (another 40 percent), and members of special teams (about 20 percent). In choosing subjects to be included in the sample, you would select players until the quota of each type in the sample represented the appropriate percentage. If you wanted a total of fifty responses from players, you would obtain the responses of twenty offensive players (40 percent of your total sample), twenty defensive players, and ten special-team players. Then, your sample of fifty players would reflect the percentages of offensive, defensive, and special-team players in the National Football League.

Quota sampling is slightly better than haphazard sampling, because it ensures representativeness of the sample with regard to the subgroupings specified (such as offensive, defensive, and special-team players). However, it provides no assurance that the sample is representative of all members of a population with regard to other characteristics. Therefore, generalization is still a problem, although not quite as serious a problem as with haphazard sampling. For example, perhaps a second factor that might influence football players' attitudes is the geographic area of the country in which they play. Consequently, if your sample included only players on the New York Jets and New York Giants football teams, even though the sample had an appropriate representation of offensive, defensive, and special-team players, it would include only players from a very small section of the United States. The sample, while representative with regard to one set of characteristics, would be nonrepresentative with regard to geographical area.

Random Sampling

There are three types of random sampling, and all of them are superior to either haphazard or quota sampling. Each type is appropriate in certain settings or contexts. The first of these techniques is called *simple random sampling*. With this technique, every member of the population has an equal chance of being selected for the sample. An example of a simple random sampling procedure is the typical lottery. Here, each member of the population is represented by a lottery ticket. Every member has one, and only one, ticket. Simple random sampling involves the selection of individuals from the lottery pool in a way that does not discriminate.

Suppose we wanted to choose for an experiment a sample from a class whose population was one hundred students. Say we wanted to select ten subjects to participate in the study. If we used simple random sampling, each and every student would have one chance out of a hundred of being selected for the study when the experimenter selected the first subject.

The second random sampling technique is *stratified random sampling*, which combines random sampling with quota sampling.

This procedure involves dividing the population into subgroups along a dimension we know to be strongly related to the dependent variable we are studying. Suppose, for example, we were interested in the reading scores (dependent variable) of students who participated in a particular reading program. If we believed that the students' race might be a powerful influence on whether they profited from the reading intervention, we might wish to be sure our sample accurately reflected the proportion of each ethnic group in the population. Suppose our population in a particular school district consisted of 40 percent black students, 40 percent white students, and 20 percent Mexican-American students. To employ a stratified random sampling procedure, we might begin by obtaining a computer printout of all of the students in the school district categorized by race. We then would conduct a lottery, such as the one described in the simple random sampling procedure, for each race separately. The major stipulation is that the final proportion of each race in the sample must approximate the representation of that race in the population. If we wished to draw a sample of one hundred students, we would randomly select forty black students, forty white students, and twenty Mexican-American students. This ratio would give us a sample equivalent in racial composition to the population of students in the target school district. Note, however, that this is still a random procedure in that all members of each ethnic group have an equal probability of being selected to participate in the study.

A third type of random sampling is called *area sampling*. This approach is often employed when it is easier to specify a population in terms of geographical boundaries than it is to specify the population by obtaining a listing or roster of all its potential members. Area sampling is useful in studies requiring samples of such populations as the people who live in a particular large city, the people who live in the state of Texas, or the people who live in the Rocky Mountain states. The first step in the procedure is to break the geographical area into equal segments. These segments are treated as if they were individuals in a random sampling process. Therefore, if we were interested in randomly sampling individuals in a particular city, the city might be divided into small sections such as blocks; and the blocks might be randomly sampled, with each block selected becoming part of the sample. Then, every person who lived on each of these blocks would be included in the study. Again, this procedure maintains its random quality by allowing every block in the city an equal chance of being selected in the lottery process.

All these random sampling procedures are intended to provide a truly representative sample that will allow for appropriate generalizations to the population of interest. Poor samples, as you may recall, result in difficulties with generalizability. When a biased sample is used, the experimenter might see relationships among variables in the sample that do not reflect the relationships among those variables in the population of interest. In fact, the experimenter might see relationships that do not exist at all in real-world settings. All these problems are problems of generalizability.

Once a researcher has obtained a representative sample of the population of interest, the next task is to begin to conduct the study. The next logical issue to be considered, then, is the assignment of subjects to groups within the study.

Issues in Assignment and Design

The preceding section described how sampling procedures determine the likely degree of generalizability of a researcher's findings. In other words, sampling affects external validity (discussed in detail in chapter 7). This section deals with assignment procedures, which affect internal validity (also described in chapter 7). You learned something about internal validity in chapter 3, which discussed how random assignment of subjects to groups allows for the elimination of hypotheses that compete with or contaminate the experimental cause-and-effect hypothesis. Assignment procedures also determine what design a study possesses. In this section, various assignment procedures, the resulting designs of studies, and the implications of the assignment procedures for inferring cause-and-effect relationships are discussed in more detail.

You will remember that chapter 3 described two general types of approaches to research, observational approaches and experimental approaches. A synonym for approaches here is *designs*. Different types of designs represent different ways of conceptualizing the research study and collecting the data. As mentioned, design depends on what assignment procedure is used. As demonstrated earlier, random assignment of subjects to groups allows us to assume that the groups have been equated on all characteristics except the independent variable. Forming the groups in this manner allows us to conclude that the independent variable has produced any effects seen on the dependent variable. This is possible because random assignment reduces the likelihood that alternative hypotheses are the real cause of the observed effects. In general, then, assignment decisions influence the ability to state with assurance what is the true cause-and-effect relationship in a study. Assignment problems, on the other hand, can cloud the ability to make appropriate estimates of the relationships among the variables measured and manipulated in a study.

You can see, then, that internal validity, assignment procedures, and design are closely related. We have already noted the differences between observational and experimental designs. There is yet another dimension along which designs can be categorized; they can be between-subjects or within-subjects designs.

Between-subjects designs are also called *independent groups* designs. In this approach, separate groups are formed and a different level of the independent variable is administered or provided to each group. Therefore, each subject in an independent groups study sees only one level of the independent variable during his or her participation in the study. If there are four levels of the independent variable, then each subject sees (or "experiences" or "is involved in") one level; and only one fourth of all of the subjects see a particular level.

The second type of design, the within-subjects design, is also called a *repeated measures* design. In a repeated measures design, each subject is exposed to more than one level of the independent variable.

As a simple example of the difference between designs, consider a study to find out whether subjects like Coke more than Pepsi. There are two levels of the independent variable—Coke and Pepsi. The dependent variable is satisfaction, or how good the Coke or Pepsi tastes. A repeated measures approach to this study would let all the subjects taste Coke and Pepsi, ask each one how much he or she enjoyed the taste, and then compare the ratings given to Coke with the ratings given to Pepsi. You can see that each subject would taste and rate both brands.

By contrast, an independent groups approach to this example would involve obtaining a sample of subjects and assigning subjects to one of two groups. One group would taste only Pepsi, and the other would taste only Coke. Subjects would rate their liking for the particular soda they tasted (the dependent variable), and the ratings obtained from Coke tasters would be compared with the ratings obtained from Pepsi tasters.

Independent Groups Designs

With an independent groups design, two basic methods of assignment can be employed. The simplest is the *simple random assignment* procedure. In the example above, where subjects were randomly assigned to either the Coke group or the Pepsi group and allowed to taste only one soda, simple random assignment was used. In such instances, some procedure for assigning subjects to groups (such as the flip of a coin) is employed. The experimenter might arbitrarily decide that if the coin comes up heads, the person will drink Coke, whereas if the coin comes up tails, the person will drink Pepsi. The experimenter then could have the subjects arrive one at a time and could flip a coin to determine which soda they would drink. Or the experimenter might obtain a list of the subjects' names and go through the coin-flipping procedure before the subjects even arrived. Then, as subjects arrived and gave the experimenter their names, the experimenter would look to the list to see whether the coin-flipping procedure had randomly assigned them to the Coke group or the Pepsi group. They might be sent to either a room wherein all subjects would drink Coke or a room wherein all subjects would drink Pepsi.

Another simple random assignment procedure often employed to assign subjects to one of several groups is to consult a table of random numbers. Such tables are usually computer generated, and the arrangement of digits in the numbers is entirely random. There are many ways of employing random number tables to assign subjects to groups, and we will not consider them in depth here. For an example of a table of random numbers, consult Appendix E.

As discussed in chapter 3, the implementation of random assignment procedures prevents contamination of a study by any biases that might result from differences between the samples of subjects assigned to the levels of the independent variable. That is because random assignment procedures provide groups that are equivalent in terms of subject characteristics such as sex, intelligence, age, IQ, personality factors, and motivation. The only warning to be heeded in simple random assignment procedures is that if the number of subjects assigned to each level of the independent variable is very small, the likelihood exists that random assignment might not have the desired effect of equating the groups on all relevant subject characteristics. Therefore, the experimenter should exert every effort to enlist a large number of subjects so that when they are assigned to independent groups, the experimenter can have confidence that the groups are equivalent on relevant characteristics. This point was demonstrated in the box on random assignment in chapter 3.

The second type of assignment procedure for an independent groups design is called *matched random assignment*. Matched random assignment procedures are employed when the experimenter has reason to believe he or she can identify a variable that is strongly related to the dependent variable in the study. An example is a case in which a teacher is investigating various instructional styles and the dependent measure is the amount of material learned in a course. A factor known to be strongly related to school performance is students' motivation. In this instance, the researcher might choose to use student motivation as a matching variable.

Suppose, for example, the researcher is looking at the effectiveness of lecture methods of instruction versus group discussion methods of instruction. The independent variable is the method of instruction, and the two levels of this independent variable are lecture and discussion. The investigator can take the sample of subjects he or she has selected and rank them from highest to lowest on level of motivation. The experimenter then can take the two students whose motivation is highest and flip a coin to assign them to different levels of the independent variable. Perhaps if the coin comes up heads the higher of the two scores will go to the lecture group and the lower to the discussion group. The experimenter then proceeds to the third and fourth most highly motivated students and again conducts the coin flip. If the flip comes up tails, the higher motivated of these two students will go to the discussion group and the other to the lecture group. The experimenter goes through the entire list flipping a coin for each pair of students until all are assigned to either the discussion or the lecture group.

One of the benefits of this procedure is that the two groups will have virtually identical mean levels of motivation. However, the procedure is still essentially random, because the coin flip determines whether the higher motivated student in each pair is assigned to lecture or discussion conditions. In general, matched random assignment is indicated only if the experimenter is certain that the matching variable is strongly related to the dependent variable in the study. Even in these instances, there is reason to suspect that a simple random assignment procedure might be preferable; consequently, researchers are typically required to make a case for their choice when they use matched random assignment instead of simple random assignment in their studies. If there is doubt in the researcher's mind as to whether matched random assignment should be employed, the rule of thumb is to use simple random assignment. In fact, to the extent that the matching variable and the dependent variable are not related, the matching procedure is either ineffective or slightly harmful in the investigation.

The example above only considered matched random assignment of subjects to two levels of the independent variable. If a study involved many levels of an independent variable, essentially the same procedure would be followed. The number of subjects in each grouping (called pairs in the previous example) would be equal to the number of levels of the independent variable. Suppose, for example, we wished to test a particular drug, and we decided to administer the drug in six different dosage levels. If we ranked all subjects to be involved in this study on a particular matching variable, we then could select the top six scores on the matching variable and conduct some random procedure (such as rolling a die) to determine which of the six groups the highest scoring subject would be assigned to. We could then roll the die again to assign the second highest scoring subject, and so on. When each of the six subjects had been assigned to one of the six conditions, we would then move to the second grouping of six subjects. Note that in our rolling of the die, if the same number came up on the third roll as on the first roll, we would not assign the third subject to the same condition as the first. We would simply roll the die again, assigning only one subject to one condition until all six subjects had been assigned, each to one of the six conditions.

Repeated Measures Designs

In the two assignment techniques just described, each subject was assigned to one condition or level of the independent variable, and he or she experienced only that condition. As mentioned earlier, a second approach to conducting experiments is to have subjects participate in more than one level of the independent variable. (Remember the example in which each subject tasted both Coke and Pepsi.) When these designs are used, subjects are not assigned to groups; rather, the crucial design feature is the order in which conditions (or levels of the independent variable) are presented to subjects.

In repeated measures designs, a critical problem involves the possibility that *order effects* might contaminate the results—that is, that the order in which the levels of the independent variable are presented might affect subjects' reactions to them. Order effects can be due to factors such as fatigue, novelty, or familiarity with the equipment or procedures in the experiment. Any of these factors can facilitate or weaken performance. An example of a facilitative order effect can be seen in a study in which the dependent variable involves reaction time to a stimulus—for example, the dependent variable may be the speed with which the subject presses a brake pedal after a light turns red in a driving simulation mechanism. The first few trials might produce slow reactions, because of the subjects' lack of familiarity with the task. In this case, any level of the independent variable that is presented first to a subject is at a disadvantage to other levels. Conversely, if we were comparing the taste of several brands of hot dogs, it seems possible that the fourth or fifth hot dog eaten by a subject would be rated as less tasty (because the subject is full) than the same hot dog would have been rated had it been the first one eaten.

Another, similar type of order effect is the *carry-over effect*. Carry-over effects occur when performance in one condition is influenced not only by the level of the independent variable of that condition, but also by the conditions that preceded it. For example, if we were interested in small children's pleasure in various toys, we might promise a child a puzzle, a ball, a jump-rope, and a bicycle. The order in which the toys are suggested to the children may have no impact on the children's ratings except that any toy that immediately follows the bicycle is rated substantially lower than it would normally be rated, because all other toys are so clearly less preferred than the bicycle.

A prime requirement of any repeated measures design is that order effects be controlled as carefully as possible so that the results of the study will not be affected. This can be accomplished by either of two assignment procedures. The first possibility involves random assignment of the order in which the levels of the independent variable are presented to each subject. This way, all levels (conditions) have the same chance of being assigned any position in the order of presentation (first, second, third, and so on); and each condition has an equal chance of following any other condition. If the randomization procedure accomplishes the desired effect, no condition will be unduly influenced by order effects.

61

The second technique for neutralizing order effects is called *counterbalancing*. Counterbalancing is more systematic in that it does not rely on randomization to achieve the desired effect. In counterbalancing, the experimenter first constructs all possible orders of presentation. In the example involving toys for children, the following twenty-four orders of presentation of the puzzle (p), ball (ba), bicycle (bi), and rope (r) are possible:

p	ba	bi	r	ba	bi	p	r
p	ba	r	bi	ba	bi	r	p
p	bi	ba	r	ba	p	bi	r
p	bi	r	ba	ba	p	r	bi
p	r	ba	bi	ba	r	p	bi
p	r	bi	ba	ba	r	bi	p
bi	ba	p	r	r	ba	bi	p
bi	ba	r	p	r	ba	p	bi
bi	p	ba	r	r	bi	ba	p
bi	p	r	ba	r	bi	p	ba
bi	r	p	ba	r	p	ba	bi
bi	r	ba	p	r	p	bi	ba

The number (n) of possible orders is given by the formula $n!$ (read "n factorial"). "Factorial" means to multiply the number by every lower integer until the number 1 is reached. In the example above, the number of orders was given by 4! (or $4 \times 3 \times 2 \times 1 = 24$). If we had five toys, we would have had 5! ($5 \times 4 \times 3 \times 2 \times 1$), or 120 possible orders.

Having determined the orders, we can use one to present the toys to the first child, another to present the toys to the second child, and so on until each order of presentation has been given once and only once. If more subjects are required, the procedure can be repeated for subjects 25 through 48.

While this discussion of random assignment of stimuli and counterbalancing dealt only with levels of independent variables, these concepts will also be dealt with later (in chapter 10) in the discussion of control procedures for variables other than the independent variable.

Additional Readings

Slonim, M. J. *Sampling in a nutshell*. New York: Simon & Schuster, 1960.
Williams, W. H. *A sampler on sampling*. New York: John Wiley, 1978.

More Complex Research Designs

Chapter Preview

Extending the logic of studies that employ only one independent or predictor variable, this chapter discusses instances in which the effect of more than one independent or predictor variable is considered. The main effects of these variables as well as the interaction effect of variables in combination are elaborated on. Finally, the effect of independent or predictor variables on multiple dependent measures (multivariate designs) is considered.

Until this point, the discussion of experimental research techniques has considered only studies that included one independent variable and one dependent variable. Similarly, the consideration of observational, or correlational, techniques has dealt with instances in which only one predictor and criterion variable were considered. (In a correlational study, the purported cause in the cause-and-effect relationship under study is called the *predictor* variable; the effect variable is called the *criterion* variable.) This simplicity has been maintained in order to clarify points regarding reliability, validity, selection, assignment, and other issues in a simple and straightforward manner. However, research in the social sciences rarely consists of univariate (one-variable) research. Rather, studies often attempt to look at the phenomenon under consideration in the context of the richness and complexity of the real world. Consequently, we will now attend to increasing the complexity of our research designs to more satisfactorily approximate the complexity of behavior in real-world situations.

Why do some students obtain high grades in courses while others obtain lower grades? We can consider this a hypothetical research question and develop univariate research techniques to assess the factors that might lead to good or bad performance in a course. However, even before we begin these studies, we know that success or failure in a course is a function of many variables interacting with one another to produce the observed outcome. For example, any serious observer of the educational process knows that students learn better when the course is taught in an appropriate and effective manner, whereas students' performance will deteriorate if the course is ill prepared and ill presented.

A second factor influencing students' performance is their background. Examples of background include intelligence, motivation to take the course, experience with the material the course will cover, and pressures that might be operating to encourage better performance (for example, the need to take a test over the course material to gain admission to medical school).

A host of extra-university influences also may affect the amount students learn. For example, a student may be forced to hold a full-time job in addition to being responsible for his or her class work. This will probably reduce the amount of energy he or she can devote to studying, which will probably decrease the amount he or she learns. Similar factors include marital difficulties, professional difficulties, and a host of others. Given this tremendous array of probable influences, how realistic is it for us to consider the influence of one variable on an outcome such as school performance? As it turns out, it is still possible to look at the influence of one variable on another variable; but for a number of reasons (some of which are elaborated on in the remainder of this chapter), it is preferable to consider the operation of multiple predictor variables and assess their effect on some criterion measure.

Factorial Designs: Multiple Independent or Predictor Variables

If researchers wish to consider more than one independent or predictor variable in a study, they become involved in *factorial designs*, in which two, three, or more independent or predictor variables are considered simultaneously. As suggested earlier, this type of design is a better approximation of real-world conditions. Researchers recognize that, in any given instance, a behavior can be influenced by many factors; consequently, experiments are designed to look at the operation of more than one independent or predictor variable at one point in time. Factorial designs, then, use more than one independent or predictor variable, or factor.

The first rule to be observed in factorial studies is that all levels of each independent or predictor variable be combined with all levels of the other independent or predictor variables in the study. The simplest type of factorial study is called a 2 × 2 factorial design. (This is read "2-by-2 factorial design.") The first 2 indicates that there are two levels of the first independent or predictor variable; the second 2 indicates that there are also two levels of the second one. A somewhat more complex study is a 2 × 2 × 2 factorial study. In this case, there are three independent or predictor variables, each with two levels. We could use this latter design to study the example discussed earlier about the effects of motivation, intelligence, and background on performance in school. This represents a correlational study, but remember that experimental studies can also use factorial designs.

Suppose we selected a group of students who were above average in intelligence and another group of students who were below average in intelligence. Intelligence would be the first factor, and the two levels could be described as above average and below average. The second factor, motivation, might be assessed by asking students to respond to a question such as, "I have a strong desire to take this course." Subjects who indicated a high degree of motivation could be considered highly motivated, whereas those indicating a low amount of motivation would be considered poorly motivated. The second factor, then, is motivation, and the two levels are high and low motivation. The third variable, or factor, might be background, or preparation. Suppose we were interested in a course in engineering, and we believed subjects who knew calculus would perform better in the class than those who did not know calculus. We could simply ask subjects whether they had taken a calculus course. Subjects who said they had taken a calculus course could be considered part of the well-prepared group of subjects, and those who said they had not taken such a course would be considered part of the ill-prepared group. Now we can look at the influence of three factors on a criterion measure—the amount of knowledge gained in a particular engineering course.

Before proceeding any further, we should consider the following question: "Have we randomly assigned subjects to the various conditions for these variables?" The answer is obviously no; we have chosen subjects according to three subject variables. Remember the warnings given regarding the use of subject variables rather than true experimental variables (that is, variables for which groups have been formed by random assignment). Those warnings related to the simple univariate observational studies described in chapter 3, but the same warnings apply to factorial studies.

A researcher can also look at more than two levels of a predictor variable in factorial studies. The previous example described a 2 × 2 × 2 factorial design in which the first variable was intelligence, the second variable was motivation, and the third variable was background. We can increase the number of levels of those subject variables in the following manner. Suppose we form our intelligence groups according to IQ scores. One group has IQ scores of 120 and higher, the second has scores between 119 and 100, the third has scores between 99 and 80, and the fourth has scores less than 80. In this case, intelligence still is the first predictor variable; but instead of having two levels, it now has four. Similarly, suppose that for preparation or background, we ask subjects to tell us the number of calculus courses they have taken. We then might have some subjects saying two, some saying one, and some indicating they have taken no calculus courses. Our study now has been changed from a 2 × 2 × 2 factorial study to a 4 × 2 × 3 factorial study. Our first predictor variable (intelligence) is now broken into four categories; and our third predictor variable (previous experience with calculus courses) now includes three levels rather than two.

Interpreting the Results of Factorial Studies

Suppose we decide to look only at the effects of intelligence and motivation on the grades students receive in a particular course. If we consider two levels of the variable motivation (high motivation and low motivation) and two levels of the variable intelligence (above-average intelligence and below-average intelligence), we have a 2 × 2 factorial study. Our criterion variable is the amount of material learned in the course. This is obviously the simplest of all factorial studies.

As with a univariate study, our aim is to find out whether the groups formed according to levels of the predictor variable are different from one another on the criterion variable. With our 2 × 2 factorial study, this can be done twice, once for each of the subject variables of motivation and intelligence. The results of these comparisons are known as *main effects*. A researcher obtains one main effect for each of the predictor variables in the study. Again, the interpretation of main effects is identical to the interpretation of differences in means between groups in univariate studies. At this point, we have conducted one study and have seen the effects of two predictor variables on a particular criterion variable. You can see that by employing this factorial design we can double the amount of information we obtain while still conducting only one study.

In addition to this multiplication of information, researchers also obtain a new kind of information from factorial studies. This new type of information is known as an *interaction effect*—the effect of the predictor variables in combination with one another. This effect is different from the main effects, which consider each of the predictor variables in isolation from the others. Consequently, we obtain three pieces of information from a 2 × 2 factorial study: two main effects and one interaction effect.

Table 5–1 presents some results of a hypothetical study of the relationship of intelligence and motivation to classroom performance. The numbers in the table refer to mean final exam scores for subjects in each of four groups—above-average intelligence with high motivation, below-average intelligence with low motivation, above-average intelligence with low motivation, and below-average intelligence with high motivation. As seen in the table, the main effect for motivation is obtained by comparing the column mean for the high-motivation

69

Table 5–1   Results of a Hypothetical 2 × 2 Factorial Study

	High motivation	Low motivation	Mean of each row Main effect for intelligence
Above-average intelligence	94	82	88
Below-average intelligence	82	70	76
Mean of each column Main effect for motivation	88	76	

group with the column mean for the low-motivation group. You can see that there is a twelve-point difference in these means. The appropriate statistical comparisons probably would find this difference to be statistically significant.

A comparison of the means of the two rows of scores yields the main effect for intelligence. You can see that the mean for people with above-average intelligence is 88; and for people with below-average intelligence, the mean is 76. As with motivation, we would suspect that a difference this large would be significant.

To assess whether an interaction effect has occurred involves the use of statistical procedures beyond the scope of this text. However, for our purposes, a graph can help in this determination. We can assume an interaction effect has occurred if the results of the study are graphed and the lines on the graph are not parallel. Figure 5–1 presents the results displayed in Table 5–1. (The box entitled "Graphing Interactions" explains how Figure 5–1 was constructed.) A glance at the figure reveals that the lines are parallel. Therefore, we can assume that there is no interaction effect in the present study. Our conclusion would be as follows: In relation to classroom grades, the main effect for motivation is that more highly motivated students perform better than poorly motivated students; and the main effect for intelligence is that more intelligent people perform better than less intelligent people. However, these two variables produce no interaction effect on the criterion variable.

To examine how variables can produce an interaction effect, let

Graphing Interactions

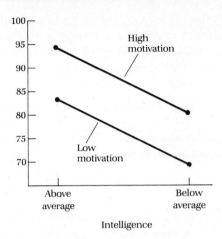

Figure 5-1 Graph of Results Shown in Table 5-1

Before proceeding any further, let us examine how to graph results to help us find out whether an interaction has occurred. (Graphing will be covered in more detail in chapter 6.) The first step is to label the y-axis (the vertical line) with the scale of the criterion measure. As you can see in Figure 5-1, our scale ranges from 70 to 100. The only rule to be observed here is that the numbers on the scale should include every value obtained in the table of data. The next step is to choose one of the predictor variables (in this case, subject variables) and label the x-axis (the horizontal line) with the levels of that predictor variable. For our results, intelligence was chosen to be the variable on the x-axis. Had motivation been chosen, it would have made absolutely no difference in our conclusions.

The next step is to take the scores for one level of the other predictor variable (in this case, motivation) and place those values above the appropriate levels of the other predictor variable (the one on the x-axis). In considering the high-motivation scores, we note that the mean score for students with above-

(continued)

average intelligence and high motivation is 94. At the level of 94 on the y-axis, we place a dot over the above-average mark on the x-axis. Similarly, above the below-average mark on the x-axis, we place a dot at the value of 82, the mean of students with below-average intelligence and high motivation. We then connect these two dots and label the resulting line "high motivation," because it represents the high-motivation scores at both levels of the other predictor variable, intelligence.

In a similar manner, we will now consider the low-motivation condition and note that students with above-average intelligence and low motivation obtain an average score of 82; we place another dot over the above-average mark on the x-axis, at a value of 82. Above the below-average mark on the x-axis, we place a dot at a value of 70. This is the mean for students below average in intelligence and low in motivation. We connect these two dots and label the line "low motivation." We now have the graph presented in Figure 5−1. Again, inspection of that figure reveals that the predictor variables have no interaction effect, because the lines are parallel.

us consider another study. Figure 5−2 presents a display of the results obtained by Aronson, Willerman, and Floyd in a study conducted in 1966. In this study, subjects listened to tape-recorded interviews of people whose answers made them seem either average or superior in ability. At the end of some of the interviews, subjects heard crashing and then heard the interviewees say they had spilled coffee on themselves. Researchers wanted to find out if subjects would respond differently to a blunder (spilling coffee) by a superior person than to a blunder by an average person. The dependent variable, then, is the amount of liking subjects expressed for interviewees.

There are two independent variables in the study. The first is whether the person is described as superior or average. For this variable, there are two levels. The second independent variable is whether or not the person commits a blunder. This second independent variable also has two levels. Therefore, in looking at this study, we are considering a 2 × 2 factorial design that involves two true independent variables. Subjects were randomly assigned to respond to one of the four possible combinations of the independent variables. As mentioned, Figure 5−2 displays the results obtained by Aronson and his colleagues. As we can see from the graph, the lines

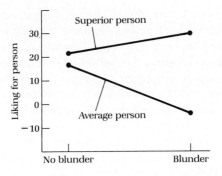

Source: Aronson, Willerman, and Floyd (1966), p. 228.

Figure 5–2   Interaction Between Committing a Blunder and Type of Person

that depict the possible interaction effect are not parallel. Statistical analyses of the data demonstrated that there was an interaction effect. In fact, subjects did tend to respond differently to superior people who committed a blunder than to average people who committed a blunder. When an average person committed a blunder, it tended to decrease subjects' liking for that person. However, if the person was perceived as superior, then the effect of a blunder was to modestly increase the liking subjects expressed for that person.

Let us look at the main effects of the independent variables. The main effect for whether or not there was a blunder was not significant. You can see this by comparing the average score of the two dots immediately above the no-blunder condition with the average score of the two dots above the blunder condition. These average scores on the dependent measure are very close to one another. As to whether the person was described as superior or average, we see a great difference in the mean scores for these levels. Finding the main effect for the type of person involves comparing the average of the two dots joined by the line labeled "superior person" with the average of the two dots joined by the line labeled "average person." The difference is very large (approximately eighteen points on the dependent measure), and statistical analyses demonstrate a significant effect for this variable. Therefore, our conclusions in this case are the following: (1) Whether a person has blundered or not has no significant effect on overall ratings of liking. (2) Overall, superior persons are rated as being more likable than average persons. (3) There is an interaction effect that can be described as the combined influence of type of person and blunder on liking. In other words, while the study found no dif-

73

ference for a blunder when viewed across the full range of subjects, closer inspection revealed that blunders did have an impact, and that the impact traveled in more than one direction. The direction of the impact depended on whether the person who committed the blunder was seen as average or superior.

What we can learn from this study is that by considering interaction effects, we can obtain information impossible to obtain by conducting separate univariate studies. Further, when interaction effects exist, and researchers are unaware of them, the straightforward interpretation of main effects is misleading. However, since the researchers are unaware of the interaction, they cannot detect their error in inference.

Mixed Designs

One final point should be made about factorial designs. In the first example, which considered the effects of intelligence and motivation on class grades, we used observational (subject) variables—not true experimental variables—as predictor variables. In the second example, which considered the effect of a blunder and of type of person on liking, both independent variables were manipulated. Consequently, there we were dealing with a true experimental study. It is possible to conduct factorial studies that use a mixture of true experimental and observational variables. These are called *mixed designs*.

When dealing with mixed designs, the major point to be remembered is that the interpretation of the main effects should follow all the traditional rules of thumb discussed in chapter 3. Remember that the interpretation of the meaning of a researcher's findings is based on whether the independent variable has been truly manipulated by the researcher (and therefore is a true experimental variable) or whether it is a subject variable. The effects of subject variables on dependent variables cannot be interpreted as causal, because of the existence of rival or competing hypotheses, as discussed earlier. When using mixed factorial designs, researchers can properly infer cause-and-effect relationships between experimental independent variables and dependent variables, but not between correlational predictor variables and criterion variables. Further, interaction effects in mixed designs should always be interpreted as if they were observational in nature, rather than truly experimental.

We considered research designs dealing with one independent variable and one dependent variable much earlier in this book. So far, this chapter has discussed the effect of multiple independent or predictor variables on a single dependent or criterion variable. The next section will describe studies in which multiple dependent variables are used. These studies can have either single or multiple experimental or observational predictor variables. Studies of this sort are becoming more and more popular in the social sciences because of researchers' increasing awareness that any cause probably has multiple effects.

Multivariate Techniques

When researchers speak of multivariate techniques they typically refer to studies that employ multiple dependent variables. An example of this sort of study might involve a researcher interested in estimating the impact of sleeping pills on individuals. Let us consider the independent variable in this study to be the number of sleeping pills taken. We will employ four levels of that independent variable in our hypothetical study. The three treatment levels will involve subjects' taking one, two, or four sleeping pills a night. The control condition will involve subjects' taking no sleeping pills.

Obviously, one dependent variable for this study will involve the effectiveness of the pills (the amount of time required to fall asleep after taking some). However, we know that sleeping pills have many side effects, some of which are very undesirable. Therefore, as a second dependent variable, we will consider the amount of time it takes subjects to get ready for work the morning after taking sleeping pills. To measure this variable, we can record the number of minutes between the alarm clock's ringing in the morning and the subject's walking out the door. This measure is meant to give us an index of any carry-over drowsiness related to taking a larger number of sleeping pills. This side effect should be viewed as a liability of taking the pills; it is a variable people should consider before making a decision to take the medication. Finally, a second, related detrimental side effect might be attitude changes on the part of subjects. Consequently, we will consider a measure of depression as the third dependent variable in this study.

In our study, then, we have one independent variable, number of sleeping pills taken per night; and there are four levels of that independent variable. The first level is the control condition; here, subjects take no real sleeping pills but perhaps an inert pill (a placebo). The second level is one sleeping pill; the third level is two sleeping pills; and the fourth level is four sleeping pills a night. The multiple dependent measures are the time required to fall asleep, the time required to get ready for work the following morning (a negative outcome), and the amount of depression experienced (another negative outcome). To conduct this study, we would recruit a sample of insomniacs and then randomly assign these people to one of the four levels of the independent variable.

Figure 5−3 presents a set of hypothetical results for our study. You can see that taking any amount of sleeping pills enables individuals to get to sleep much more quickly. However, the differences among the means of the groups that took one, two, and four pills are very, very small. Consequently, taking two or four pills does not save much time in getting to sleep. Inspection of the second dependent variable (the time required to get ready for work the following morning) reveals that the placebo and the one-pill condition are about the same, whereas the two-pill condition adds a total of about fifteen minutes to the time required. In the four-pill condition, subjects do much more poorly on this measure. The average person requires almost fifty minutes more to get ready for work than individuals in the placebo or one-pill condition. Similarly, looking at the results for depression, you can see that the placebo, the one-pill, and the two-pill groups all seem about equal on level of depression, whereas the four-pill group shows a considerably greater amount.

In summary, it appears that subjects who are insomniacs can get to sleep much more quickly by taking pills; but they can get to sleep almost as quickly by taking one pill as by taking more than one. In addition, it appears taking one pill has no detrimental effects on the amount of time it takes subjects to get ready for work the following morning, and there is no evidence that level of depression is increased by taking one pill. Taking two pills is very similar in effect to taking one pill, with the exception that the two-pill group required more time to get ready for work in the morning. In addition, the amount of increase in time required to get ready for work is sizably larger than the amount of time saved by falling asleep faster when two pills are used instead of one pill. Finally, taking four pills is obviously not a good idea. The amount of time saved in going to sleep after taking four pills instead of one or two is extremely small. In addition, the side effects are clearly detrimental for this group. Consequently, taking more than two sleeping pills would not be advised based on the results of this study.

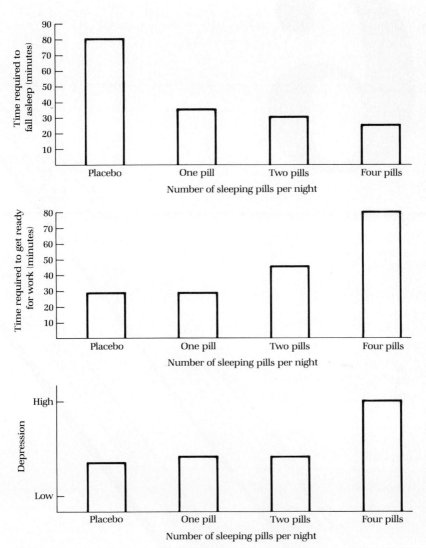

Figure 5-3 Results of Hypothetical Study Using Multivariate Techniques

Additional Readings

Keppel, G. *Design and analysis: A researcher's handbook* (2nd ed.). Englewood Cliffs, N.J.: Prentice-Hall, 1982.

Kirk, R. *Experimental design* (2nd ed.). Belmont, Calif.: Brooks-Cole, 1982.

Displaying Data: Figures, Tables, and Graphs

Chapter Preview

A number of ways to summarize, group, and display quantities of data are explained in chapter 6. The chapter starts by describing how to present a group of scores on one dimension. Ways to graphically characterize relationships between two or more variables are then characterized. Finally, locating the position of an individual score within a group of scores is discussed.

Presenting Frequency Data

You may recall that chapter 2 described various scaling methods. One such method used a nominal scale. Collecting nominal data simply involves noting differences; no assumptions are made regarding the meaning of those differences. That is, the differences are not quantitative in nature. Examples of nominal data include people's sex, their college major, the days of the week, the various religions, and so on. The most common method for presenting such data employs the frequency table.

Suppose we asked subjects the question, "What television show do you watch most often?" Since the question involves only listing the answers, the results could be presented in a frequency table, which simply would note the frequency with which each program was mentioned. Table 6–1 presents the fictitious results of such an analysis. The table, called a one-way frequency table, is the simplest way to

Table 6–1 One-Way Frequency Table

Program	Score
M.A.S.H.	25
Little House on the Prairie	21
Muppet Show	20
Mork & Mindy	17
Vegas	17
WKRP in Cincinnati	15
Monday Night Football	14
Soap	13
Monday Night Baseball	9
Wide World of Sports	5

Table 6–2 2 × 2 Matrix Frequency Table

Type of television program watched

Frequency of engaging in sports

	Once a week or more	Less than once a week
Sporting events	21	7
Other shows	20	81

present data. A slightly more complex method for presenting data is a frequency table that deals simultaneously with two factors. An example is Table 6—2, a 2 × 2 matrix frequency table. This example includes data that measure relationships between variables we think may be meaningfully related.

Let us look more closely at Tables 6—1 and 6—2 in relation to the needs of an advertiser of sporting goods. If advertisers have reason to suspect that people who engage in weekly athletic activities are much more likely to buy sporting goods than those who do not, then they might be interested not only in how many people watch sporting events versus other shows but also in how frequently these people engage in sporting activities. Thus, in addition to asking which television shows subjects watched, a researcher investigating these questions would also ask subjects whether they engaged in sports as part of a normal week's activities. The 2 × 2 matrix presented in Table 6—2 presents data that might result from this researcher's efforts. You can see that using these data would lead advertisers to very different conclusions regarding where advertising money might be most profitably invested than using the data in Table 6—1. Table 6—1 indicates that more people would be reached by advertisements in other shows than by advertisements in sporting events. However, Table 6—2 suggests that by advertising in three low-rated sporting events, advertisers could reach as many individuals who engage in sports weekly as they could if they spent the additional money to advertise in seven highly rated nonsport shows, whose popularity probably makes their advertising time expensive. Advertisers might look at these data and decide that their dollars could be more wisely spent by advertising only in the sporting events.

Again, this decision to focus on advertising during sporting events is only appropriate insofar as the assumption is correct that people who engage in weekly sports activities do indeed buy more sporting goods than people who engage in sports less frequently. However, we can see that by linking these two logically related variables, advertisers obtained a different picture than by simply looking at one variable in isolation. Frequency tables of this type also can often help researchers in making practical decisions.

Of course, frequency tables can be expanded so that the number of categories per variable is increased. If we wanted to look at a third type of television program (such as news events), we could simply add another category to change from a 2 × 2 matrix to a 3 × 2 matrix.

81

Similarly, if we wished to know *what* sports people engaged in, rather than simply how often they engaged in sports, we could construct our matrix to include many types of sporting activities. The resulting matrix might include preferences for viewing sporting events, news events, or other shows as well as preferences for engaging in water sports, indoor court sports, outdoor non-water sports, or other sports (a final catch-all category). This is a 3 × 4 matrix (three types of television shows, four types of sports). Finally, we can look at more than two variables in frequency tables. For example, the simple 2 × 2 matrix can be converted to a 2 × 2 × 2 matrix simply by the addition of a third variable, such as the sex of the responding person. Therefore, our 2 × 2 × 2 frequency table could include two choices each for type of television show, involvement in sports, and sex of responder.

There are several points to be kept in mind when assigning nominal data to frequency tables. The first is that the categories should be exhaustive. That is, each observation or data point must fit into only one category, and the categories should account for all the observations. A second important rule is that categories should be mutually exclusive and independent. This means not only that every observation must be assigned to one category and only one category but also that assigning an observation to a category must in no way influence the assignment of any other observation to a category. Frequency tables are preferable to lists of data because they can convey information more efficiently.

Ordered Lists

When a researcher is dealing with ordinal data (data that can be rank-ordered in some nonarbitrary fashion), it sometimes becomes more meaningful to order the data and to present an ordered list of the results. Table 6 — 3 presents such a list of students' scores on a test from a research methodology course. Scores are ordered from highest to lowest and are based on a possible point total of 150. The major advantage of the ordered list method of presentation is that it allows the user to calculate the range of scores quickly. In this case, the highest score is 130 and the lowest is 54, yielding a range of 76. Further, if there are unusual gaps in the data, they can often be detected by a glance at an ordered list.

A slightly more sophisticated method of presentation is the frequency distribution. The frequency distribution shows the number of

Table 6-3   Ordered List of Test Scores

130	108	100	92	80
125	108	100	91	72
124	107	99	91	71
115	107	99	89	67
115	106	98	87	66
114	105	97	85	64
113	103	96	85	60
111	101	96	84	54
109	100	93	83	

cases falling within each class interval, or given range of scores. We can summarize the frequency distribution of the scores in the research methods class in the following manner. First, we look at the entire range of scores; in this case, the range is 76. We can choose to group scores into any desired interval size. For example, we could group the data into seven intervals, each with a size of eleven units. Seven eleven-unit intervals can encompass a range of seventy-seven scores; and since we have a range of seventy-six scores, our study will fit nicely into this configuration. Similarly, we might have chosen to have eleven intervals, each seven units in length. The choice of the size of a class interval is somewhat arbitrary and depends on the organization that seems most helpful to the researcher and the reader of the study.

Since the highest score in Table 6-3 is 130, we will make the first interval encompass scores of 120 to 130, which involves eleven scale points. Moving eleven units down the scale from 120 places us at a score of 109; therefore, from 109 to 119 will constitute the second class interval. The third class interval extends from 98 to 108, and so forth. The class intervals are listed in Table 6-4. If we had chosen to construct class intervals of seven points, the first class interval would have extended from 124 to 130; the second would have extended from 117 to 123; and so forth.

After having determined which scores will be included in particular intervals, the next step is to proceed down the ordered list and count the number of scores that fall in each interval. Looking at the figures in Table 6-3, and employing seven intervals of eleven units each, we note that three scores (130, 125, 124) fall in the first class interval, which extends from 120 to 130. In the column in Table 6-4 labeled "Frequency," we see this fact recorded. Proceeding down the list, you can see that six scores (115, 115, 114, 113, 111, and 109) fall in the second interval, and so forth.

Table 6-4   Class Intervals, Score Frequencies, and Class Interval Midpoints

Class interval	Frequency	Class interval midpoint
120-130	3	125
109-119	6	114
98-108	14	103
87-97	9	92
76-86	5	81
65-75	4	70
54-64	3	59

Graphical Presentation of Data

Graphs are usually two-dimensional representations or pictures of data. The basic frame on which a graph is based consists of a horizontal line, called the x-axis, and a vertical line, called the y-axis. Graphs are used to describe distributions in several ways.

Histograms and Frequency Polygons

One type of graphical presentation of a collection of data is called a *histogram*. A histogram is one of the easiest ways to present a distribution of data graphically. The x-axis represents the midpoints of the class intervals obtained earlier from the frequency distributions. It will become evident later that the midpoint of the interval is important here, as we are searching for the x value that best represents that interval. Points on the y-axis correspond to the number of subjects in each of these intervals.

To illustrate, we can construct a histogram for the data in Table 6-4 in the following manner. The first task is to determine the midpoint of each class interval. Our first class interval ranges from 120 to 130; its midpoint is 125. We could obtain this value in several ways. The most straightforward involves listing in order the numbers from 120 to 130 and determining which of these numbers is exactly in the middle. Since our class interval consists of eleven units, the sixth unit represents the midpoint. Therefore, the value of 125 is the middle of the interval. If an interval has an even number of elements (such as ten), the midpoint is halfway between the middle two scores. If our

84

first class interval had ranged from 121 to 130, it would have contained ten interval points, and the midpoint would have fallen halfway between the fifth and sixth scores. In this example, the fifth score would have been 125 and the sixth score would have been 126, so the midpoint would have been 125.5. You can see that midpoints can be scores no particular individual could have obtained, since there is no way of obtaining a half-unit in the test-scoring procedure represented in Table 6−4.

Once the midpoint for each class interval has been determined, as shown in the last column in Table 6−4, the next step is to mark the x-axis of the graph with these midpoints. The typical procedure is to put the smallest class midpoint closest to the y-axis and to make the intervals equidistant from one another, as shown in Figure 6−1. As seen in Table 6−4, the smallest class interval midpoint is 59; so that value is placed at the point on the x-axis closest to the y-axis. The second midpoint is 70, which is placed next closest to the y-axis. This procedure is followed until all midpoints have been placed on the x-axis. The y-axis represents the frequency of subjects scoring in a particular class interval. You will note that in Figure 6−1, the y-axis is marked with units ranging from 0, the minimum possible frequency (or a category wherein there were no members), up to 14, the highest frequency listed in Table 6−4. The next step involves taking the frequency for each class interval and placing a point or mark directly above the midpoint for the class interval at the frequency obtained for that interval. Therefore, over the value of 59, we place a point at 3 units; and over the value of 70, we place a point at 4 units. After completing this procedure, we have a point at the appropriate frequency for each class interval midpoint.

The next step is to determine the actual limits of the class intervals. The apparent limits for the lowest interval are 54 and 64; a score of 64 would be classified in the lowest interval, while a score of 65 would be classified in the next higher interval. That means the real upper limit for the lowest class interval is halfway between these two points, at a score of 64.5. Using the same logic, we note that 75.5 is the real limit between the interval that extends from 65 to 75 and the interval that extends from 76 to 86. By subtracting 64.5 from 75.5, we find that the class interval widths still are eleven units, which conforms to our previous determination regarding the number of elements in an interval. We can obtain the upper and lower real limits for each class interval in the same way. Note that in order for the class interval from 54 to 64 to contain eleven elements, the lower real limit

85

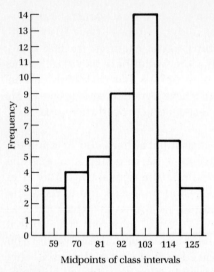

Figure 6–1 Histogram of Test Scores from Table 6–4

of that interval must be 53.5. Similarly, the upper real limit of the interval that encompasses 120 to 130 is 130.5.

Now we can complete the histogram by drawing a horizontal line extending from the lower real limit of a class interval to the upper real limit of the interval at a height on the y-axis that corresponds to the frequency of that interval. For example, a horizontal line is drawn from an x value of 53.5 to an x value of 64.5 at the height that corresponds to a frequency of 3. Similarly, a horizontal line is drawn from an x value of 64.5 to an x value of 75.5 at a frequency value of 4, and so forth. All that remains is to drop vertical lines from the upper and lower real limits for each interval to the x-axis, and the resulting bar graph will resemble that shown in Figure 6–1.

A second type of pictorial representation of a distribution is the *frequency polygon*. A frequency polygon is similar to a histogram in that the x- and y-axis are labeled in the same manner. The frequency value of each class interval is plotted immediately above the midpoint of the interval by means of a dot, and then these dots are connected to form a line graph, as shown in Figure 6–2.

Plotting Bivariate Distributions

Undoubtedly the most common form of pictorial presentation of data involves graphing the relationship between two variables by let-

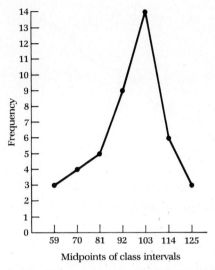

Figure 6-2 Frequency Polygon of Test Scores from Table 6-4

ting the scale points represent various levels or quantities of each variable. The resulting graph demonstrates the relationship between these two variables. In graphs of this sort, the most frequently employed descriptive statistic is the mean.

Figure 6-3 presents a very simple graph that relates height to weight in a typical college class. The height of individuals (measured in inches) is presented on the x-axis, whereas the average weight of the subjects of each particular height is presented on the y-axis. The averages for each weight are connected sequentially by a straight line. Graphs of this sort are frequently employed in the social sciences.

Figure 6-4 demonstrates that a graph can depict more than one relationship. In this case, the relationship between height and weight is presented for both males and females in a hypothetical college class.

This section has demonstrated that histograms and frequency polygons can graphically present data along one attribute, or dimension. They are the graphic counterparts of the ordered list. The section then described a second type of graphic presentation that allows researchers to demonstrate pictorially how two variables are related to one another. This latter situation, in which two variables change in concert with one another, is called *covariation* between the variables. Chapter 2 introduced the correlation coefficient as a measure of relia-

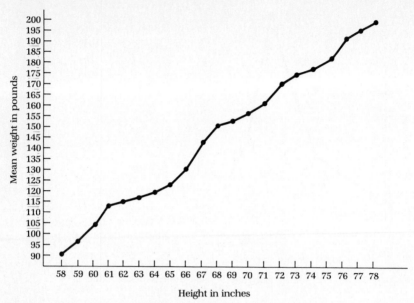

Figure 6–3   Graph of Height and Weight for All Subjects

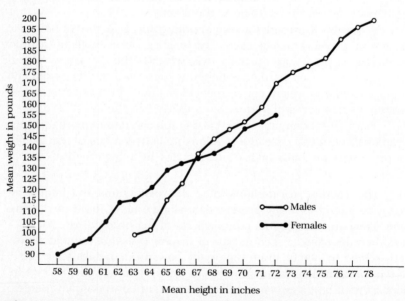

Figure 6–4   Graph of Height and Weight for Each Sex

bility. The correlation coefficient can also be used to express the covariation between two variables. Remember that correlation coefficients can have a maximum value of +1.0 and that a .00 correlation coefficient indicates that no relationship exists.

Scatter Plots

Correlation coefficients can be displayed pictorially by means of scatter plots. Scatter plots are graphs on which the two scores *a particular subject* obtains on two variables are used to locate a position on the graph for that subject. For example, if we thought two variables, such as a person's income and the amount of money he or she spent each year on luxury items, were covariants, we might obtain an impression of whether or not our hunch was correct by constructing a scatter diagram of the relationship between the two variables. We would do that by selecting one variable to be on the x-axis and placing the smallest obtainable x value closest to the y-axis, with larger x values placed progressively farther to the right. In this example, we will place the value for amount of money spent on luxuries on the y-axis, with the lowest value as close to the x-axis as possible. The place where the x-axis and y-axis cross is called the *origin* of the graph. It is possible for a subject to have no income and to spend no money on luxuries, and such a person would be positioned at the origin. Once an individual's position has been located on the graph, we typically represent that subject with a dot or a small x.

Figure 6−5 presents a scatter diagram of the relationship between income and amount of money spent on luxuries for a sample of subjects. You can see that there is a positive relationship between these two variables: that is, people who earn more money tend to spend more money on luxuries. There are several formulae to compute the exact values of the correlations. They will be presented and explained in chapters 11 and 12. For now, it is only important that you be able to distinguish among graphs that show positive relationships, negative relationships, and no relationship among variables.

Negative relationships are those in which higher scores on one variable are associated with lower scores on the other. Figure 6−6 presents a graph based on the speeds of students who participated in several races in a track meet. A runner's speed in a race (in meters per second) is compared with the length of the event. You can see that as the length of the race increased, the average speed of the runners decreased, signifying a negative relationship.

89

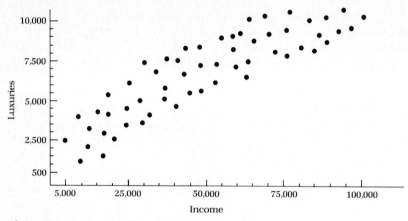

Figure 6–5 Scatter Plot of Relationship of Income to Amount of Money Spent on Luxuries

Figure 6–7 presents a few scatter diagrams with the correlation coefficient (r) for each plot included at the top of the graph (for example, $r = .00$). You will note that positive correlations are associated with distributions that extend from the lower left-hand corner of the graph to the upper right-hand corner. Negative correlations tend to go from the upper left-hand corner of the graph to the lower right-hand corner. When there is no correlation, no discernable pattern is evident.

Measures of Individual Position

The last topic in this chapter uses the information presented about graphing to present measures of central tendency and measures of variability. The purpose of this section is to determine ways in which we can assess the position of an individual score or subject within a distribution of a group of scores or subjects.

We will start with the simplest measure, *uniqueness*. Uniqueness is typically considered when the scale of measurement employed is nominal. To say that a person is the only Republican in a room says something about his or her uniqueness. By the same token, to say that a woman is one of the hundred most outstanding woman business leaders in the country gives information regarding her position relative to other comparable individuals.

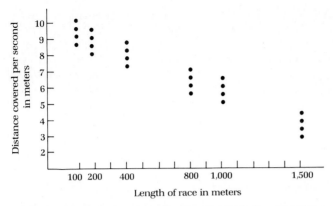

Figure 6–6 Scatter Plot of a Negative Relationship Between Runners' Speed and the Length of a Race

If we are using an ordinal scale, we can go a step further in quantifying an individual's position by noting his or her rank with regard to the target dimension. If we know the businesswoman mentioned above is ranked as the third most successful businesswoman in the nation, we have more sophisticated knowledge than was provided by the measure of uniqueness, which only told us that she was in the top hundred. Obviously, rank values are superior to measures of uniqueness, since they convey more precise information. However, it is equally obvious that the meaning of a rank value depends on the number of individuals in the distribution of interest. For example, suppose our businesswoman was ranked hundredth among businesswomen. That would mean something very different if there were only a hundred businesswomen in the nation than if there were 100,000 businesswomen. Thus, the rank alone may not give us all the information we need.

A more appropriate index than rank alone is percentile rank. Percentile rank provides researchers with even more information about the relative position of an individual within the distribution. The percentile rank provides an index of the position of a score in terms of the percentage of smaller scores in the sample. To compute the percentile rank, simply divide the rank of the subject by the number of people in the distribution. For example, a woman ranked thirtieth in a distribution that included a hundred women would have a percentile rank of 30 (30 ÷ 100). On the other hand, a woman ranked thirtieth in a distribution made up of 10,000 women would

91

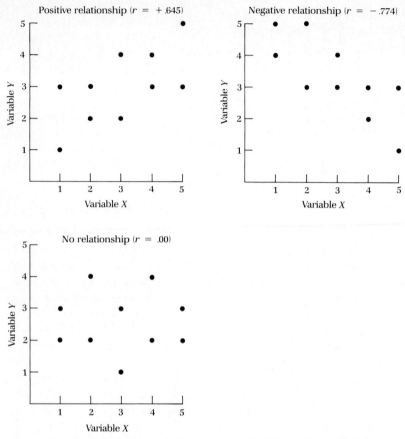

Figure 6– 7   Scatter Plots of Types of Relationships Between Variables

have a percentile rank of 0.03. That is, only 0.03 percent of the population of interest would have achieved a higher rank than this woman.
(By higher in this case, we mean a small-numbered rank such as 1, 2,
or 3.) You can see that percentile rank is an extremely precise index of
an individual's position in a distribution.

   A final measure of individual position used in the social sciences
is the standard score. The standard score is defined in terms of the
mean and standard deviation of the distribution of interest. The most
common type of standard score is called the Z score. Z scores are
computed by use of the following formula:

92

$$Z = \frac{X - \overline{X}}{\text{s.d.}}$$

In this formula, X is the individual score whose position in the distribution we are attempting to assess; $\overline{X}$ is the mean of the distribution of interest; and s.d. is the standard deviation of that distribution (you'll remember the formula for the standard deviation was given in chapter 2). We can compute the Z score for a given value if we know the mean and standard deviation of the distribution to which that score belongs. Consequently, we can compute the Z value for the height of a man if the average height of men in the distribution and the standard deviation of heights in that distribution are known.

Figure 6−8 presents the normal distribution (or normal curve), an assumed distribution of scores that is often employed in studies in the social sciences. The x-axis of the normal distribution represents Z scores, and the y-axis represents frequencies. The mean of the normal distribution is zero, and the standard deviation is equal to one Z-score unit.

As you can see by looking at Figure 6−8, the greatest number (highest frequency) of subjects should obtain the score that is the mean for the population. As we move substantially above or below the mean, we see fewer and fewer subjects obtaining the deviant score values represented by these points.

The normal distribution is a useful tool because it allows researchers to convert Z scores to percentile ranks. By inspecting Figure 6−8, you can see the percentile equivalent for each point on the x-axis of the normal curve. You will note that the percentile units are bunched around the mean of the distribution and that as you go further from the mean, the percentile ranks spread out considerably.

The other lines on the graph below the normal curve present some common tests that have been related to the normal distribution. For example, if you knew your score on the SAT test, you could convert that score to a Z score. This is because the graph reflects the mean and the standard deviation of SAT scores. Once your SAT score had been converted to a Z score, you could look up the corresponding percentile rank value. After doing this, you would know how your score ranked in the distribution of scores on the SAT. If, for example, your SAT score on the verbal subscale was 600, you would be at the eighty-fourth percentile. Employing a similar logic, if you scored 92 on the Stanford-Binet IQ test, you would be at the thirty-first percentile.

93

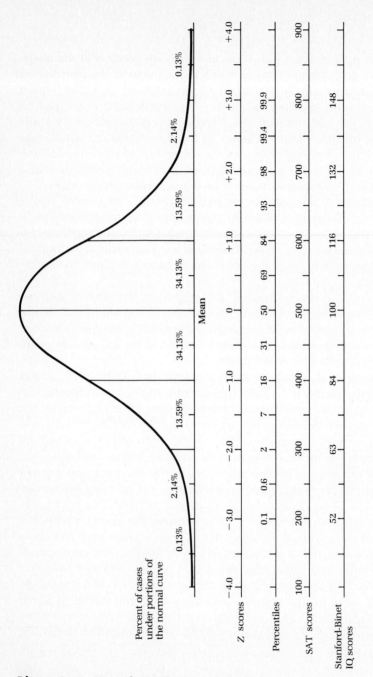

Figure 6–8 Normal Distribution or Curve

The box entitled "Interpreting a Score: Z-Score Exercise" will give you some practice in using the normal distribution.

Interpreting a Score: Z-Score Exercise

Fourth-grade students—10,000 males and 10,000 females—were given verbal and quantitative achievement tests. Let us assume that the scores on the verbal and quantitative tests are normally distributed, which will allow us to utilize Figure 6−8 to interpret the results. The means $(\overline{X})$ and standard deviations (s.d.) are as follows:

	Verbal	Quantitative
	Male $\overline{X}$ = 94	Male $\overline{X}$ = 110
	s.d. = 9	s.d = 8
	Female $\overline{X}$ = 103	Female $\overline{X}$ = 100
	s.d = 9	s.d = 9

Answer the following questions:

1. Suzie had a score of 112 on the vertbal test. How many girls did better than she? How many boys had a higher score than she?

2. What percentage of the boys scored 102 or better on the quantitative test?

3. What percentage of the boys scored between 85 and 103 on the verbal test?

4. What percentage of the boys scored between the mean of the girls and the mean of the boys on the verbal test?

5. A score of 118 on the quantitative test is at what percentile for boys? For girls?

6. If Sally Watkins had a score of 121 on the verbal test, what score would her twin brother Jim have to make on the verbal test to have the same percentile rank among boys as she has among girls? What is that percentile rank?

7. Two *scores* on the verbal test are so extreme (low and high) that a total of less than 5 percent (4.54 percent) of the boys fall above or below them. What are those scores?

Validity of Research Projects

Chapter Preview

Chapter 7 begins with a reminder that reliability is a prerequisite for validity in both individual measures and research projects. Forms of face validity, criterion validity, and construct validity of measures are then considered, and difficulties in assessing a measure's validity are elaborated on. The chapter explains how an investigation of the relationship among variables can be compromised by threats to the internal, external, construct, and statistical conclusion validity of an experiment. A great deal of attention is given to internal validity, while external and construct validity receive a moderate amount of attention.

In chapter 2, we considered two topics that apply to any measurement—reliability (or repeatability) and validity (or accuracy). In addition to considering the reliability and validity of a particular measure, we can consider the reliability and validity of an experiment. This chapter will briefly describe the concept of reliability, and then it will consider issues involved in validity. Reliability is a necessary, but not a sufficient, prerequisite for the validity of either a measure or an experiment. The issues involved with validity are much more complex and subtle than the issues involved in whether or not a measure or an experiment is reliable.

Reliability

We considered the reliability of a particular measure in chapter 2. We will now turn to a consideration of the reliability of a particular investigation. When scientists conduct a study, they assume that, if they repeat the study following the same procedures, employing the same types of research subjects, and analyzing the data in a similar manner, they will obtain results very similar to those obtained the first time the experiment was performed. This assumption—that research findings are repeatable—is referred to as the *replicability* of investigations. Whenever researchers repeat exactly an experiment that was conducted earlier, they are involved in performing a replication of the study. The results of experiments are said to be reliable if researchers are able to replicate the findings in subsequent studies.

While it is not uncommon for social scientists to fail to replicate a particular investigation, we would hope that, as a general rule, the results of studies could be replicated by other investigators performing similar tasks and employing similar procedures. To the extent that strict replications are unable to produce consistent results, researchers are forced to conclude that no sensible conclusions can be reached from these studies' findings.

It may be interesting to note that failure to replicate is not necessarily bad. Researchers often gain additional insight into their topics of investigation by considering minor changes in their studies— changes that can either aid or hinder efforts to replicate previous findings. Consequently, while researchers may hope to replicate the results of previous studies, failures to replicate can sometimes actually aid their understanding of the area under study. For example, a researcher might wonder if a particular form of psychotherapy produces greater change than drug therapy in the treatment of depression. If psychotherapy is in reality only slightly more effective than drug therapy, the researcher can expect to find instances in which psychotherapy is superior and others in which the two methods appear about equally effective. That happens because the slight difference between the two therapies is sometimes evident and sometimes not quite apparent. This failure to replicate signals a small effect size, not a research problem.

Up to this point, the effort to replicate has been described as an identical implementation of the procedures and methods employed in previous research. Later we will consider attempts to replicate called conceptual replications. A *conceptual replication* is an experiment that yields results similar to those from a previous experiment, but that differs from that experiment in its operational definitions of the variables involved, the characteristics of the subjects employed, or other supposedly irrelevant aspects of the study. Conceptual replications help researchers obtain a feeling for whether the findings of previous studies were due to the relationships among the variables involved or whether the findings might simply have resulted from seemingly irrelevant factors involved in the original study.

As a general summary of current research practice in the social sciences, it seems appropriate to note that there are far fewer replications of findings in the research literature than one would hope to find.

Validity

Validity of a Measure

Once again, the definition of validity involves accuracy. You might reasonably wonder, "Accuracy with respect to what?" The accuracy of a measure involves several types of validity. The first type to be considered here is *content validity*. Content validity is established by showing that test items are a representative sample of a larger group of items from which the experimenter could have selected. There are many ways of asking a particular question in a test item. An experimenter interested in measuring assertiveness might simply ask, "How assertive are you?" Alternatively, the researcher might ask, "Would you tell a person who cut in front of you to please go to the end of the line?" The researcher might also ask, "If you received a well-done steak in a restaurant when you had ordered a rare steak, would you ask the waiter to return it?" Each of these three questions seems to assess whether or not a person is assertive, but they do it in different ways. Each has content validity, because each represents what a researcher feels should be measured under the domain of assertiveness.

A type of validity similar to content validity is *face validity*. Face validity tells us whether a measure appears (on the face of it) to measure what it is supposed to measure. For example, if I were testing someone for a secretarial job, to test their typing, shorthand, and filing skills would be reasonable, since those are the tasks associated with secretarial positions. The test has face validity, because it looks as if it is measuring applicants' skills on dimensions thought to be relevent to the target job. This is the least sophisticated form of validity, and most psychologists are not satisfied if their measures have face validity alone.

Another type of validity is called *criterion validity*. There are two types of criterion validity; concurrent validity and predictive validity. *Concurrent validity* is studied when one test is proposed as a substitute for another. For example, if a psychologist is interested in obtaining a shorter, easier-to-adminster intelligence test to use in place of the Stanford-Binet intelligence test, he or she might select a subset of the items on the Stanford-Binet and administer both this new short form and the original long form to a group of subjects. To the extent that the set of scores from the short form is roughly the same as those from the long form, the short form is said to have concurrent validity. Further, the researcher has some reason to believe that the short form serves as an adequate replacement.

The second type of criterion validity is *predictive validity*. Predictive validity involves determining the value of a test by using it to predict performance in some future event. For example, we could determine the predictive validity of the Scholastic Aptitude Test (SAT) of college ability by finding out whether subjects who score higher on the SAT perform better in college than subjects who score lower. To the extent that those relationships are observed between present behavior (the SAT scores) and future behavior (performance in college) we conclude that the SAT possesses predictive validity.

100

The last type of validity of a measure to be considered here is *construct validity*. Whenever a test is to be interpreted as a measure of some attribute or quality, the problem faced by the investigator involves the issue of construct validity. You may wish to refer to the box in chapter 1 entitled "Methods of Knowing" and note that a test takes place on the level called "observations" and the attribute or quality to be measured exists on the level called "generalizations." Construct validity has to do with how well the operational definition used at the "observations" level reflects the attribute or quality at the theoretical, "generalizations" level. For example, an investigator interested in how accurately the Stanford-Binet intelligence test measures the theoretical construct "intelligence" is concerned with the construct validity of the test.

Let us take a moment to consider how construct validity differs from the types of validity already discussed. Content validity simply involves defining what type of questions are appropriate. To have face validity, the test need only look as if it is appropriate. Criterion validity involves defining the measure of performance that represents an appropriate measure to be used to assess the validity of a given test. Here, we know that if a measure agrees with some other measure, it has concurrent validity; if it allows us to predict some future event, it has predictive validity. With construct validity, the problem is somewhat more complex.

Many constructs in the social sciences are impossible to specify with any one measurement technique (the criterion validity approach). Similarly, it is often impossible to exhaustively delineate the content of certain theoretical entities (the content validity approach). Cronbach (1971) notes that construct validity is assessed by a procedure wherein no one measure can be identified as an adequate criterion for construct validation efforts. Therefore, multiple measures of a particular construct are often needed to determine if a new test indeed possesses construct validity. One must think of construct validity within the theoretical scheme an experimenter is considering. From this perspective, one might define the construct validity of a test as "the extent to which performance on a test fits into a theoretical scheme about the attribute the test tries to measure" (Gleitman, 1981, p. 107). You can see that construct validity is more difficult to define clearly than the other types of validity, but many researchers feel it is the most important type of validity.

101

Construct validity is particularly important for the more theoretically oriented social scientists. While natural scientists deal with constructs such as valences, electromagnetic fields, and quarks, social scientists are concerned with concepts such as intelligence, social class, and political constituencies. Once these concepts are adequately specified, scientists can begin their efforts to find relationships among theoretical variables ("Does frustration lead to aggression?").

This chapter is concerned with the proper specification of constructs that will later become the terms employed in scientific theories. Students who wish to consider the subtleties of the procedures involved in establishing the construct validity of theoretical entities in the social sciences should consider the multitrait-multimethod approach (Campbell & Fiske, 1959) and how it is applied in construct validation studies (Cook & Campbell, 1979).

All the aforementioned approaches to establishing validity can be employed for any measure. Again using the example of a measure of assertiveness, let us consider how we might test the validity of subjects' responses to the single question, "How assertive are you?" On the face of it, a subject would seem to be indicating his or her level of assertiveness in a reply to that question. Therefore, we can conclude the question has face validity. However, most would agree that this is not sufficient evidence to give a researcher much confidence in this index of assertiveness.

Consequently, we might note the behavior of a group of subjects in a particular experimental situation in addition to asking the subjects how assertive they are. By noting if subjects who say they are assertive tend to behave more assertively in the experimental situation than subjects who say they are not very assertive, we can obtain some concurrent validation of the self-report index. In addition, if we ask students to answer the question "How assertive are you?" and then *later* note their behavior in some situation that calls for assertiveness, we may be able to establish predictive validity. Finally, we might be able to obtain many different measures of assertiveness that range over a variety of instruments and techniques; for example, we might ask a few close friends of each subject how assertive the subject is, have the subject play a role that requires assertive behavior, and obtain an unobtrusive measure of assertiveness such as the one obtained through the telephone call technique mentioned in chapter 2. If we note a consistent pattern of relationships between subjects' responses to the question of how assertive they are and all the other measures, we will tend to trust the construct validity of the single assertiveness question.

As you can see, a researcher looks at various forms of validity for a particular index. To the extent that any measure possess all these types of validity, the researcher trusts not only the measure but also the results of studies that employ the measure.

Validity of an Experiment

Just as we can employ procedures to assess the validity of a particular measure, so also can we consider the validity of a scientific investigation. Four types of validity can be considered in determining the effectiveness of any scientific study: *internal validity, external validity, construct validity*, and *statistical conclusion validity*. The considerations included under statistical conclusion validity are beyond the scope of this book; they are described in texts on statistics and in advanced texts on research methodology, which consider statistical issues in depth. The interested reader is referred to Cook and Campbell (1979) for a thorough treatment of topics related to statistical conclusion validity.

Internal Validity

Remember that true experimental studies attempt, by using random assignment, to manage the experimental situation in such a way that differences in the dependent variable can be related to the operation of the independent variable. Internal validity concerns our ability to unequivocally assert that the independent variable (and only the independent variable) caused the differences in the dependent variable shown by different groups in a study. That is, internal validity allows us to state confidently that the independent variable was indeed the cause of the differences noted in the dependent variable. This is because internal validity involves our ability to rule out competing interpretations for a particular finding. These competing interpretations, you may recall, are sometimes called *rival hypotheses*.

In order to appreciate why experimental studies enable researchers to eliminate rival hypotheses, we might consider an observational, or correlational, study and note how many interpretations other than the one we favor might explain the differences in the dependent variable. Insofar as we cannot rule out the various

103

interpretations that compete with ours, we cannot be sure the relationship observed between the independent variable and dependent variable is indeed a causal one. We can examine the rival hypotheses by means of an example wherein threats to internal validity are not well controlled.

Let us consider an instance in which an investigator wishes to determine if a program designed to reduce prejudice is effective. In this instance, the independent variable is a lecture on prejudice for grammar school students. For the dependent measure, the researcher will use a standard self-report test of prejudice. To conduct the study, the researcher selects a group of students from a local grammar school and administers the prejudice questionnaire to all of them. A week later, all the students receive the lecture on prejudice and, after the lecture, again are tested. The next step is to find out whether the prejudice scores collected before the intervention (call them the pretest scores) are substantially higher than scores obtained following the lecture (the posttest scores). The researcher might conclude that, if the posttest responses are lower than the pretest responses, the intervention has reduced subjects' prejudice. As you can see, what the researcher has done is assume that changes in the dependent variable were caused by the introduction of the independent variable. But what possibilities other than the operation of the independent variable on the dependent variable might explain the observed relationship? The following section explains several such threats to internal validity (from Campbell & Stanley, 1963).

Threats to Internal Validity

History

History refers to any event that occurs between the first and second measurements in the study but that is not a part of the independent variable. For example, suppose the lecture on prejudice—and the posttest—had been given right after the television movie *Roots* was first aired. Might we not expect that a substantial number of students in the class had seen *Roots* and that changes in their prejudice scores from pretest to posttest might have been a result of having seen the movie? In this case, the historical event—the showing of *Roots*—coincided with the introduction of the independent variable. We could not rule out the possibility that the differences in the dependent variable were caused by *Roots* rather than the independent variable in the study. Therefore, the rival hypothesis resulting from history could not be ruled out with the design employed in this study.

Maturation of the Subject

Maturation refers to any normally occurring change an individual experiences simply as a function of the passage of time. The best examples of maturation can be seen where people are undergoing rapid changes at particular points in their lives. An obvious example relates to physical growth in children. Suppose the prejudice researcher decides to study physical strength in children by using a design similar to the one used to study prejudice. Pre and Post measures of strength are gathered on all subjects, and a treatment intervention—a weight-lifting program—is to be evaluated. However, this intervention lasts for a year. At the end of this period, how will the researcher know whether the weight-lifting program was responsible for any increases in childrens' strength or whether the increases could have been expected to occur naturally as the children grew?

In the prejudice example, it seems unlikely that individuals' levels of prejudice would change dramatically over the period of one week because of maturation effects. However, strictly speaking, we cannot rule out the possibility that maturation might have occurred. Maturation is different from history in that history is related to the occurrence of a particular event at a particular point in time, while maturation refers to somewhat predictable changes that occur in all human beings.

Instrument Decay

There are instances in research in which the calibration of a measuring device is altered during the course of an experiment. A simple example might involve a scale in an experiment to measure the effectiveness of a weight reduction program. A calibration problem would exist if, for example, a subject was weighed at the beginning of the experiment and again a week later and the scale read first 100 pounds, then 105 pounds, with the difference in weights due totally to mechanical difficulties with the scale. You can imagine how this would affect the experiment. Suppose the program was really quite effective and that subjects lost an average of five pounds the first week. A subject who actually had lost five pounds would register no weight loss on the scale, because of its mechanical malfunctioning.

105

Because of this instrument decay, the researchers might conclude that the independent variable—the weight reduction treatment—had no effect on the dependent variable—the amount of weight lost. That would be an inappropriate conclusion.

With regard to the prejudice example, you can see that a self-report instrument would not suffer exactly this sort of decay. However, a somewhat similar problem could have occurred if the children asked to rate their level of prejudice did not fully understand the self-report when they first filled it out. The treatment program, the lecture on prejudice, might have made clear to the students the true nature of prejudice, thereby causing an instrumentation change that altered the way subjects conceived of their level of prejudice. That is, the lecture might actually have caused students to *interpret* the questions differently. An instrumentation effect such as this has been reported by Howard, Ralph, Gulanick, Maxwell, Nance, and Gerber (1979) and is referred to as response-shift bias. The subjects in the prejudice study might have experienced such a response shift. At any rate, the research design employed does not allow us to rule out that possibility. Therefore, the rival hypothesis of instrument decay cannot be eliminated as a possible explanation for the relationship between the independent and dependent variables.

Testing Effects

Testing effects occur when the previous taking of a test systematically alters subjects' responses to subsequent administrations of that test. A good example of such effects involves the testing of individuals' ability to solve mathematical word problems, such as the one in the accompanying box. You probably know that in most word problems there is a key relationship or insight that enables us to set up the appropriate equations that, in turn, enable us to solve the problem. It often takes a good deal of time to think over the problem and discover an insight that will result in the solution. However, after we have puzzled over and solved a problem, we might well remember the particular insight we used at some later date. Therefore, if I administered a word-problem test as a pretest measure and later employed the same test as a posttest measure, subjects might remember their insights the second time they took the test, making the posttest an easier task. This would be especially important if the test was timed. Subjects would need much less time on the posttest, and so

106

A Mathematical Word Problem

Train #1   Train #2

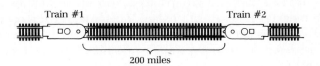

200 miles

Two trains, each traveling at 100 miles per hour, are two hundred miles apart and are approaching one another on a collision course. At this point, a bird starting at train #1 flies toward train #2 at 250 miles per hour. As soon as the bird reaches train #2, it turns around immediately and flies back to train #1. Upon arriving at train #1, the bird turns and flies to train #2 again. This procedure is repeated until the trains collide. When the trains collide, how far has the bird traveled? (Spend some time trying to solve the problem before reading further.)

This problem can be difficult to solve if you attempt to calculate how far the bird travels on each successive trip from one train to the other. However, it becomes rather simple if you approach it by asking "How long before the trains collide?" This insight enables you to solve the problem (and, perhaps, similar problems) much more quickly. A subject who achieves such an insight at the pretest in a experiment will perform better on the posttest; this represents a testing effect.

they could attempt many more problems than they had on the pretest.

Again returning to the prejudice example, we might not be surprised to find that simply answering the questions on a prejudice questionnaire might stimulate subjects' thinking about their attitudes toward other groups. This process, in turn, might result in their becoming somewhat less prejudiced. In this case, the pretest would have produced effects that showed up in the posttest; but the researcher might erroneously conclude that changes in the dependent variable were caused by the independent variable rather than by the testing effects.

107

Statistical Regression

Another threat to internal validity is represented by statistical regression artifacts. Statistical regression is a problem in studies that employ extreme groups—groups made up of individuals selected because they are atypical with regard to a particular dimension. The problem of statistical regression involves the fact that scores from people selected for membership in a study *because* they scored extremely high or low tend to move closer to the population mean on a second testing.

For example, suppose I tested every individual in the United States on bowling ability. My pretest might be to have everyone bowl one game. If I had every person in the nation bowl one game, I would not be at all surprised to find a small number of subjects, perhaps ten or fifteen, who bowled perfect games (a score of 300). Now, imagine that I had formed the hypothesis that eating an extremely large meal before bowling might cause a decrease in performance. To test this hypothesis, I might be tempted to have these bowlers overeat and then have them bowl another game. Here is the problem: It is virtually assured that the average bowling score of this group will not be 300, as it was in the pretest. This is because bowling 300 is an extremely rare event that requires, in addition to considerable skill, a tremendous amount of luck. The chance that an individual will bowl back-to-back 300 games is very, very small. Consequently, we can be sure that the average posttest score for this group will be much lower than 300 (perhaps about 230). If I naively interpreted these results, I might erroneously conclude that the overeating had produced the lower scores. The truth is, however, that I cannot tell how much of the decrease from 300 to 230 was due to the independent variable (the overeating) and how much was due to the natural tendency of extreme subjects to regress toward the mean of their group.

With regard to the prejudice example, if the researcher gave the lecture only to a group of individuals whose pretest prejudice scores were extremely high, we might expect their scores to be somewhat lower on the posttest simply because of the effect of regression toward the mean. Again, employing extreme groups results in inability to tell whether the differences between pretest and posttest are due to statistical regression effects or to a true effect of the independent variable.

Experimental Mortality

Problems of mortality can arise when subjects drop out during the course of a study. I might conduct an experiment to discover whether a certain vitamin supplement increases intelligence. But let us assume that the vitamin really has no effect on intelligence at all. If I measure subjects' intelligence both before and after they receive the vitamin supplement, I should note no change in the group's average intelligence. But suppose the most intelligent subjects think the study is stupid and drop out. What might occur? If I forget to remove the scores of the subjects who have dropped out from the average of the pretest intelligence scores, I might erroneously conclude that the vitamin actually has reduced subjects' intelligence.

The observant student may have realized that if random assignment of subjects to levels of the independent variable had occurred in all these studies, all the threats to internal validity would have been adequately controlled. You should review each of the threats individually and think about how the problems of internal validity could have been solved if treatment and control groups had been formed through random assignment procedures.

Selection Biases

The last threat to internal validity to be considered here can occur when a control group is formed by some procedure other than random assignment. Selection bias assumes major importance in the next chapter, which considers quasi-experimental designs.

If, in the prejudice example, the researcher gave the treatment to the most prejudiced subjects and had the least prejudiced subjects serve as a control group, the comparison of the groups would be contaminated by selection bias effects. Even if the treatment had no effect on subjects' levels of prejudice, the changes in the groups' mean prejudice scores might be misinterpreted as suggesting the existence of a treatment effect. Think of the treatment group as people who scored extremely high on prejudice. Regression effects, you will recall, predict that their posttest scores will be somewhat lower because of the effects of regression toward the mean. For the same reason, the control group's scores should move in the opposite direction. This movement, which brings the groups' mean scores closer together, could be misinterpreted as a real treatment effect. Any time

109

comparison groups are formed by nonrandom assignment procedures, the effect of selection biases presents possible rival hypotheses that cloud any interpretation of the findings.

External Validity

External validity deals with the extent to which a researcher can generalize across various kinds of persons, settings, and times based on the evidence from a particular study. That is, a researcher might conclude from a totally internally valid experiment that variable A causes variable B in a particular experimental situation. The next question the researcher might wish to consider is, "How general is this observed relationship between variable A and variable B?" For example, a researcher might note that in a particular research setting at a particular time, greater aggression was observed in subjects with increased frustration than was observed in a nonfrustrated control group. Most scientists would wonder if this relationship between frustration and aggression would also exist with other operational definitions of frustration or if it was specific to the operational definition of frustration employed in this study. Similarly, the subjects in this study might all have been students in a public grammar school in a large city. Would frustration also lead to aggression in adults? Does frustration lead to aggression in both males and females? Would frustration lead to aggression in suburban or rural children? These are all issues of external validity.

Unlike internal validity, with which it was possible to list potential threats and determine whether they had been adequately controlled, external validity cannot be unequivocally determined for a particular study. That is because external validity, or generalizability, must always be considered with respect to the particular group to which we wish to generalize. We would not be surprised to find that while a particular study helped to predict the behavior of adults in a specific situation, it did not help predict how children would act in that same situation. We know from experience that children often react differently from adults.

The closest we can come to having confidence in the external validity of a particular study is to clearly specify the population of subjects, situations, settings, and times to which we wish to generalize. An example provided by Cook and Campbell (1979) may be

110

instructive. Suppose a new television show was introduced that was aimed at teaching basic arithmetic to seven-year-olds in the United States. Here, a target population to which we wish to generalize— seven-year-olds in the United States—has been defined. If we had some means of adequately obtaining a representative sample of seven-year-olds across the United States, and if we could perform an internally valid true experiment, we could ascertain if the television program did increase the subjects' basic arithmetic skills. If our sampling techniques were appropriate, we would also have confidence that the study had external validity with regard to the target population.

However, notice this somewhat puzzling possiblity. Suppose you were the principal of a grammar school that taught only boys. You might look at that internally valid study and wonder whether the cause-and-effect relationship it had found would hold for your particular situation. To the extent that your population of students is dissimilar to the sample of subjects employed in the experiment, the results of the experiment might not be generalizable to your students. That is, the experimental results might not represent what would occur if you tried to employ the methods used in the study.

For instance, suppose the study found that the basic arithmetic program improved problem-solving skills by an average of ten problems on the particular test used as the dependent measure. It is possible that this finding might have resulted from female students' increasing their scores by twenty problems on the test, while males did not increase their arithmetic skills at all. When the data for both boys and girls were considered together, what looked like a ten-problem increase across all students was really a surprisingly large effect for girls and no effect at all for boys.

Therefore, you, as a school principal who really is only interested in whether the program works for male students, might be misled by the results of the study. If you implemented the program used in the study, you would be surprised to find it had no effect at all on male students. You can see that in this instance it was assumed that the results were generalizable to a broad range of subjects because of the heterogeneity of the students who were sampled in the original study. However, this heterogeneity masked a lack of relationship between the variables in the study (the program on basic arithmetic skills and increased problem-solving ability on a test) for certain subpopulations (male students).

111

While it is possible that results appropriate for heterogeneous groups do not hold for more homogeneous subgroups, the problems of external validity typically go in the other direction. That is, researchers typically tend to use limited samples of subjects, situations, and settings. For example, they might sample students at a particular university, and these students' characteristics might represent only a limited sample of the characteristics that could possibly be sampled. The question of external validity then becomes, "Does this research, which was conducted on a limited sample of people, generalize to individuals who are outside the range of the restricted sample?"

Suppose research is being conducted on students in a psychology class at Harvard University. The researcher is probably dealing with a homogeneous sample of intelligence scores, because it is unlikely that many people of average and low intelligence are represented in the typical class of Harvard students. The study may be internally valid and may even be externally valid for highly intelligent subjects. However, if the relationship among variables observed by the researcher holds only for people of high intelligence, and is different for people of average or low intelligence, the results of the study might be totally misleading if generalized to the total range of intelligence scores of the general population of university students.

The various types of threats to external validity will not be described in detail in this book. The interested reader is referred to Cook and Campbell, 1979, pp. 73 – 74, for a consideration of the specific factors that threaten the external validity of studies.

We will, however, consider certain techniques whereby studies' external validity can be increased. First, as suggested earlier, in certain studies, researchers know they wish to generalize to specific target populations of persons, settings, and times. When the target populations can be clearly specified, the major consideration in increasing external validity is to ensure that samples be respresentative. We considered ways in which sampling can be done to ensure representativeness in chapter 4.

In other instances, researchers may not have specific populations in mind. This is the case when researchers are developing a general theory they hope will apply to a broad range of humans. In addition, in many specific instances in applied research, it is impossible to specify beforehand the range of populations and settings to which the results might be generalized. In instances such as these, several techniques can be employed to optimize the likelihood of obtaining results that might generalize to a broad range of populations. Essentially, these techniques call for researchers to test their theories in the broadest and most heterogeneous situations possible.

That is, early in a research program, the researcher should deliberately sample broadly with respect to factors such as types of persons, types of settings, geographical sections of the country, and other dimensions that might, if narrowly sampled, limit the generality of the findings. Having done this, the researcher should undertake a second stage wherein the results of the earlier studies can be reanalyzed (or additional studies conducted) to test whether the general findings hold for limited samples and for homogeneous subgroupings that were part of the larger, more heterogeneous study. This procedure allows the researcher to initially make a very general statement regarding the relationships among the variables and then later to specifically test whether the generalizability of these results is limited by certain characteristics of subgroups or settings.

Let us consider again the generalizability of our earlier example—the program in basic arithmetic skills. The results of the study might be stated something like this: "While this program yields a salutary effect overall, the effect is extremely pronounced in females and insignificant in males." This more precise statement regarding the relationships among the variables in the study is much more useful to individuals seeking to apply the results and is a more accurate representation of the implications of the study for practitioners.

Construct Validity

In chapter 1 and earlier in this chapter, the role of theory in the social sciences was mentioned. As noted, it is impossible actually to do research on the theoretical level. Rather, the first step in empirically testing theoretical ideas involves creating operational definitions we believe will measure the theoretical constructs of interest. Internal validity deals with our ability to make valid inferences about causal relationships among the variables as they are operationalized in the study. External validity deals with our ability to generalize these relationships among variables to other populations of subjects, different experimental settings, different points in time, and so on.

Yet another type of validity is construct validity, which deals with the relationships among variables as operationally defined and

Theoretical level:	Intelligence	Learning
Operational level:	Score on WAIS IQ test	Grades

Issues of internal validity: Did differences in IQ really produce differences in grades?

Issues of external validity: Would the same relationship between IQ and grades have been observed if different students, age levels, backgrounds, etc., had been employed?

Issues of construct validity: Did differences in IQ scores really reflect differences in intelligence, or did they reflect some other theoretical construct (such as test-taking ability)?
Did differences in grades reflect true differences in learning, or were they due to some other factor (such as how well the teacher liked the student)?

Figure 7–1   Analysis of a Research Question

manipulated in particular experiments and with their relationship to the theoretical propositions we believe the results represent. Construct validity deals with the degree to which the results of experiments are appropriately *theoretically* interpreted. Our observation of relationships among variables as they are manipulated in particular studies may reflect the operation of theoretical relationships in the world. To the extent that we are able to correctly identify the theoretical relationships reflected in the relationships observed in our studies, we have made valid construct inferences.

As with internal and external validity, threats to construct validity do exist. However, because of the complex nature of many of these threats, they will not be described in detail here. (The interested reader is referred to Cook and Campbell, 1979, pp. 64 – 68.) To give an idea of the types of problems associated with construct validity, an example will be presented.

Figure 7 – 1 presents an analysis of a research question. As it is expressed at a theoretical level, the question is, "Does high intelligence lead to greater learning?" At the level of the concrete operational definitions employed to test the possible theoretical relationship, the question is, "Are differences on the WAIS IQ test related to the grades students receive in a particular class?" The figure includes questions related to the validity of the research. The questions of internal and external validity were discussed earlier. You can see that the questions related to construct validity deal with whether activities

114

on the concrete operational level really relate to the theoretical constructs of interest to the researchers. Have they performed an experiment that clearly reflects the operation of those and only those theoretical variables with which they are concerned?

Additional Readings

Campbell, D. T., & Stanley, J. C. *Experimental and quasi-experimental designs for research.* Chicago: Rand-McNally, 1963.
Cook, T. D., & Campbell, D. T. *Quasi-experimentation: Design and analysis issues for field settings.* Chicago: Rand-McNally, 1979.

Quasi-Experimental Designs

Chapter Preview

While the true experiment is the preferred design, researchers often find themselves in situations where practical concerns preclude true experimental approaches. In such situations, quasi-experimental designs are sometimes preferred to simple observational procedures. Chapter 8 describes several quasi-experimental designs: nonequivalent control group design, simulated before-after design, regression-discontinuity design, interrupted time-series design, multiple time-series design, partial correlation approaches, and time-lagged correlation approaches. Situations in which each of these approaches might be appropriate are characterized. Finally, the unique strengths and liabilities of each method are delineated.

As this text has frequently noted, observational approaches typically make little or no effort to rule out explanations that compete with the research hypothesis as an interpretation of the phenomenon under investigation. On the other hand, experimental approaches, through the mechanism of random assignment, attempt to eliminate all competing explanations except the experimental hypothesis. As you might have guessed from the title of this chapter, there is a group of research designs that can eliminate some, but not all, of the competing explanations. These approaches are known as the quasi-experimental designs.

Why would a researcher ever use a quasi-experimental approach, when the experimental approach is superior? An appropriate answer is that a researcher should never use a quasi-experimental approach if an experimental study can be conducted. Unfortunately, it is not always possible to conduct an experimental study. In such cases, a quasi-experiment is generally preferable to an observational study. The following sections are intended: (1) to introduce the reader to classes of quasi-experimental designs; and (2) by using the information on threats to valid inference introduced in chapter 7, to give a brief sketch of the relative strengths and liabilities of each approach.

Nonequivalent Control Group Design

In a number of designs, comparison, or control, groups are included, but the control and experimental groups are not formed by random assignment. Consequently, we cannot be sure that the experimental and control groups are equivalent. Since these initial group differences might be at least partially responsible for differences between the groups on the dependent variable, they remain as uncontrolled rival hypotheses. Table 8–1 presents a typical nonequivalent control group design. As you might suspect, the intention is to compare changes in experimental group subjects from pretest to posttest with similar changes in control group subjects. You may recall that this same design—with random assignment of subjects to groups—controls for all threats to internal validity. Without random assignment, how does this quasi-experimental approach fare with regard to threats to internal validity?

No simple answer to this question can be given. The result depends on how the nonequivalent groups were formed. For exam-

Table 8–1   Nonequivalent Control Group Design

	Pretreatment Measure	Treatment	Posttreatment Measure
Experimental group	O_1	X	O_2
Control group	O_1		O_2

ple, if I were interested in the effects of a propaganda movie on the political attitudes of students in an introductory psychology course, I might choose the students in an introductory sociology class as a control group. Suppose my pretests are administered after class one day for both groups. The experimental group is shown the movie immediately, while the control group simply waits an equivalent amount of time, either talking or sitting quietly. Then, the posttest is conducted before the subjects are dismissed. Intuitively, you might suspect that history, maturation, instrumentation, and similar effects would be about equal for each group. And your intuitions might be correct. We could never know for sure, but that intuitive guess seems reasonable in this instance.

However, contrast that situation with a study in which I considered the effect of change of U.S. presidential administrations on the amount of violence in U.S. cities. If my control group consisted of cities in England, or France, or any other country, could I have any confidence that history effects, for example, for the two groups of cities were equivalent? You can see that the degree to which a nonequivalent control group can control for threats to internal validity is logically a function of just how similar or dissimilar the control group is to the experimental group.

A second general type of threat to nonequivalent control group approaches is a class of interactions of particular threats (such as instrumentation, maturation, and so on) with differences between groups that are due to selection effects. For example, suppose a selection bias results in groups that receive very dissimilar scores on the pretest. Say the experimental group scores much lower than the control group. Then, instrument decay causes differences between pretest and posttest scores; but the instrument decay produces greater effects on low pretest scores than on higher pretest scores. Figure 8–1 represents the data that might be produced by such an effect, *even if there is no treatment effect*.

119

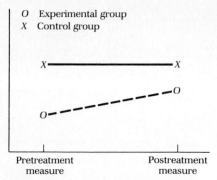

Figure 8–1 Misleading Data from a Nonequivalent Control Group Study

Note: Interaction of selection bias with instrument decay causes an effect that may be mistaken for a treatment effect.

Suppose these data relate to treatment subjects who are receiving remediation for some problem. You can see that the results might be mistaken as a true treatment effect. This is precisely the problem encountered when programs are targeted toward people in special need in a particular area of their lives, such as social welfare programs. It is difficult (and sometimes unethical) to withhold treatment from some people, which would be required if random assignment were to be employed. However, finding a nonequivalent control group that is equal at pretest to the experimental group on the dependent variable is often impossible. Consequently, nonequivalent control groups are sometimes the only option available. In such cases, the interaction of selection with other effects can always present threats to valid inference.

Simulated Before-After Design

The simplest example of simulated before-after design involves identifying a group of subjects, *all* of whom are to receive an intervention. We then randomly divide this group into two parts. Half the subjects will be pretested but will not be posttested (this is our control group). The remainder of the subjects will not be pretested but will be posttested (this is our experimental group). Comparisons between control group prescores and experimental group postscores provide an estimate of the treatment effect.

The obvious advantage of this technique is that the groups are equivalent at pretest, since we randomly divided the subjects into groups. Further, since our comparison is performed on scores that represent the first and only time each group is measured, testing effects are controlled also. This latter strength would not exist if all subjects were pretested and posttested and we compared the pretest scores of one randomly selected group with the posttest scores of the other group. Therefore, if random assignment to a group that will not receive treatment is impossible, and if testing effects represent a real threat, then the simulated before-after design may be of value.

However, this simulated before-after design is open to history, maturation, and other threats to which true experimental designs are immune. Again, if it is possible to perform a true experiment, doing so is preferable to conducting a quasi-experiment.

Regression-Discontinuity Designs

Regression-discontinuity designs are especially appropriate "when people or groups are given awards or those in special need are given extra help [and] one would like to discover the consequences of such provisions" (Cook & Campbell, 1979, p. 137). Let us examine the logic behind this design. Suppose a special award, or perhaps a remedial program, is given to a particular subset of a sample of subjects *because* they scored among the highest (in the award case) or lowest (in the remedial program case) of the subjects in the sample. If we wished to determine if the award or the remedial program had an impact on individuals' subsequent behavior, a regression-discontinuity design might be appropriate.

Figure 8–2 provides two sets of hypothetical data for a study wherein salespeople who performed poorly one year (1982) were given a sales training program to improve their performance the following year (1983). The upper panel presents data that would suggest the program was ineffective, while the data in the lower panel would be interpreted as demonstrating that the training had been successful. In other words, if the program was totally ineffective, then the plot of 1982 sales with 1983 sales would show a linear (straight-line) relationship, as depicted in the top panel of Figure 8–2. If the sales training program did have an effect, then there would be a break in this line, as depicted in the lower panel of Figure 8–2. The break would occur

121

Quasi-Experimental Designs

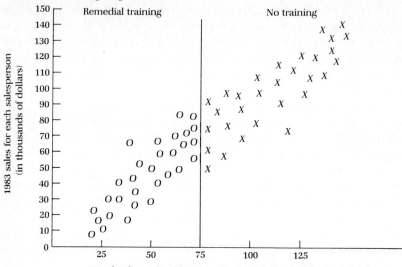

a. Ineffective Training Program

b. Effective Training Program

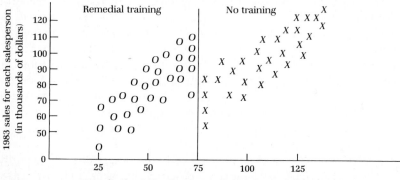

Figure 8–2 Two Sets of Hypothetical Data for a Regression-Discontinuity Study

at the cut-off point ($75,000 in 1982 sales) between those who received the intervention and those who did not.

There are several potential problems with regression-discontinuity designs, as with all quasi-experimental approaches. A first problem involves the possibility that the cut-off score between groups was not adhered to rigidly. In the sales training example, suppose a few salespeople who had sales between $75,000 and $85,000 in 1982 expressed an interest in attending the training program, and company officials wished to allow them to attend. Similarly, a salesperson who sold $70,000 worth of products in 1982 might be adamant about not attending the training program; and the company might be tempted to allow him or her to decline to participate. Whenever the cut-off score is not rigidly adhered to, the regression-discontinuity design is weakened. If crossovers must occur, the researcher should not include the data from crossover subjects in the study. But even with these data not included, the design is weaker than one in which crossovers are prohibited and all subjects are included.

A second difficulty with regression-discontinuity designs involves the very fact that remedial programs or awards are often given to extreme groups. If, for example, researchers were examining the effect of being a national merit scholar on subsequent academic performance, they would have to realize that only individuals with the highest academic scores had been selected as award winners. This would result in a very narrow range of scores among the treatment group subjects. For statistical reasons, having a restricted range of scores in either the treatment or control group presents problems for the regression-discontinuity design. (You will note that this restriction of range problem is not always applicable in regression-discontinuity designs. In the data on salespeople presented in Figure 8−2, both groups had reasonably broad ranges of scores in 1982—the remedial group ranged from $25,000 to $75,000, while the no-training group ranged from $75,000 to about $130,000.)

Interrupted Time-Series Design

Sometimes control subjects are simply unavailable for a study. As you will see in more detail in chapter 9, when researchers conduct single-subject studies, they can eliminate certain rival hypotheses by taking many more observations of the phenomenon of interest. Interrupted time-series designs require that multiple observations of the phenomenon of interest be obtained both before and after the introduction of the intervention. The basic design of the interrupted time series is presented in the upper panel of Table 8−2.

Table 8–2 Interrupted Time-Series Design and Multiple Time-Series Design

a. Interrupted Time-Series Design

	Preintervention Measures	Intervention	Postintervention Measures
Experimental group	$O_1 O_2 O_3 O_4 O_5$	X	$O_6 O_7 O_8 O_9 O_{10}$

b. Multiple Time-Series Design

	Preintervention Measures	Intervention	Postintervention Measures
Experimental group	$O_1 O_2 O_3 O_4$	X	$O_5 O_6 O_7 O_8$
Control group	$O_1 O_2 O_3 O_4$		$O_5 O_6 O_7 O_8$

A study by Caporaso (1974) provides an example of an interrupted time-series design. In this study, the researcher considered the impact of the formation of the European Economic Community (EEC) on the development of various interdependencies among the countries involved in the EEC. This was accomplished by observation of activities on several dimensions for the member nations from 1950 to 1970. The EEC was formed in 1958, and so that became the critical year in the study. If a reasonably stable pattern of activity appeared to exist in the years 1950 through 1957, and if the activity dramatically increased in 1958 and persisted at that level for the next several years, might not one infer that it was the formation of the EEC that was responsible for the dramatic increase?

When using an interrupted time-series design, collecting several preintervention observations aids the researcher in asserting that testing, maturation, and instrumentation effects are not very likely rival hypotheses. However, the interrupted time-series design is particularly susceptible to history effects. We know that the formation of the EEC is not the only important historical event to occur around 1958. With the launching of the Sputnik satellite, Soviet Russia served notice that it was ready to challenge the Western powers for leadership in space exploration and, quite possibly, the lead in technological innovation in general. This visible sign of a Soviet threat in an important military and economic domain might have spurred greater interdependency among Western European nations. This scenario suggests that the observed increases, which the study attributed to the forma-

124

tion of the EEC, might be due to Soviet space advances. You can see that this historical event serves as a rival interpretation to the experimental hypothesis.

Multiple Time-Series Design

The multiple time-series design represents a logical improvement on the interrupted time-series design. The lower panel of Table 8−2 represents this approach. The essential improvement over the interrupted time-series design lies in the inclusion of a comparable control group. This control deals with the history effects that serve as plausible rival hypotheses in interrupted time-series designs.

A study by Campbell and Ross (1968) represents an excellent example of the use of the multiple time-series approach. In 1955 the state of Connecticut implemented a crackdown on automobile speeding violators. Obvious dependent measures to assess the impact of such a program are the number of traffic accidents in a year, the number of traffic fatalities, the number of traffic citations issued for speeding, and so on. What might serve as an appropriate control group? All the other forty-seven states might be employed as the control group. However, the weather conditions are very different in different parts of the country. For example, the winter of 1955 might have been extremely severe in the New England states but relatively mild in other parts of the country. Consequently, the traffic accident figures for Connecticut might have been inflated that year relative to those for other regions of the country. Consequently, it makes more sense to employ states adjacent to Connecticut (Massachusetts, New Jersey, New York, and Rhode Island) as a pool of control states.

That is what Campbell and Ross did. By employing the pool of control states, the multiple time-series design dealt more effectively with history effects that might be responsible for changes in dependent measures. Campbell and Ross noted that severe weather and improved safety features might be plausible explanations of changes in a dependent measure, unless a suitable control group was employed.

Figure 8−3 presents the figures for Connecticut and the control states on traffic fatalities for the years 1951 through 1959. You can see that in the first year after the crackdown (1956), the Connecticut fatality rate began a slow decline, while the control group fatality rate

125

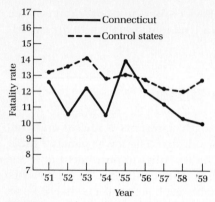

Figure 8-3 Traffic Fatality Rates Reported by Campbell and Ross

Source: Campbell and Ross (1968), p. 44.

remained about the same. This pattern suggests that the speeding crackdown might have produced a slight effect on the number of traffic fatalities.

Partial Correlation Approach

Chapter 7 pointed out that true experimental designs (those involving random assignment) eliminate threats to valid inference of cause-and-effect relationships. However, when random assignment is not possible, researchers face the potential problem that some uncontrolled third variable might be responsible for the observed relationship between the two variables of interest. Thus, problems with inferring cause-and-effect relationships are sometimes called third-variable problems. Such problems do not occur in experiments involving random assignment because, as you know, groups formed by random assignment are theoretically equivalent on all possible extraneous variables. When random assignment cannot be used, a technique called *partial correlation* offers a way to statistically control for certain third variables. A partial correlation is a correlation between two variables of interest, with the influence of a specific third variable removed from the original correlation.

For example, numerous researchers have found a correlation between the grades students receive in a particular class and the

126

students' ratings of the instructor. That would seem to suggest that instructors, by giving higher grades to students, could encourage their students to evaluate their performance as teachers more favorably. If this were so, the causal influence would be such that the grades assigned to students actually would influence the ratings instructors received. However, a third variable might be responsible for that apparent causal relationship. For example, it seems likely that if a teacher taught the class very well, the amount of material learned by students would be greater, encouraging the teacher to assign higher grades. Similarly, if students were taught better and learned more material, they might rate the teacher more highly. Therefore, you can see that while a correlation between grades and ratings might result from a direct causal influence from one variable to another, as shown in Figure 8−4a, it might also result from some third variable's influence on the two variables of interest, as shown in Figure 8−4b.

It is possible to test whether Figure 8−4a or 8−4b is the appropriate view by computing the partial correlation of grades and satisfaction with the influence of teaching performance removed. Suppose the regular correlation between grades and satisfaction is .60. If the partial correlation is very small, such as .00 to .10, Figure 8−4b is more likely to reflect the flow of causal influence in this case. If, however, the partial correlation remains high (stays close to .60), Figure 8−4a is more likely to be the more accurate pattern. In this latter case, the use of a partial correlation has allowed us to rule out a particular third variable as the cause of an observed correlational relationship.

However, the problem with partial correlations is that there exists an unknown number of potential third variables other than

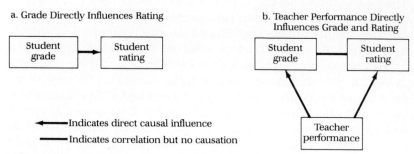

Figure 8−4 Possible Relationships among Student Grade, Student Rating of Teacher, and Teacher Performance

teaching quality (such as students' intelligence, teachers' personalities, students' motivation to take the course, and so on). Any of these variables might influence both grades and satisfaction and be the "real" cause of the correlation between them. In practice, it is impossible to identify, measure, and calculate the partial correlation for each of these potential third variables; so, in general, partial correlation represents a partial solution to the third-variable problem with correlational data. However, there are some instances in which the number of plausible third variables may be quite limited; and in such instances, partial correlation can be appropriately used.

Time-Lagged Correlations and the Direction of Causality

Just as random assignment in true experimental designs allows experimenters to rule out potential third-variable problems, it also adequately handles issues of the direction of causal influence. That is, in true experiments we are confident that the differences in the levels of the independent variable produced the observed differences in the dependent variable and that the differences in the dependent variable could not have been responsible for the differences in the levels of the independent variable. A moment's reflection will reveal that the proof for these assertions rests on our belief that a cause must precede its effect in time. It defies logic to think of an effect's occurring prior to its cause.

The correlational procedures that capitalize on this logical relationship between causes and effects are the time-lagged approaches. The logic behind time-lagged procedures is simple. We might believe there is a causal relationship between two variables. But it might be unclear whether variable A produced the effects observed in variable B, or variable B caused the effects observed in variable A. Time-lagged approaches require measuring both variables at two different points in time. If variable A causes variable B, the correlation between variable A measured at time 1 and variable B measured at time 2 should be higher than the correlation between variable B measured at time 1 and variable A measured at time 2. The thinking behind this procedure is that if A causes B, the time 1 level of A should be a good predictor of the time 2 level of B, whereas if B does not cause A, the time 1 level of B should not necessarily suggest any particular inci-

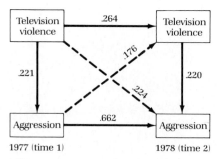

1977 (time 1)   1978 (time 2)

Figure 8 – 5 Results of Time-Lagged Study of the Relationship Between Violence Watched on Television and Aggression Reported by Peers

Source: Data from Eron and Huesmann (1980).

dence of A at time 2. Figure 8 — 5 presents the results of a time-lagged study on the relationship between adolescents' watching violent programs on television and peer ratings of the aggressiveness of these adolescents' behavior. Comparison of the correlations represented by the dotted lines in the figure is the crucial comparison.

While the reasoning behind the time-lagged approach is logical, in practice, demonstrating a difference between these two correlations is extremely difficult. Consequently, while the promise of establishing the direction of causality between two variables through time-lagged procedures is attractive, in practice, the findings all too often are inconclusive.

Additional Readings

Cook, T. D., & Campbell, D. T. *Quasi-experimentation: Design and analysis issues for field settings*. Chicago: Rand-McNally, 1979.

Glass, G. V., Wilson, V. L., & Gottman, J. M. *Design and analysis of time-series experiments*. Boulder, Colo.: Colorado Associated University Press, 1975.

Single-Subject Research

Chapter Preview

To this point, our research designs have focused on patterns observable in groups of subjects. We now consider what can be learned from passive observation of a single subject (a case study) and active manipulation used with one individual (a single-subject experiment). The advantages of using reversal techniques and systematically varying baseline lengths to help eliminate the plausibility of various rival hypotheses are enumerated. Several continuing problems for single-subject research (such as carry-over effects) are also considered.

You will remember that our major purpose in conducting research is to recognize patterns of behavior and/or to determine causal relationships in our interest area. Knowledge about patterns of behavior can be secured through the use of many techniques. In applied areas of the social sciences, such as clinical psychology, the use of case studies—wherein a single person with a particular problem or a single organization with a particular set of problems is studied intensively—has been a productive way of obtaining knowledge. Case studies are passive and observational in nature and relate in many ways to the other observational research methods dealt with earlier (chapter 3). The major similarity is that no attempt is made to rule out rival hypotheses (such as history effects, maturation effects, and so on). Therefore, while the behavior exhibited by the subject in the case study is very similar to his or her behavior in real-life settings, ascribing the specific causes of that behavior is extremely difficult, because many uncontrolled rival hypotheses exist. Remember that chapters 3 and 7 described how researchers could conduct true experimental studies. The strength of true experiments is their ability to control for many threats to validity, which remain present in observational studies. Chapters 3, 4, and 7 described some procedures characteristic of experimental studies, told how we could logically rule out rival hypotheses in experimental studies, and explained why this gave experimental studies an advantage over observational studies.

As mentioned, the case study deals with a single subject and makes no strong attempt to rule out the rival hypotheses discussed earlier. There are, however, a number of experimental designs that consider only one subject, rather than groups of subjects, but that *do* attempt to rule out plausible rival hypotheses. This chapter will elaborate on a few of these single-subject designs and describe how they control for the threats to valid inference in an experiment. This single-subject approach to research was first used extensively by B. F. Skinner and his colleagues and became important in clinical psychology with the growing popularity of behavior therapy in the 1960s and 1970s. The theoretical positions of behavioral approaches are uniquely suited to the demands of single-subject research. Consequently, behavioral approaches to clinical psychology have flourished by employing single-subject research designs.

Competing hypotheses are eliminated by true experiments in two ways: through the use of random assignment of subjects to conditions and through the inclusion of control groups for comparison purposes. It is obvious that these requirements cannot possibly be met in single-subject research. Consequently, new methods for eliminating rival hypotheses must be considered for single-subject research designs. In a general sense, all single-subject research involves the use of repeated measures studies. For this reason, we should keep in mind the discussion of assignment techniques in chapter 4, which considered how the order of presentation of stimuli or conditions could be used to control for contamination in studies.

The logic of single-subject research can be demonstrated by a simple example. Assume that a researcher has designed a treatment to increase the amount of interaction a worker has with his or her colleagues in a business organization. Suppose this investigator wishes to determine the intervention's effectiveness on one person with a pattern of low interaction with colleagues before recommending the intervention's wider use in the organization. A very simple and straightforward research design the experimenter might consider using involves a *baseline* observational period, during which the researcher would observe the subject to obtain an idea of the usual frequency of the target behavior (prosocial interaction, in this example). After sufficient observation of the subject, the experimenter might feel a stable estimate of the person's prosocial behavior could be formed.

The experimenter might then initiate a period—the *experimental* period—in which techniques for increasing prosocial behavior would be initiated. Let us say that this technique involved requiring every worker in the experimental subject's work setting to write down at the end of each day both his or her interactions with the subject and his or her reactions to those interactions. These reports could be evaluated by the experimenter each day, and the reports that highlighted and reinforced prosocial behavior on the part of the subject could be placed in the subject's mailbox at the beginning of the next day. The experimenter would continue to observe the amount of prosocial behavior in which the subject engaged during the experimental period.

Suppose the researcher noticed that the subject engaged in considerably more prosocial behavior during the experimental phase of the study than during the baseline phase. Would the experimenter be justified in concluding that the treatment was responsible for this increase in prosocial behavior? Definitely not! There are several

133

potential reasons for the increase in prosocial behavior that are not related to the experimental hypothesis (the hypothesis that the treatment produced the change in behavior).

At this point, you should be able to cite a number of rival hypotheses that contaminate this study. Take a few moments now to list potential contaminants. Do not read any further until you have identified at least four.

Some of the contaminants that are uncontrolled in the previous example are effects caused by history, maturation, instrument decay, testing, and regression. Given these numerous threats to valid inference, we could have very little confidence in the study as it is currently described. However, the addition of one simple feature can eliminate many of these threats, as will be described in the next section.

Reversal Designs

The example above used a baseline period and an experimental period. We can refer to baseline periods as "A" and to experimental periods as "B". Using these designations, we can consider the example above an AB design—that is, a baseline period followed by an experimental treatment period. Single-subject *reversal designs* involve the addition of a third time period that follows B (the experimental period). This third period is another A, or baseline observation, period.

This return to a second A period is known as the *reversal phase* and is a critical aspect of most well-designed single-subject experiments. Reversal designs can become even more elaborate; a second reversal can be included by addition of a second experimental phase to the design, which then becomes an ABAB design. Figure 9−1 presents data that might have been obtained from the study on increasing prosocial behavior had an ABAB design been employed.

Inspection of Figure 9−1 shows that the subject engaged in very little prosocial behavior during the initial five-day baseline period. The intervention was initiated on the morning of day 6, and you can see that there was an immediate and dramatic increase in the amount of prosocial behavior on days 6 through 10. Had the experiment been terminated at this point, the researcher might have suspected that the increase in prosocial behavior was due to the introduction of the

134

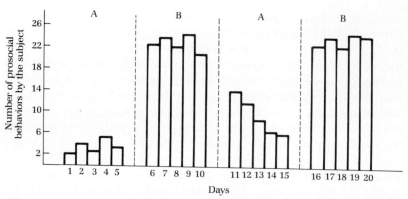

Figure 9-1 Results of Single-Subject ABAB Design

experimental intervention. However, the subject might simply have been growing more comfortable with coworkers and might thus have experienced the increase in prosocial behavior even if the intervention had not been initiated (although this is an unlikely possibility). In this case, the subject's higher comfort level (a maturation-like effect), rather than the experimental treatment, might have been responsible for the increases in prosocial behavior between days 6 and 10.

Similarly, the differences between days 1 through 5 and days 6 through 10 might have been due to changes in the observer. That is, perhaps the rater was initially unskilled at noticing the frequency of prosocial behavior but between day 5 and day 6 became aware of a large number of behaviors that he or she had not realized were prosocial. In this case, some behaviors counted on days 6 through 10 also had occurred on days 1 through 5 but had not been counted on those days. This instrument decay could have been responsible for the observed increases on days 6 through 10 and remains an uncontrolled rival hypothesis. There are other uncontrolled threats, but we will not go into them here.

Now, suppose that on day 11 the procedure for providing feedback to the subject was discontinued; days 11 through 15 represented a reversal period (a return to the A condition). Inspection of days 11 through 15 reveals that the frequency of prosocial behaviors decreased and almost returned to the original baseline level. This phenomenon allows us to reject the hypotheses that compete with the experimental hypothesis. It appears that the experimental treat-

135

ment was indeed responsible for the increase in prosocial behavior. Our confidence would be further bolstered by a second reversal. That is, if a return to the treatment condition for days 16 through 20 produced an immediate increase in prosocial behavior, we would have further evidence that the increases in prosocial behavior resulted from the experimental intervention. While this second reversal is not, strictly speaking, necessary to rule out the competing hypotheses, it does provide further evidence that the experimental treatment was responsible for the noted changes.

A further point deserves mention: In many cases in which single-subject research is carried out, the researcher may experience ethical reservations about leaving the subject after withdrawing the treatment condition (as would be the case with an ABA design). Chapter 13 will present a full discussion of ethical issues in research. However, it should be noted here that if the subject has agreed to participate in the study in order to increase the behavior produced by the experimental treatment, then there may exist an ethical responsibility for the researcher to leave the subject with the treatment as the final state of affairs. In that case, the ABAB design enables the experimenter to terminate the experiment knowing the subject has profited from the experimental intervention.

Variables in Combination

Up to this point, we have considered using a single-subject design to study one variable. We will now focus our attention on single-subject designs in which more than one variable is considered in a particular study. In order to consider more than one variable in a single-subject study, it is necessary to consider the effect of each variable singly and then all variables in combination. This procedure allows us to assess not only the separate impact of each variable but also the summed effect of all the variables on the behavior of the research subject. The logic behind considering variables in combination in single-subject experiments is similar to the logic behind considering the interaction effect in group research. That is, we look at the effects of variables singly and then in combination with one another to ascertain how their effects mesh to produce an influence on the dependent variable.

Several points should be made before we proceed. First, a cardinal rule of single-subject research is that changes can be made in only one variable at a time. That is, when we move from one time period to another in a single-subject study, the changes between those periods should involve only one variable—never more than one. It also should be apparent that, even if we know the behavioral change that results from the introduction of one variable and the behavior change that results from the introduction of a second variable, we cannot assume the effect of both variables is necessarily the sum of the two individual effects. Further, if the effect of both variables (for example, variables B and C together) is no greater than the effect of one of these variables alone (for example, variable B), we conclude there is no *combination effect*. That is, the total effect of BC can be explained by the effect of B alone.

Suppose, for example, we consider an ABAB design, as described above. In this instance, A is the baseline condition, while B is an experimental condition involving some variable we wish to understand—for example, the effect of verbal reinforcement on an assembly-line worker's productivity. The dependent variable might be the number of items produced by the worker, while the B treatment is the verbal reward (praise) the worker receives. Suppose we also are interested in whether monetary rewards influence the number of articles produced by the worker. We might consider this monetary reward as variable C. By using an ABAB design, we can ascertain whether variable B (praise) influences the productivity of the worker. If we immediately follow the last B treatment with a combined BC treatment (as shown in Figure 9—2), we can ascertain whether the addition of mon-

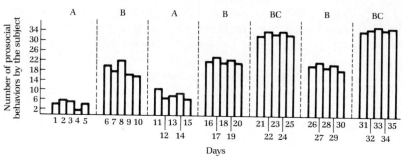

Figure 9—2   Results of Sequence 1

137

Table 9–1   Interaction Design for Single-Subject Research

	First Baseline	Treatment	First Baseline	Treatment	Combined Treatment	First Treatment	Combined Treatment
Sequence 1	A	B	A	B	BC	B	BC

	Second Baseline	Treatment	Second Baseline	Treatment	Combined Treatment	Second Treatment	Combined Treatment
Sequence 2	A	C	A	C	BC	C	BC

etary reinforcement adds to the worker's productivity. If this combined treatment is followed by a single treatment B (praise alone), we have met the requirement of a reversal. Following the logic outlined earlier, we might perform another reversal and return to the BC treatment condition once again.

Table 9–1 elaborates the sequence of events just described and labels it sequence 1. The results of sequence 1 demonstrate that variable B (praise) has an influence on the worker's productivity. Further, the addition of the combined treatment, BC, shows that variable C (monetary reward) also adds to the performance of the worker. Have we met all the requirements that would allow us to assess the combined impact of the variables? While we have met most of the requirements, we have failed to meet one. Specifically, the combined treatment effect should exceed the simple effect of *either* variable. While we have shown that the BC effect exceeds the B effect, we have not yet demonstrated that the BC effect is greater than the C effect.

Employing the same logic as in sequence 1, we will now introduce a second sequence (sequence 2), which consists of ACAC followed by BC (the combined treatment) followed by a reversal to the single treatment C and another reversal to the combined treatment BC. With the addition of sequence 2 (as set out in Table 9–1), we have a complete design for ascertaining whether the combined treatment effect of BC (verbal praise and monetary reward) exceeds the effect of either variable considered by itself. Figure 9–3 presents hypothetical results for sequence 2. According to the figure, the effect of the combined treatment (BC) was not any greater than the effect of treatment C alone. Had we not run sequence 2, we would not have been aware

138

that the total BC effect could be attributed to the effect of treatment C alone.

It appears, then, that verbal praise adds nothing to *this worker's performance* over and above what monetary reward provides. However, it should be noted that in the absence of monetary reward, verbal praise does have an effect. Consequently, it would be incorrect to infer that praise has absolutely no effect on performance. A more accurate statement would be this: In the absence of monetary reinforcement, praise increases performance; however, when monetary reinforcement is present, praise provides no additional increment to the behavior.

Limitations of Single-Subject Reversal Research

There are two major limitations to reversal research employing single subjects. The first problem involves *carry-over effects*, which were mentioned in chapter 4. Carry-over effects are often noticed when treatment sessions are followed by reversal to baseline situations, but when the subject fails to return to the original baseline level of performance. There are many reasons for carry-over effects, and it is difficult to specify precisely what is carried over from one period of an experiment to another. The problem of carry-over effects seems to be closely related to the fact that many studies on human subjects are carried out precisely because the subjects involved in the studies would like to change their behavior in a particular manner. If the treatment intervention provides the subject with the insight, skills, or

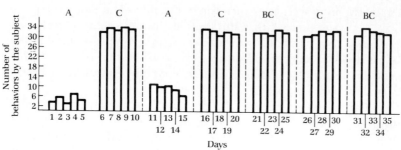

Figure 9–3   Results of Sequence 2

confidence required to bring about the desired changes, then we should not be surprised to find that the subject maintains the behavioral change even after a return to a baseline condition. For instance, in the example given earlier in the chapter, a subject was given feedback on his or her prosocial behavior in an organization. It would not be surprising to find that this worker's attitude toward his or her coworkers had been substantially altered by the increased frequency of prosocial behavior during the treatment period. This being the case, the subject might maintain those improved attitudes during the reversal to baseline period; and the amount of prosocial behavior in the baseline period might be higher than expected because of these improved attitudes and relationships. It is precisely such carry-over effects that—while desired in most practical interventions—create problems with clearly interpreting the results of single-subject research and with unequivocally identifying cause-and-effect relationships in it.

The second major difficulty with single-subject research involves problems of external validity, or generalizability. The multiple-subjects designs considered earlier in this book also had problems of external validity. These problems involved our ability to determine whether the findings had been influenced by other factors in the study (such as use of different types of subjects, different settings, or different measures). Single-subject research shares all the aforementioned problems and has yet another external validity problem. The problem relates to the fact that multiple-subjects research, when properly done, involves the specification of a particular population of subjects and employs sampling techniques to ensure that generalization to that population is appropriate. In single-subject research, no population is specified, and no adequate sampling techniques are employed to ensure generalizability. Therefore, the possibility is always present that the findings in any single-subject study are unique to a particular individual and do not represent the potential behavior of any other human beings. While this is an overstatement of the problem's magnitude, in a strictly conceptual sense, it does represent a possibility.

Simply stated, then, the generalizability of single-subject research is always in question. However, there is a rather straightforward solution to problems of this sort—the immediate replication of single-subject studies on other subjects. If similar patterns of results are obtained from subjects dissimilar to the original subject, the researcher can begin to suspect that the generality of the finding is not as limited as might have been supposed.

Multiple-Baseline Designs

The earlier discussion of reversal designs stated that using reversals is necessary to eliminate rival hypotheses, such as those represented by effects of history, maturation, testing, and so on. However, as just noted, when reversals are employed, carry-over effects often prevent a return to baseline behavior. Since it is sometimes difficult to return to baseline behavior in reversal designs, several designs have been developed to eliminate rival hypotheses without using reversals. These *multiple-baseline* designs can be most easily understood as replications of single-subject techniques wherein the length of the initial baseline period varies for each subject.

Figure 9—4 demonstrates a possible ordering of the introduction of a treatment intervention for five different subjects, each with a baseline period of a different length. If the relationship between base-

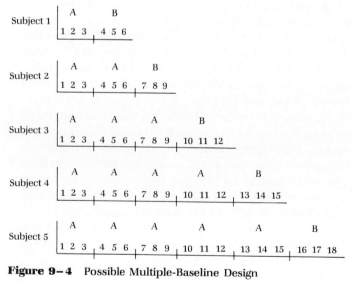

Figure 9—4   Possible Multiple-Baseline Design

141

line levels and treatment levels of the dependent variable are similar in each of these cases, the researcher can reasonably eliminate rival hypotheses without having used a reversal.

One need not think of multiple-baseline designs as only appropriate for research with individual subjects. An example of the use of the multiple-baseline design in other types of studies might involve the introduction of sales-promoting activities into subgroups of an organization. Suppose a retail sales corporation is interested in the feasibility of promoting sales by using specific management techniques. Rather than introducing the intervention techniques throughout the entire organization simultaneously, the corporation might find that introducing the techniques in stepwise fashion to various subgroups within the organization would allow for a more systematic and definitive assessment of the intervention's effectiveness.

To understand this, imagine that management, convinced of the value of the techniques, implements the intervention for all units simultaneously. If the commencement of the intervention coincides with a sharp upturn in the business cycle, it will be impossible to say whether the increase in sales is due to the intervention or to the change in the business cycle. In this instance, since sales have increased, management may not particularly care whether the cause of the gain is correctly attributed. But scientists must be concerned that they draw only scientifically appropriate conclusions. Therefore, a social scientist acting as a consultant to this firm might suggest that the various departments within the organization implement the intervention at different points in time. Sales in each of these departments would be monitored for varying lengths of time, and these varying times would serve as baseline periods.

Figure 9–5 presents hypothetical data that the consultant might obtain as a result of implementing the intervention at differing points in time for various departments within the corporation. Using this design provides several important gains. First, if the intervention does not seem to be working after the first few departments have implemented it, the program can be modified and improved or even terminated. Second, by noting the general trends in all subdivisions within the company, the researcher can separate out, to some extent, the fluctuations in the business cycle. This allows the researcher to assess the impact of the intervention more precisely.

Another way in which multiple-baseline approaches can be employed is to let stimuli or inanimate objects be the primary unit of study. Suppose, for instance, we were involved in marketing a line of textbooks for Scott, Foresman and Company. Perhaps a member of our sales staff suggests that we might increase sales by periodically sending the names of various institutions currently using our company's books to other college teachers. A list of books that we might advertise in this manner should be gathered. The semesters in which the list of schools using these books is circulated to faculty might be staggered so that one or two books are selected to be highlighted each semester. In this case, it is important to note that increases in sales should occur in the semester *following* the distribution of the list of schools currently using the book.

Figure 9–6 presents hypothetical data we might have gathered if we had carried out such an experiment. Inspection of the data

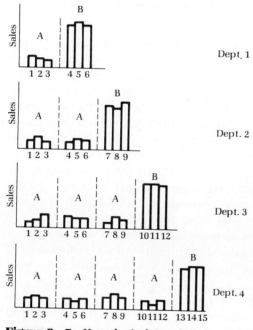

Figure 9–5 Hypothetical Results of a Multiple-Baseline Study Using Departments Within a Corporation

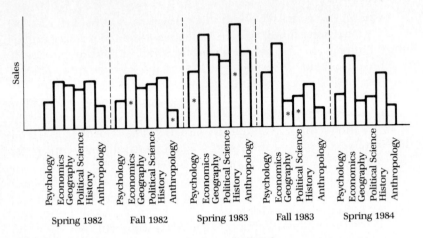

* Semester in which list of schools using book was distributed.

Figure 9–6 Hypothetical Results of a Multiple-Baseline Study Using Textbooks

reveals that our enterprising advertising worker's idea does not appear to have had a demonstrable impact on the sales of books in the semester immediately following the circulation of the lists. The data demonstrate that if we had circulated lists for all the books in the Fall 1982 semester, we might mistakenly have believed that the strategy had been successful. This mistaken belief would have been based on the fact that all the books demonstrated a moderate increase in sales in the Spring 1983 semester. However, a more careful inspection of the total pattern of results demonstrates that the gains made by the two books advertised in Fall 1982 were no larger than would have been expected for any book in the Spring 1983 semester. More importantly, the strategy of advertising other books in the Spring 1983 and Fall 1983 semesters appears to have had no impact on the sales of those books. Using this multiple-baseline procedure has allowed us to be reasonably confident that the strategy did not succeed in improving the sales of the books.

We should note that a reversal design is inappropriate for a study of this sort. If Scott, Foresman and Company is marketing good books, and if we succeed in encouraging teachers to try teaching their courses with Scott, Foresman books, we can expect that a substantial number of these teachers will continue to use the books in subsequent semesters because of their quality. Therefore, if we returned to

144

the baseline condition we could not expect book sales to return to their baseline level of sales. Of course, all of this depends on the advertising campaign's having achieved an increase in the use of the target books, which it did not do.

Additional Readings

Hersen, M., & Barlow, D. H. *Single case experimental designs: Strategies for studying behavioral change*. New York: Pergamon Press, 1976.
Sidman, M. *Tactics of scientific research*. New York: Basic Books, 1960.

10

Contamination Problems and Control Procedures

Chapter Preview

Ways in which the reactions of persons involved in a study can contaminate and even invalidate the study's findings are discussed. Experimenter expectancy effects are described and possible control procedures suggested. Several subject-generated contamination problems are also considered, along with techniques for dealing with these difficulties. Finally, contamination effects and control procedures for order effects and progressive error are discussed.

Chapter 2 introduced criteria for evaluating the appropriateness of measures and observations. Specifically, it discussed the reliability and validity of measures. This chapter will consider some of the problems that arise when we attempt to obtain reliable and valid data. It has long been known that the act of observation can, itself, produce influences that tend to invalidate the data obtained. The concept that necessary limits to the validity of any measurement are caused by the measurement process itself was first identified by the physicist Werner Heisenberg, who formalized his observation in the "principle of uncertainty." The phenomenon by which the process of observation influences the data obtained is probably more pronounced in the social sciences than in the physical sciences, since social scientific investigations usually involve a study of human beings. The reactions of humans to the experience of being observed and experimented on can produce several unintended and potentially contaminating effects.

An earlier chapter dealt with threats to internal validity (such as history effects, instrumentation effects, and so on). As you recall, these threats can represent obstacles to valid inference in research efforts. In addition to these sources of contamination, other effects can alter findings and potentially invalidate results. A few of these contaminants are explained in the following sections. Several control techniques developed in response to the problems of various types of contamination will also be considered, and their importance for various research procedures in the social sciences will be probed.

Experimenter Expectancy Effects

An experimenter may prefer that the results of a study take one direction rather than another, and this bias may actually influence the results obtained in the study. For example, perhaps an educational researcher believes lecture techniques rather than class discussion techniques represent the optimal classroom teaching method. A study conducted by this individual might find the lecture technique superior to the discussion technique, whereas an investigator who preferred the discussion format might have obtained exactly the opposite result. How might such confusing differences in results occur?

148

The existence of these experimenter expectancy effects suggests that experimenters, far from being passive observers in their studies, are active agents who can influence the outcomes of their experiments in any number of ways. This does not imply that experimenters intentionally distort their results; rather, this process can occur in spite of experimenters' conscious efforts to be fair and accurate in their experimental efforts. Even when they try to be unbiased, experimenters can still cue subjects in subtle and unintended ways that indicate what hypotheses they would like to see supported. Insofar as subjects can discern these subtle cues and alter their behavior in a way that *actually brings about* the hoped-for results, the experimenters are altering the subjects' behavior despite their best efforts to be objective and unbiased.

An intriguing example of how an experimenter can influence results is the story of Clever Hans. Clever Hans was a horse that supposedly was able to perform mathematical computations. Clever Hans' owner would give Hans a mathematical problem, and Hans would answer by tapping his foot until he reached the appropriate number. Many, many people who observed Hans actually believed that he could perform these mathematical feats, and only much later was it discovered that the trainer would look at Hans as he approached the correct answer to the problem and that this look served as the cue for Hans to stop tapping his foot. The important point to be remembered here is that the owner of Hans was *not* attempting to deceive anyone—he was, in fact, totally unaware that he was giving Hans the correct answer. Similarly, there are virtually limitless ways in which experimenters can unintentionally cue their subjects as to the set of results they would like to obtain. Subjects, then, may actually change their behavior in an experiment according to their perception of how the experimenter would like the results to come out.

Experimenter expectancy effects also can influence the study at other stages. In general, when formulating conclusions, researchers analyze all the data they have obtained in a study. However, in some instances, data are obviously contaminated and should be removed from consideration. Experimenter expectancy effects can enter the picture when decisions about discarding data must be made, because sometimes it is unclear whether data might be contaminated and thus whether they should be removed from the study.

149

Experimenters are trained to detect cues that will help them make such determinations. For example, suppose students have been asked to rate a teacher on a scale that goes from 1 (poor) to 10 (excellent). If a student has simply marked response 1 for every item, the experimenter *might* assume that this person has not really reacted to the experience of the teacher in the classroom but rather has simply tried to perform the ranking task as quickly and effortlessly as possible. The question then arises, should this subject's data remain in the study? We can make a case that data of this sort are probably invalid and should be eliminated from the study. However, the researcher might be more likely to make such a case in some situations than in others. Suppose the experimenter's hypothesis involved a prediction that ratings would be very good for this particular teacher. The researcher might be tempted to look more closely at data that disconfirmed this hypothesis. Disconfirming data might then be more likely to be eliminated.

Conversely, if a subject has provided ratings of 10 for every item for this teacher, a case could be made that the teacher is indeed an outstanding, unique individual and that the student truly believes the teacher deserves the highest possible rating on every dimension. However, the experimenter who began with the belief that the teacher would be highly rated might be especially likely to adopt this perspective. Therefore, the researcher would be likely to leave these data in the study.

The problem here often revolves around the question of how deeply an experimenter will pursue the question of whether data should be left in the study or taken out. The most appropriate statement to be made on this topic is that it may be an understandable human tendency to look more closely for assurances that data should be left in when they support our hypotheses than for reasons that data should be eliminated when they tend to disconfirm our hypotheses.

The problem cuts still deeper, because experimenters are keenly aware of the fact that results that support their hypotheses are much more likely to be published than ambiguous results or results that do not support their hypotheses. The tremendous amount of time, effort, and personal involvement in most research studies creates pressures that make it very difficult for experimenters to maintain their objectivity. Further, the pressures are increased by the "publish or perish" philosophy that has permeated academic life of late. Because there is

150

ample documentation of unconscious and unintended experimenter bias effects—and some evidence of conscious deception and distortion of experimental effects—researchers must always be careful to employ whatever control procedures are available to minimize the chances that such effects will influence their data.

There are several ways in which experimenters can increase the chances that experimenter expectancy effects will not influence their results. One way involves the experimenter's designing his or her own experiments and then soliciting the aid of colleagues to conduct these experiments; in return, the designer can conduct the experiments of others. What experimenters exchange here is the time and effort involved in conducting a study conscientiously and honestly. Obtaining positive findings is not necessarily in the best interest of the person actually conducting the experiment and working with the subjects. Therefore, the chances of conscious or unconscious distortion of results are probably far less than when experimenters conduct studies they have designed themselves.

Similarly, the chances that expectancy effects will influence decisions about which data will be left in a study can be minimized by experimenters' setting up clear decision strategies before they ever see the data subjects provide. That is, a researcher might decide that if a subject gives the same response to every item—no matter which experimental treatment group the subject is in or which response category the subject is choosing—those data will be discarded. Decisions made beforehand in this way and carried out faithfully allow experimenters to gain greater confidence that they are not allowing their expectancies to influence the data. Other procedures for reducing experimenter expectancy effects are discussed later in the chapter.

Subject Effects

Human beings are incredibly diverse. It is not only true that no two people are exactly alike but also true that no one is exactly the same person at any two points in time. For example, if you poked your head into my office one day and said "Good morning, Dr. Howard," I might respond, "Hello, how are you?" But suppose you greeted me in the same manner a week later. It is not outside the realm of possibility that I might respond, "Get out of here, you turkey!" How is

151

a science to make sense of these two diverse reactions by the *same* person under almost the *same* conditions? The answer is very complex and, unfortunately, incomplete because of our sciences' current, limited knowledge of human action. The final chapter of this book will sketch some partial answers as programs of research for the future. For now, we need only consider that, just as experimenters can influence the findings of their studies, research subjects can and do exert their individual influences on the data they provide and thereby influence the outcomes of studies.

Social scientists would like to use ideal subjects in their studies—that is, subjects who respond honestly and appropriately to the conditions and instructions presented to them. To the extent that subjects are trying to "look good" to the experimenter, "figure out" what the experiment is about, or actually influence the outcome of the study, they are providing biased data. The next section will discuss the findings of several research programs that consider ways in which human subjects are less than ideal in research investigations; in other words, the section will describe some sources of contamination subjects can bring into studies. Experimental control procedures designed to lessen the effects of these biases are also discussed.

Response-Style Effects

Almost everyone has a long history of trying to be the best person he or she can possibly be. Very few of us are consciously trying to fail or look bad in what we do or say. In fact, long years of practice have helped us to develop the skills involved in putting our best foot forward. It should not be surprising, then, that subjects may tend to respond to ambiguity in experiments by presenting the best possible picture of themselves.

For example, do you know what your IQ is? Well, people involved in the measurement of intelligence tell us that a person can never know his or her intelligence score with absolute certainty. With sufficient testing, the best we might have is a high degree of confidence that our intelligence lies within a given range of IQ scores.

For example, you might come to learn that you can be 95-percent certain that your IQ lies somewhere between 110 and 120. In that case, if I asked you "What is your IQ?" what would you answer? You would not be unusual if you gave a response closer to 120 than to 110.

This tendency to present oneself positively can be viewed as a source of contamination in studies.

There would be no problem if all subjects presented themselves equally favorably, but this is not the case. We also know that subjects are not equally positive in their self-presentations; some people consistently give themselves the benefit of the doubt and present themselves as positively as possible, whereas other individuals are consistently more critical of themselves.

The best solutions to the problems of positive subject self-presentation vary according to the objectives and goals of the study. Suppose, for example, that I am interested in ascertaining whether two assertiveness training procedures improve subjects' abilities to respond appropriately to situations requiring assertive responses. If I employ proper *design controls*, the problems of subject self-presentation strategies can be controlled. Suppose I take a group of potential subjects and randomly assign them to one of three groups: assertiveness training (a standard experimental group); bibliotherapy (a group that reads a book on assertiveness, offering an alternative for subjects who want to change but do not want more active treatment); and a group that does nothing related to change in assertiveness (a no-treatment control group). At some point in the future, all subjects will be measured for their levels of assertiveness.

Several very important points should be made:

1. *Any* measure of assertiveness can be influenced by self-presentation biases.
2. Therefore, we cannot be confident that any score or group mean represents an absolute level of assertiveness.
3. In spite of this, because of random assignment of subjects to groups, we can assume that all groups are equal on all factors except the independent variable (including the tendency to present themselves in a positive manner).
4. Therefore, while assertiveness scores are inaccurate because of subject self-presentation biases, the groups are about equally influenced by these biases.
5. Thus, comparisons among group mean levels of assertiveness are appropriate.
6. This is true because differences in mean assertiveness scores for the groups reflect the effects of the independent variable (assertiveness training versus bibliotherapy versus control) on the dependent variable (assertiveness scores).

153

You can see that design control strategies can often handle problems of subject self-presentation bias, just as they were shown to handle other potential threats—such as effects of history, maturation, testing, and so on—in chapter 7.

A second approach to handling positive self-presentation strategies involves measuring the subjects' levels of particular biases at the same time the construct of interest is being measured. Then, in any one of a number of ways, each subject's score on the construct can be adjusted by that subject's probable amount of positive self-presentation bias. For example, suppose I measured three subjects' assertiveness levels and the levels at which they tend to give socially desirable responses (a self-presentation bias). For simplicity, let us assume that both scales range from 1 to 10, with a 10 on the assertiveness scale identifying a person who is totally assertive and a 10 on the social desirability scale indicating a person who always gives the more socially desirable response. Let us also assume that an assertive response is almost always a socially desirable response, since to say that you would not be assertive in a particular situation would be to admit a certain degree of social imperfection. Now, suppose I told you that subject 1 had an assertiveness score of 5 and a social desirability score of 0, subject 2 scored 5 on assertiveness and 5 on social desirability, and subject 3 scored 5 on assertiveness and 10 on social desirability. Your problem as a researcher would be to decide how assertive the three subjects really are. How could you decide?

A first strategy might be to assume that the assertiveness measure is a perfectly accurate and unbiased index of the construct of assertiveness and to conclude that, since all three subjects obtained the same score on the assertiveness measure, they are equal. This approach simply opts to ignore the effects on assertiveness ratings of subjects' giving socially desirable responses. An alternative approach is to assume that subjects' tendency to respond in a socially desirable manner might have influenced their assertiveness scores. What we might do in this instance is to raise the assertiveness score of subject 1, leave the assertiveness score of subject 2 unchanged, and decrease the assertiveness score of subject 3. The rationale behind this procedure involves attempting to approach the "true" assertiveness score of each subject—the score we hypothetically would have obtained if the subjects had not shown dissimilar tendencies to respond in a socially desirable manner. But another problem immediately arises. How much should the observed assertiveness scores be adjusted? Should

154

the adjusted scores for subjects 1, 2, and 3 be 6, 5, and 4; or 7, 5, and 3; or even 10, 5, and 1? Unfortunately, the actual procedures employed to adjust scores are beyond the scope of this book. The point to be remembered is that, in spite of the apparent difficulties, scientists attempt to isolate probable contaminants of their empirical findings and correct the observations for these potentially biasing influences.

In the previous example, two separate tests were administered—one for assertiveness and one for social desirability. It is also possible to include measures of subject response-style tendencies within the actual test of the construct of interest. For example, the Minnesota Multiphasic Personality Inventory (MMPI) has a "lie scale" obtained from subjects' responses to various test items. The lie scale identifies inconsistencies in responses that may be due to various self-presentation biases on the subject's part. The other scales (for example, neuroticism and psychoticism) are then interpreted with this lie scale score in mind.

Other Contaminants

Several types of contaminants that subjects may introduce into a study do not fall under the category of response-style effects. While it would be impractical to detail all these potential pitfalls here, describing a few of them briefly may prove informative. A more thorough treatment of these topics can be obtained in advanced texts on experimental design, such as Cook and Campbell (1979).

In experiments, subjects are often assigned to various treatment groups or to control groups. Since subjects usually have some idea of what topics the study deals with and what types of treatments might be involved, we might wonder about subjects' reactions to the particular treatment to which they are assigned. We then should wonder if these reactions might contaminate the results obtained in some important manner.

For example, suppose I am interested in determining whether a particular training package is effective in increasing sales for a group of salespeople. I might give the training to half of the salespeople in a particular company and have the remainder serve as a no-treatment control group. If the assignment of subjects to conditions is random, we might believe that comparisons between treatment and control groups will be uncontaminated by threats to internal validity. However, consider the plight of the poor control subjects. People whom

155

they work with (possibly even compete against) are being given special training to help them improve their work performance. What makes matters even worse is that the choice of which workers receive the training is unrelated—and must, from the researcher's point of view, be unrelated—to any meaningful criteria for selection into the program.

From the control subjects' point of view, then, the decision to withhold the treatment from them was capricious. How might such a reaction influence a particular control subject? Some might become angry and simply give up trying to sell as hard as they had tried in the past, saying something like, "Well, if they won't help me sell more, why should I kill myself trying?" On the other hand, other control subjects might become angry and redouble their efforts, thinking, "Since they [the treatment subjects] are getting help, I'd better pull out all the stops and sell all I can, or I might lose my job." These differing reactions might lead some subjects to sell less and others to sell more. If these differing effects were about equal, in a sense the two types of reactions would cancel each other out, and the resulting average level of performance of the control group would be unaffected. If that were the case, the problems for the internal validity of the study would be minimal.

Unfortunately, long experience with research in real-life settings suggests that subjects' reactions rarely cancel each other out. Rather, control groups tend to show typical patterns of reacting to the experience of being control subjects. This is so because people often tend to respond in a similar manner to a particular experience and also because often they can talk to one another and thereby influence each other's reactions to being control subjects.

When control subjects tend to redouble their efforts and actually improve their performance, they are engaged in *compensatory overachievement*. The opposite effect, deterioration of performance, is called *resentful demoralization*. It might prove instructive to consider the performance of control groups that demonstrate both types of effect and to examine the resulting problems for the conclusions of a study. Let us return to the sales training program mentioned earlier and consider two hypothetical cases—one in which the training *is* effective and one in which it *is not* effective. Figure 10−1 presents hypothetical sales per year per salesman (in thousands of dollars) for treatment and control group subjects when the treatment was effective (left-hand column) and when it was ineffective (right-hand col-

156

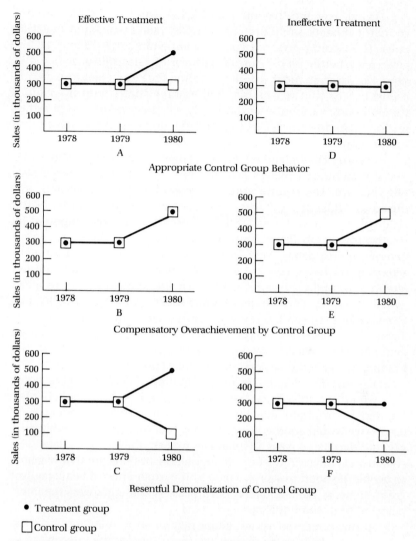

Figure 10–1 Hypothetical Results of Sales Training Program

umn). The magnitude of the treatment effect, as shown in the left-hand column, is an increase in sales of $200,000 per year. The top row of graphs demonstrates the results of the study when the control group behaves appropriately.

157

Let us assume that the training occurred at the end of 1979, so that its effects could only show up in 1980 results, not in earlier ones. The figure provides hypothetical results for 1978 and 1979 to give you a better picture of the pattern of sales performance over time. However, in most studies, baseline data such as these are not available. For that reason, we will assume that I (and my clients, the company's executives) have only the 1980 results from which to draw conclusions regarding the effectiveness of the sales training program.

Remember, the correct interpretation of the results should be that the training increased sales for the treatment group by $200,000 per year over the control group for the left-hand column and produced no difference between treatment and control groups in the right-hand column. Those are indeed the conclusions supported by the top row in the figure (graphs A and D), where the control group behaves appropriately. Now, look at the second row, where compensatory overachievement takes place. Here, the left-hand column (graph B) would lead us to believe that the treatment had no effect (which is wrong); and the right-hand column (graph E) would lead us to conclude that the training produced a deterioration in sales performance (which is also incorrect). In the bottom row, where resentful demoralization occurs, we might conclude from graph C that the training was effective (which is technically correct), but we would also estimate that the magnitude of the training effect was $400,000 per year, which is a substantial overestimate. In graph F, instead of drawing the appropriate conclusion—that the training produced no effect—we would conclude erroneously that the training resulted in a gain of $200,000 per year. (Remember, we can only see 1980 data.) The conclusions to be drawn from these demonstrations are that whenever people respond inappropriately to the experience of being control group subjects, contamination is introduced that endangers the internal validity of the findings.

At this point, the astute reader might reason that if the baseline data were available to the researcher, more appropriate interpretation of the research data might result. For example, in light of the baseline data, graph F might be interpreted as suggesting that the training produced no effect (treatment group sales were $300,000 per year for 1978, 1979, *and* 1980) and that the control group demonstrated the effects of resentful demoralization (control group sales were $300,000 per year in 1978 and 1979 *but only* $100,000 in 1980). These conclusions are, of course, correct. While that line of logic seems good, though, it fails to hold up under closer scrutiny. For example, we assumed that the absence of a treatment effect and the presence of resentful demoralization explained the data presented in graph F; but suppose the following scenario were true instead. The training was effective in producing a $200,000 per year increase in sales; but in 1980, there was a substantial downturn in sales in the industry as a whole. Salespeople who operated at the same level of efficiency in 1980 as in previous years experienced a decline in 1980 sales of $200,000. If we constructed a graph of those data, it would be identical to graph F. Which set of conclusions is correct? Did the training produce no effect and the control group's performance deteriorate? Or was the training effective and sufficient to offset a simultaneous downturn in sales, as reflected by the $200,000 decline in sales of an appropriately functioning control group? Unfortunately, the data provide no sure way of choosing one plausible alternative scenario over the other. Therefore, the conclusion of the preceding paragraph remains true: When control subjects demonstrate compensatory overachievement or resentful demoralization, we have problems interpeting the data.

Gaining experimental control of inappropriate reactions by control group members is a very difficult task. In many instances, the difficulty can be reduced by isolating treatment group subjects from control group subjects. Minimizing the amount of interaction among control group members can also help. While these clearly are only partial solutions, they can serve to lessen the severity of the contamination.

A related procedure is to employ a *placebo* control group rather than a no-treatment control group. A placebo control provides subjects with some experience that the experimenter believes will have no real effect but that gives subjects the mistaken impression that they are receiving a treatment. Believing they are receiving treatment, placebo control subjects are less likely to experience reactions such as resentful demoralization and compensatory overachievement. Placebo control groups are frequently employed in psychotherapy research, where techniques such as use of "support groups" are employed as general placebo conditions against which more specific therapy approaches are compared.

More generally, if subjects' knowledge of what experimental treatment they are receiving might influence their reactions in the study, the researcher should employ a *single blind* control procedure. Originally developed for drug research studies, a single blind procedure involves, for example, placing subjects in groups that receive various types of medications, various dosage levels, or placebos—but not giving them any information or clues as to which group they belong to. That is, subjects have no idea whether the pills their group receives contain a strong dose of medication, a weak dose of medication, or no medication at all.

Similarly, as you recall from the discussion of experimenter effects earlier in this chapter, an experimenter's knowledge of what treatment a subject receives can produce unintended effects. In cases where this might occur, a *double blind* procedure can be employed. Here, in addition to subjects' not knowing which treatment they are receiving, the researcher is also unaware of which treatment a subject is receiving. This withholding of information from the researcher can be easily carried out in a drug study by making all pills look identical. However, in other instances, such as psychotherapy research, it is much more difficult to disguise a placebo so that the researcher will not recognize it as one.

You may have perceived that a number of ethical difficulties are implicit in the last few examples. Rather than ethical problems, being addressed as they arise, they are treated as a group in chapter 15.

Order Effects

The consideration of within-subjects designs in chapter 4 gave some examples of studies in which subjects were exposed to several experimental treatments in the course of an investigation. That discussion emphasized that the order in which treatments (or stimuli, or the like) are presented can influence the subjects' reactions to them. If a particular treatment is always presented first, and if subjects respond more favorably (or less favorably) to any treatment given first, superior (or inferior) ratings might not be a true reflection of the worth of that particular intervention but rather might be due to the intervention's being assigned to first position in the order of presentation. The point is that the researcher has no way of knowing which of these possibilities was the true cause, or if both produced effects. The confusion of order effects with treatment effects always leads to confusion in interpreting findings.

The order effects we will consider here are *practice effects* and *fatigue effects*. Practice effects occur when subjects' performance shows improvement over the course of the experiment. This improvement may be due to any of numerous reasons, such as gaining increased skill in the tasks involved, greater ease in the experimental setting, more relaxed relations with the researcher, and so forth. Practice effects are generally considered to help a subject's performance over time in any experimental condition. The order effects believed to detract from subjects' performance are fatigue effects. In addition to actually becoming physically tired, subjects may become bored with the experimental tasks, find the researcher's mannerisms progressively more irritating, become uncomfortable in the experimental setting, and so forth.

Both facilitative and detrimental effects represent examples of *progressive error*. As the experiment progresses, the findings become

Table 10–1 Within-Subjects and Between-Subjects Counterbalancing

Order of Treatments for Single Subject											
Treatment	A	B	C		C	B	A	C	B	A	A	B	C
Position	1	2	3		4	5	6	7	8	9	10	11	12

	Treatment A	Treatment B	Treatment C
Positions	1	2	3
	6	5	4
	9	8	7
	10	11	12
Average position	26 ÷ 4 = 6.5	26 ÷ 4 = 6.5	26 ÷ 4 = 6.5

Order of Treatments for Group of Subjects			
	Position 1	Position 2	Position 3
Subject 1	A	B	C
Subject 2	A	C	B
Subject 3	B	A	C
Subject 4	B	C	A
Subject 5	C	A	B
Subject 6	C	B	A

	Treatment A	Treatment B	Treatment C
Positions	1	2	3
	1	3	2
	2	1	3
	3	1	2
	2	3	1
	3	2	1
Average position	12 ÷ 6 = 2	12 ÷ 6 = 2	12 ÷ 6 = 2

distorted because of these influences. Remember that the experimenter's goal is to obtain true comparisons of experimental conditions. For this to be possible, all other factors or influences that might affect the outcome must be similar for all experimental conditions. Against the backdrop of this goal, how is the experimenter to control order effects? You may recall from chapter 4 that one way is through counterbalancing, a way of ordering the presentation of experimental conditions to make average position within the order about equal for each experimental condition. Table 10−1 presents examples of counterbalanced orders of presentation of experimental conditions. Here, balance is achieved for a particular subject in the top example and across a group of subjects in the bottom example.

In each case, the average position within the order is identical for treatments A, B, and C. That is, in the within-subjects example, at the top of the table, each treatment has an average position of 6.5; so comparisons among the three treatments will not be biased by progressive error effects. If it is not feasible to balance the order of presentation for a given subject, researchers are forced to turn to between-subjects counterbalancing, illustrated in the lower part of the table. However, both examples of counterbalancing presented in Table 10−1 are appropriate only insofar as it makes sense to expose each subject to more than one treatment condition. If this procedure is illogical in a particular experiment, the investigator is forced to employ a between-subjects design in which each subject is randomly assigned to one and only one treatment condition. The alternative to counterbalancing to achieve control over progressive error effects, called *randomization of the order of presentation* of treatments (or stimuli, or the like), also allows the researcher to gain approximately equal average positions for the various treatments. While counterbalancing is generally the preferred method when the number of assignments to be made is small, randomization becomes an increasingly more viable option as the number of assignments becomes large.

A linkage should be made at this point with the concept of instrument decay, discussed in chapter 7. You may recall that instrument decay—systematic changes in the calibration of measuring instruments or in observers or scorers—can produce changes in measurements. You may be able to see from this definition that instrument decay is really progressive error related to the actual measurement process. The point to be made here is that the solution to instrument decay is the same as outlined above for other forms of progressive error—namely, randomization or counterbalancing.

For example, suppose we conducted a study to attempt to determine whether a training program could improve interviewers' skills in conducting better personnel selection interviews. We might have each interviewer conduct a placement interview with a client both before and after the training program. These pretraining and posttraining interviews could be videotaped, and the interviewer's skills could later be assessed by trained judges who would view the videotaped interviews and provide ratings. Perhaps the judges would become bored with their rating tasks and be progressively less attentive as the judging proceeded. Being less attentive, they might notice fewer and fewer mistakes interviewers made in the interviews. The net effect might be that judges would be more lenient in rating later videotapes than they would have been earlier. (This type of instrumentation effect is common when judges are employed as rating instruments in research efforts.)

You can see that if the judges rated all the pretraining interviews first and all the posttraining interviews later, they might give higher ratings to the posttraining interviews *even if the training had no effect on interviewers' skills*. The progressive easing of the rater's judgment standards alone might produce a significant difference, which we might mistakenly believe to be a true treatment effect. As suggested earlier, a solution to this instrumentation problem is to either counterbalance or randomize the order in which pretraining and posttraining videotapes are presented to the judges. This serves to equalize the effects of progressive error (instrumentation effects, in this case). Comparisons of pretraining and posttraining ratings would therefore be unbiased with regard to contamination caused by instrumentation effects.

Additional Readings

Rosenthal, R. *Experimenter effects in behavioral research.* New York: Appleton-Century-Crofts, 1966.

Cook, T. D., & Campbell, D. T. *Quasi-experimentation: Design and analysis issues in field settings.* Chicago: Rand-McNally, 1979.

Inferential Statistics: A Conceptual Overview

Chapter Preview

Chapter 11 presents an overview of inferential statistics that stresses its importance as a decision-making device in research. Statistical methods that relate to both group mean differences and strength of relationship are presented. Other considerations for statistical significance, such as sample size, also are explained.

Until now we have considered hypothetical distributions of data that might have been obtained from various research studies and have simply made intuitive judgments as to whether those data supported the experimental hypotheses. In reality, as soon as the data are collected, experimenters turn to statistical techniques to help them answer precisely the question of whether the data support the hypotheses. As has been stressed throughout this book, the quality of the data and data collection procedures are of paramount importance in the interpretation of the meaning of the findings. The methods of inferential statistics are merely tools that help researchers answer questions such as, "Are the trends I have observed in the data sufficiently strong that I can confidently say there is a real phenomenon at work that supports my experimental hypotheses?"

No statistical method available can adequately overcome the problems associated with data obtained from poorly designed studies or poor data collection techniques. The maxim associated with computer programming applies equally well to statistics: "Garbage in, garbage out!" That is, to the extent that our data is contaminated by threats to valid inference, we will arrive at inappropriate or misleading conclusions regardless of the sophistication of the statistical analysis performed.

You may recall that we touched on statistics in chapter 2, in relation to distributions of scores. The statistical techniques discussed there—central tendency and variability—are descriptive statistics; they help researchers organize, summarize, and present data they have gathered. Inferential statistics, as the name implies, comprises techniques used as the basis for inferences from the data.

Two basic types of inferential statistics are employed by social scientists. The first type relates to group mean differences. The techniques of this type are designed to assess whether the means of two samples of data are sufficiently different that the experimenter can confidently infer that this difference reflects the operation of some non-chance phenomenon. These statistical methods are used to help answer such questions as, "Do boys obtain higher scores in mathematics on the College Board Examinations than girls?" The second type of statistics employed by social scientists relates to the strength of relationships. These techniques provide an indication of the similarity between two samples of data. For example, is there any relationship between the number of inches of rainfall per year in a particular place and the amount of grain harvested there?

166

Researchers, then, have available a number of statistical methods to use in their studies. The first major decision all researchers must confront is whether they can more appropriately answer the research question by considering differences between the means of data samples or by considering similarities between data samples. As you will see later, the decision about what specific type of statistical method will be employed is further influenced by whether nominal, ordinal, interval, or ratio scales are employed in analysis of the data. Other issues that affect the type of statistical method chosen are the number of groups or levels of the independent variable to be compared and the number of dependent measures gathered, as well as various other considerations beyond the scope of this book.

The remainder of this chapter will consider in detail one statistical method that measures group mean difference—the independent groups t-test—and one statistical method that measures strength of relationship—the Pearson correlation coefficient. In the case of the t-test, we will consider an independent variable that includes two groups and a dependent variable that uses interval data. If the dependent measure had used nominal data, we would have used a different statistical test (chi square). The computation of both the t-test and the chi square will be demonstrated in chapter 12. In reading these chapters, you will, it is hoped, come to understand *how* one proceeds from raw data collection through an analysis of the data to an interpretation of the findings of that analysis.

An Example of Group Mean Difference Statistics: The t-test

Suppose you conducted an experiment to study the effect of a particular food additive on the taste of a food. Twenty subjects volunteered for the experiment and then were randomly assigned to one of two conditions. The first condition involved the subjects' eating cereal that did not contain the food additive. The other group ate cereal identical to the cereal eaten by the first group except that it contained the chemical additive (we'll call it "cereal plus"). After eating the cereal, each group member rated his or her satisfaction with its taste on a ten-point scale (1 means "This is the worst-tasting cereal I've ever eaten"; 10 means "This is the best-tasting cereal I've ever eaten").

Table 11-1   Subjects' Ratings of Cereal Taste

	Plain Cereal	Cereal Plus
	1	6
	5	4
	3	5
	3	6
	4	8
	1	9
	2	5
	3	6
	4	6
	3	8
Mean	2.9	6.3
Standard deviation	1.22	1.51
Number of subjects	10	10

Table 11−1 presents the hypothetical results of the subjects' ratings of taste for each group. Figure 11−1 is a graphical representation of these findings. In Figure 11−1, there appears to be a good deal of separation between the distribution of responses given to the plain cereal (the solid line) and to the cereal that contained the additive (the dotted line). The purpose of any statistical method that measures group mean difference is to specify mathematically the degree to

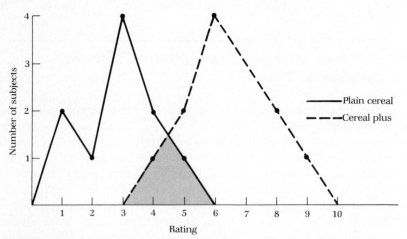

Figure 11-1   Overlap of the Distributions of the Data Presented in Table 11−1

which distributions of this sort overlap or do not overlap. The overlapping area is shaded in Figure 11−1.

In an elementary sense, the *more* the overlap (shaded area) between distributions, the *less* the chance that the statistical method will find the means of the two distributions to be significantly different. More overlap, then, implies a smaller possibility of finding a significant difference, whereas less overlap suggests a greater chance of concluding that the means of the groups are significantly different from one another.

Three factors influence whether or not a statistical method will conclude that there is a significant difference between two distributions of scores. The first factor is the magnitude of difference between the means of the two groups. In the example, the mean of the plain-cereal group was 2.9, while the mean of the cereal-plus group was 6.3. As can be seen in Figure 11−1, there was very little overlap between these two distributions, a reflection of the fact that the mean values were 3.4 points apart (6.3 − 2.9 = 3.4). Now, if we subtract two points from each score in the cereal-plus group, the difference between the two means is decreased by two points; and the difference between the two distributions is less likely to be considered significant, as shown by the increased overlap in Figure 11−2. The fact that the means now differ by only 1.4 points (4.3 − 2.9 = 1.4) is yet another

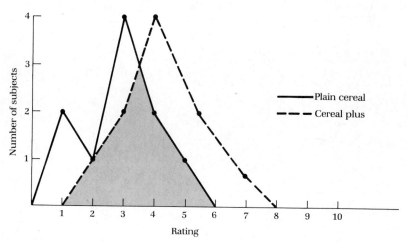

Figure 11−2 Increased Overlap of Distributions When Mean Values Are Brought Closer Together

169

indication that it is unlikely that the statistic we compute will allow us to conclude that the difference between the means of these distributions is significant.

In addition to the actual size of the difference between the group means, two other factors can influence the magnitude of the group mean difference statistic and therefore can influence whether we can conclude that the differences between the means of the distributions are significant. These two factors are the standard deviation of each distribution of scores and the number of subjects in the study. (You may recall from chapter 2 that the standard deviation can be thought of as the average distance of each score from the mean.)

When we altered the data in Table 11−1 by subtracting two points from each score of the cereal-plus group, the resulting distribution for the group had a different mean (4.3 instead of 6.3), but the standard deviation remained unchanged (1.51) and the number of subjects remained unchanged (ten per group). The difference in overlap between Figures 11−1 and 11−2 was totally due to changes in the differences between the means.

The data presented in Figure 11−3 are slightly different from the data in Figure 11−2: The mean of each distribution is exactly the same as in Figure 11−2, but the standard deviation of each distribution is substantially less than the standard deviations in Figure 11−2. Table 11−2 presents data for both figures; the data marked with asterisks in the table are illustrated in Figure 11−3. Again, notice that the means for the two sets of data are the same. The difference is that the

Table 11−2   Ratings Illustrated in Figures 11−2 and 11−3*

	Plain Cereal	Plain Cereal*	Cereal Plus	Cereal Plus*
	1	2	4	4
	5	3	2	5
	3	3	3	4
	3	4	4	4
	4	3	6	3
	1	3	7	4
	2	3	3	5
	3	2	4	5
	4	3	4	5
	3	3	6	4
Mean	2.9	2.9	4.3	4.3
Standard deviation	1.22	0.54	1.51	0.64
Number of subjects	10	10	10	10

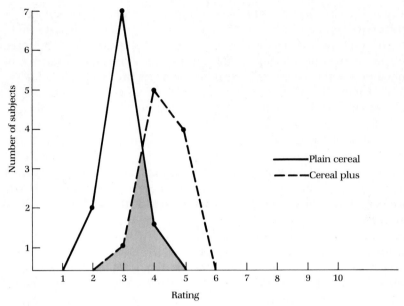

Figure 11 – 3 Overlap of the Distributions of Data Marked with Asterisk (*) in Table 11 – 2

scores in the set of data marked with asterisks have been manipulated to show a smaller standard deviation—that is, the scores in each of these distributions tend to be closer to the distributions' means.

When you compare the two figures, you can see that the amount of overlap between the distributions in Figure 11 – 3 is less than in Figure 11 – 2, in spite of the fact that the difference between the means of the two distributions is the same (4.3 − 2.9 = 1.40) in both cases. The smaller overlap in Figure 11 – 3 is due solely to the smaller standard deviations of the distributions. As a general rule, with all other things being equal, as the standard deviations of distributions decrease, the chances of finding a significant difference between group means increases.

Finally, with all other things being equal, a researcher can increase the chances of finding a significant difference by increasing the number of subjects in the study. The data in Figure 11 – 2, for example, were obtained from twenty subjects (ten in each group). If two hundred subjects had taken part in the study, and if the means and standard deviations had been identical with those represented in

Figure 11−2, then the chances of those means' being significantly different from each other would be greater than when the data came from only twenty subjects. Again, all other things being equal, obtaining data on a larger number of subjects increases the chance of obtaining a significant difference between group means.

The reason for this phenomenon is not readily apparent, and its demonstration would require a complex mathematical exposition. The logic behind the point is that the more completely we sample, the less likely we are to obtain a freak, unrepresentative finding. For our purposes, an example will make the point. If I had a die that I suspected might be loaded, I might perform a study to see if I was correct. Now, there are six sides to a die; so if the die is fair, I would expect each side to appear on top one-sixth of the time (in about 16 2/3 percent of the throws).

Suppose I tossed the die twelve times and observed the follow- ing results: Side 1 occurred two times (16 2/3 percent); side 2 occurred two times (16 2/3 percent); side 3 occurred four times (33 1/3 percent); side 4 occurred two times (16 2/3 percent); side 5 occurred one time (8 1/3 percent); and side 6 occurred one time (8 1/3 percent). As researchers, the question for us is this: What is the likelihood that those findings could reasonably have occurred if the die was fair? Remember, I expected each side to appear on top about 16 2/3 per- cent of the time. However, in some cases, that did not happen—side 3, for example, appeared on top 33 1/3 percent of the time. We should note, though, that people familiar with dice know that even with fair dice, some numbers will occur more frequently than would have been expected over short periods of time. Consequently, it is entirely possi- ble that my findings could have occurred even if the die was, in fact, fair. In other words, we have asked the question "How likely is it that certain outcomes—33 1/3 percent for side 3; 8 1/3 percent for side 5; 8 1/3 percent for side 6—would have occurred if the die was fair?" Because the unusual percentages are based on a small sample of observations (twelve tosses), it is still well within the realm of possibil- ity that these percentages are the result of chance alone.

Now contrast that hypothetical situation with the following example: instead of tossing the die twelve times, I toss it 12,000 times. I might observe the following results: side 1 occurred 2000 times (16 2/3 percent); side 2 occurred 2000 times (16 2/3 percent); side 3 occurred 4000 times (33 1/3 percent); side 4 occurred 2000 times (16 2/3 percent); side 5 occurred 1000 times (8 1/3 percent); and side 6 occurred 1000 times (8 1/3 percent). Again, if the die was completely fair, I would have expected each side to occur about 2000 times (16 2/3 percent). You can see that the *percent* occurrence of each side of the die is identical in both examples (this corresponds to the relationship between group means in the previous discussion of the t-test). The only difference between the two examples is the number of tosses of the die (this corresponds to the number of subjects in the study in the discussion of the t-test).

In the second example, in which 12,000 trials were conducted, it would have been mathematically almost impossible for one side of the die to occur 4000 times while two other sides occurred only 1000 times if the die had been really fair. Consequently, we can conclude, in this second example, that the mean occurrence of the various outcomes is significantly different from the result we would have expected to result from the operation of chance alone. Stated slightly differently, the differences observed cannot reasonably be attributed to chance. Hence, we are probably safe in concluding that the die is unfair in some way. As a general rule, with all other things being equal, the greater the number of trials (or subjects or observations), the greater the chance of finding significant differences, if they exist.

Statistical Significance

The previous discussion mentioned significant differences between group means but never defined what a significant difference was. Webster's dictionary lists among the possible meanings of the word *significant* the following: important; momentous; having special meaning; full of import. Given this common understanding of the word *significant*, it would be logical to conclude that a "significant difference" between group means is simply a large, important, or meaningful difference. However, *this is not the meaning* of the term *significant* for social scientists.

As was demonstrated by the example of the tossing of the die, to claim that a difference between group means is *statistically* significant is to assert that the observed differences between group means are not likely to be due to chance alone. Rather, the conclusion is that some nonchance factor must be operating to produce differences as large as those observed in the data. You should realize, then, that *statistical significance* represents a statement of confidence that chance fluctuations can be eliminated as the sole cause of observed differences. Significance does not address the issue of whether the differences are important, meaningful, or large in an absolute sense. There are statistical methods that *do* attempt to measure the size of an effect (such as the strength of relationship measures). A concept related to the size of an effect (called *proportion of variance accounted for*) will be considered later in this chapter.

The astute reader may have noticed that a reverse logic was employed in the previous example. I originally asked if the die was loaded. However, my procedure consisted of assuming the die was fair; noting how much the means observed in my "experiment" differed from the expected means; and then, after I had tossed the die 12,000 times, concluding that it was extremely unlikely that my unusual set of results would have occurred as a result of chance alone. Therefore, I concluded that some real factor must have been operating to produce mean differences that large. More formally stated, the basic logic of testing for statistical significance takes the following steps:

Procedure	Terminology
1. The researcher formulates a guess about some real factor that might produce an effect on some other factor. ("This die might be loaded.")	1. This possible causal relationship is called the *experimental hypothesis* or the *research hypothesis.*
2. The researcher then doubts this experimental hypothesis and predicts a set of results that should occur if the experimental hypothesis is false. ("The die is fair; so each side should appear on top equally often.")	2. The new hypothesis that directly contradicts the experimental hypothesis is called the *null hypothesis*.
3. Data are collected and analyzed statistically. The resulting statistic tells the experimenter how confident he or she can be that the observed result could have been due to chance alone.	3. The statistic tells the researcher the *probability* that the results actually observed would have been obtained if the null hypothesis was true.

An Example of Group Mean Difference Statistics: The t-test

Procedure

4. The standard confidence level in research in the social sciences requires that there be only five or fewer chances in a hundred that chance alone could have produced the observed findings.

5. A certain value corresponds to a mean difference that would occur by chance alone even if the experimental hypothesis was completely false.

6. The researcher compares the value computed from the data with the critical value obtained from the table. If the computed value exceeds the critical value, the researcher can be more than 95–percent confident that something other than chance alone was required to obtain the magnitude of mean differences observed in the data (because he or she is less than 5-percent confident that the results were due to chance alone).

Terminology

4. Another way to say "The chance of obtaining these results if the null hypothesis is true is less than five out of one hundred" is "$p < .05$."

5. This value is called the *critical value* and can be obtained from a table of critical values unique to the statistical method being employed (for example, a table of critical values of t appears in appendix E of this book).

6. In this case, the difference is said to be *statistically significant*.

Keep in mind that research in all sciences involves not certainty but probability. That is, in terms of the procedure described above, there are about five chances out of one hundred that mean differences larger than the critical value will be observed even if the null hypothesis is true. When this happens, we will conclude that the null hypothesis is false and the experimental hypothesis is true. In such a case, however, the observed differences are due solely to chance factors; and we have drawn an incorrect inference. The problem of concluding the experimental hypothesis is true when the mean difference is in fact due to chance is referred to as a *type I error*. In about 5 percent of the cases in which the null hypothesis is correct, an error of this sort will occur when $p < .05$ is used as the standard. Again, in these cases, the researcher will mistakenly conclude that the experimental hypothesis is true.

Because conclusions are never certain but rather are probabilistic, a researcher who observes a difference that is statistically significant never knows if the difference represents a real effect or a type I error; he or she can only be confident that such a difference represents a real effect a certain percent of the time. For this reason, replications are essential in the social sciences—to discover whether statistically significant effects might simply have been due to type I errors. One way to reduce type I errors is to require a more stringent critical value as the basis for concluding that a significant difference exists. For example, a researcher may be willing to tolerate only one chance in one hundred of incorrectly rejecting the null hypothesis ($p < .01$). Conceptually, this means that the researcher needs to find an even larger mean difference before he or she will be willing to conclude that a significant difference exists.

The practice of guarding against type I errors has an unintended and unfortunate consequence. In some instances, experimental hypotheses are true but result in rather small mean differences. We sometimes miss these small (but real) effects because we are demanding very large mean differences in order to be convinced that a real difference exists. These errors of overconservatism are called *type II errors*. As we reduce the likelihood of making type I errors, the probability of making type II errors must increase.

There is no "best" or "correct" setting of the relative amounts of type I versus type II errors (referred to as selecting the alpha level), although the usual convention is that an alpha level of .05 ($p < .05$) is employed. However, a researcher can choose (before the data is analyzed) to employ a different alpha level if he or she has a reason to particularly fear a type I or a type II error. For example, suppose a medical researcher wanted to compare a standard drug that reduced blood pressure reasonably well and had no side effects with a new drug that could have some negative side effects. In such a case, the researcher would want to be very confident that the new drug was demonstrably better than the standard drug at reducing blood pres-

176

sure before worrying about its side effects. In such cases, using a conservative alpha level, such as $p < .01$, might be appropriate. By choosing $p < .01$ instead of $p < .05$, the researcher ensures that stronger positive effects by the new drug will be needed to make him or her prefer it to the standard drug. These stringent standards for acceptance are justified by the negative side effects of the new drug.

Statistics That Relate to Strength of Relationship: The Pearson Correlation Coefficient

The second major category of statistical techniques measures the amount of similarity between two or more distributions of data. The fundamental purpose of this second type of statistical techniques, then, is to address the question, "How similar are these distributions of data?" You can see that this goal is different from the goal of the group mean difference statistics—to note mean differences and determine if it is feasible to attribute those differences solely to chance. We will consider the Pearson product-moment correlation coefficient as an example of the strength of relationship type of statistics.

The basic logic underlying group mean difference statistics, such as the t-test, involves the belief that if the means of two groups are different from one another on a particular dimension, this difference might be the result of systematic differences between the groups on some variable. Data from two variables can be analyzed by consideration of the connection between the variables. Do the two variables tend to increase together (as do people's height and weight) or do they tend to move in opposite directions (as do the number of hours since a person woke up and the number of minutes it will take the person to fall asleep again)? In instances such as the ones just mentioned, we are interested in the association between variables. That is, is there a systematic connection between changes in one variable and changes in another?

When an increase in one variable tends to be associated with an increase in another variable, we claim that the variables are positively associated. Conversely, when an increase in one variable tends to be accompanied by a decrease in another variable, the variables are said to be negatively associated. You will remember that such relation-

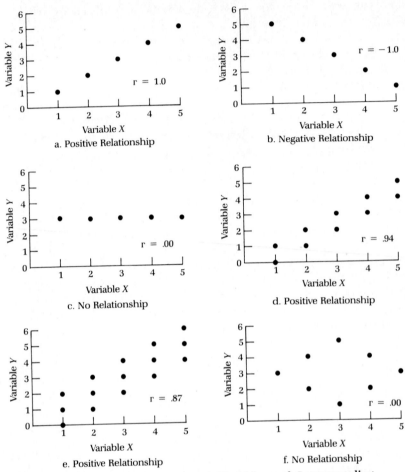

Figure 11-4 Relationships Between Variables and Corresponding Pearson Correlation Coefficients

ships can be represented graphically: Positive associations generally can be characterized as extending from the lower left-hand corner of a graph to the upper right-hand corner, while negative associations go from the upper left-hand corner to the lower right-hand corner.

Of course, relationships often are not absolute. For example, while taller people tend to be heavier than average and smaller individuals frequently weigh less than average, we can all think of exceptions to this rule. Consequently, what is needed is a way of specifying

178

the degree to which this general rule of thumb is accurate on the average. Certain types of statistical methods concern themselves with "on-the-average" associations between variables such as height and weight, intelligence and school performance, and automobile speed and gas mileage. The Pearson correlation coefficient is one such statistical method. Correlation coefficients can range from +1.0 to −1.0, with a correlation of .00 signifying that no relationship appears to exist between the two variables. Figure 11−4 presents scatter plots of data for two variables to demonstrate several types of relationships. In each instance, the Pearson correlation coefficient (r) is also provided to demonstrate the correlation associated with that relationship.

Pearson correlation coefficients can be understood at several different levels. The most obvious level of understanding—the manner in which higher versus lower scores on one variable are related to higher versus lower scores on a second variable—has already been considered. Higher scores on one variable related to higher scores on the other is a positive relationship; higher scores on one with lower scores on the other represent a negative relationship; and if no discernible pattern exists, we assume that there is no relationship between the two variables. Another, more sophisticated understanding of correlation coefficients involves the degree to which knowledge of a subject's score on one variable allows us to make more accurate predictions regarding the subject's score on the other variable.

Strength of Relationship and Predictability

Did you know that there is a strong positive correlation between the number of taverns in a city and the number of churches in that city? What does this association mean? For one thing, we should never infer that a causal link exists between two variables simply because a correlation exists between them. Therefore, we *cannot* make statements like the following: "The more time people spend in taverns, the more they are in need of repentance, which explains the greater number of churches." As far as we can tell, there is no direct causal relationship between the number of taverns and churches; rather, both may well be causally related to a third variable—the population of the city. Therefore, while a correlation exists between the number of taverns and the number of churches in a city, knowledge of this correlation is not particularly helpful in answering such questions as, "What determines the number of taverns (or churches) in a

179

particular city?'' That question asks for a causal explanation of a phenomenon, which is beyond the scope of a simple correlational relationship. However, correlation coefficients are valuable to researchers interested in prediction.

Suppose, for example, you were interested in accurately guessing the number of churches in a particular city. You could improve the accuracy of your predictions if you knew the number of taverns in the city. This point will be demonstrated in greater detail later. However, you can already see that *if* I knew a correlation existed between the temperature on the first day of the month and the price of gold on the last day of the month, I could parlay this knowledge into some handsome profits by judiciously buying and selling gold.

As an example of how much the knowledge of a correlation between two variables can enhance the accuracy of predictions, let us consider the following hypothetical task. Suppose you need to guess, or predict, the weight of particular students in your class. Further, you will not know which students' weights you are guessing until after you have made your prediction. You will not be discouraged by small inaccuracies in your predictions, but you wish to avoid at all costs predictions that are very inaccurate. Finally, overestimates and underestimates of the subjects' actual weights are equally undesirable. What is your best prediction strategy?

Before considering the best strategy, we must specify a method for precisely quantifying the accuracy of your predictions. First, we will find the difference between your guess and the subject's actual weight. This yields an inaccuracy score. We need to penalize large inaccuracies much more heavily than small inaccuracies. This can be accomplished by squaring the inaccuracy scores to arrive at a weighted inaccuracy score. (Note that by squaring each number we also remove all minus signs.) The sum of the weighted inaccuracy scores is the total inaccuracy score. Obviously, a large total inaccuracy score represents poor prediction, whereas a total inaccuracy score of zero represents perfect prediction.

Table 11−3 shows the computation of a total inaccuracy score you might obtain by blindly guessing the weights of six hypothetical subjects. (Remember, you don't know whose weight you are guessing!) The total inaccuracy score in this instance is 10,200. Now, it can be shown mathematically that generally (though not always) you can improve the accuracy of your predictions by using for each guess the average weight of your sample of subjects. Let us assume you have

180

Table 11-3 Prediction by Blind Guessing

	Subject's Actual Weight	Your Guess	Inaccuracy Score	Weighted Inaccuracy Score
Subject 1	140	130	(140−130) or 10	$(10)^2$ or 100
Subject 2	160	140	(160−140) or 20	$(20)^2$ or 400
Subject 3	180	150	(180−150) or 30	$(30)^2$ or 900
Subject 4	120	160	(120−160) or −40	$(-40)^2$ or 1600
Subject 5	200	140	(200−140) or 60	$(60)^2$ or 3600
Subject 6	220	160	(220−160) or 60	$(60)^2$ or 3600
				10,200

this information and follow this strategy. Table 11−4 presents the results. You can see that the total inaccuracy score obtained with this strategy (7000) is better than with the random guessing approach. At this point, using average weight seems to be your best prediction strategy.

We can now consider how knowing a correlation exists between the variable to be predicted and any other variable can help us make more accurate predictions. We have been assuming you knew nothing about the individual subjects in your sample. Suppose, however, that you knew subjects 1, 3, and 4 were women and subjects 2, 5, and 6 were men. For now, assume the correlation between subjects' sex and their weight is .78. (The exact procedure for calculating correlation coefficients will be discussed in detail in the next chapter.) The knowledge of this correlation between the two variables can enhance your prediction of scores in this way: Now, instead of guessing the average weight of the entire group, your best estimate is to guess the average weight of the subgroup to which the subject belongs.

Table 11-4 Prediction Using Average Weight of Sample

	Subject's Actual Weight	Your Guess	Inaccuracy Score	Weighted Inaccuracy Score
Subject 1	140	170	−30	900
Subject 2	160	170	−10	100
Subject 3	180	170	10	100
Subject 4	120	170	−50	2500
Subject 5	200	170	30	900
Subject 6	220	170	50	2500
Total weight	1020			7000
Average weight	170			

Table 11−5 **Prediction Using Average Male and Average Female Weight of Sample**

	Subject's Actual Weight (and Sex)	Your Guess	Inaccuracy Score	Weighted Inaccuracy Score
Subject 1	140 (F)	147	−7	49
Subject 2	160 (M)	193	−33	1089
Subject 3	180 (F)	147	33	1089
Subject 4	120 (F)	147	−27	729
Subject 5	200 (M)	193	7	49
Subject 6	220 (M)	193	27	729
Total weight	440 (F)			2734
	580 (M)			
Average weight[a]	147 (F)			
	193 (M)			

[a] Rounded to nearest whole number.

Specifically, when you predict a subject's weight, you will no longer choose 170 (the average weight of all subjects); but instead you will guess 147 if the subject is a woman and 193 if the subject is a man (since 147 pounds and 193 pounds are the average weights of women and men in the sample). Table 11−5 presents the total inaccuracy score when the predictions reflect knowledge of the subjects' sex. As you can see, the total inaccuracy score went from 7000 to 2734—an increased accuracy of 4266 units. This represents an increase of 61 percent (4266 ÷ 7000) in the accuracy of the predictions!

It can be shown mathematically that the percentage increase in the accuracy of predictions is equal to the square of the correlation coefficient (r^2). In this case, the correlation coefficient (.78) squared equals .61—the amount by which you can improve your best prediction strategy if you have knowledge of the relationship between the variable to be predicted (subjects' weight) and some correlated variable (subjects' sex).

Several additional points should be made clear.

1. The increase in predictive accuracy operates in the same manner whether the relationship between the two variables is directly causal (as is probably the case with subjects' sex and weight) or is not directly causal (as with the number of taverns and churches in a city).

2. Negative correlations are as good as positive correlations in increasing predictive accuracy, since, for example both $(-.5)^2$ and $(+.5)^2$ equal .25.

3. There are a number of statistical techniques that measure strength of relationship besides the Pearson correlation coefficient. Their similarity derives from the fact that they describe the strength of the relationship between variables and consequently allow researchers to make more accurate predictions about one variable if they possess knowledge of subjects' scores on another variable.

Additional Readings

Moore, D. S. *Statistics: Concepts and controversies.* San Francisco: W. H. Freeman, 1979.

Huck, S. W., Cormier, W. H., & Bounds, W. G. *Reading statistics and research.* New York: Harper & Row, 1974.

Tanur, J., et al. *Statistics: A guide to the unknown.* San Francisco: Holden-Day, 1978.

Huff, D. *How to lie with statistics.* New York: W. W. Norton, 1954.

Computation and More Complex Examples in Statistics

Chapter Preview

This chapter demonstrates the computations involved in three statistical techniques: t-test for independent groups, Pearson product-moment correlation coefficient, and chi-square. Many of the issues involved in selecting the appropriate statistical method are enumerated. Finally, several advanced statistical procedures—such as analysis of variance, multivariate analysis of variance, multiple correlation, partial correlation, and time series analysis—are presented and their functions described. Examples of each approach are explored. Finally, the importance of computers for research in the social sciences is discussed.

Chapter 11 provided a conceptual overview of the two main types of inferential statistics employed by social scientists. In this chapter, a few sets of data will be analyzed to provide you with a feel for the relationship of various patterns of results to the statistical values obtained from these data. The final section of the chapter considers a few more sophisticated statistical techniques to demonstrate how statistical refinements can be wed to design modifications to deal creatively with some of the vexing methodological difficulties described earlier in the book.

Computation of t

Chapter 11 discussed an example that involved randomly assigning subjects to two groups, one that tasted plain cereal and one that tasted cereal with additives (cereal plus). The subjects' ratings were presented in Table 11—1, reproduced here as Table 12—1. In this case, a t-test for independent groups is an appropriate tool to help us answer the research question: Are the groups' mean ratings of satisfaction with the taste of the cereal significantly different from one another? Or are the observed differences small enough that we cannot confidently rule out chance as their sole cause.

The formula for t is:

$$t = \frac{\overline{X}_1 - \overline{X}_2}{\sqrt{\left[\dfrac{\Sigma X_1{}^2 - \dfrac{(\Sigma X_1)^2}{N_1} + \Sigma X_2{}^2 - \dfrac{(\Sigma X_2)^2}{N_2}}{(N_1 + N_2) - 2}\right] \times \left[\dfrac{1}{N_1} + \dfrac{1}{N_2}\right]}}$$

The numerator of the formula simply asks us to calculate the difference between the means for the two groups. The denominator, called the *standard error of the difference*, is related to the amount of variability within each group of scores, a concept mentioned in chapter 11. The denominator also reflects the size of the samples of subjects involved (N_1, N_2). The actual steps performed in the calculation are found in the box entitled "Calculation of Independent Groups t-test."

As demonstrated in the box, the t-value for the data in Table 12—1 is −5.31. The minus sign simply means that the mean of level 2 is greater than the mean of level 1. In order to determine if this value is

Table 12–1 Subjects' Ratings of Cereal Taste

	Plain Cereal	Cereal Plus
	1	6
	5	4
	3	5
	3	6
	4	8
	1	9
	2	5
	3	6
	4	6
	3	8
Mean	2.9	6.3
Standard deviation	1.22	1.51
Number of subjects	10	10

significant, we must see if it exceeds the critical value—the value required to enable us to conclude that the observed difference is large enough that chance alone can reasonably be ruled out as its sole explanation.

We obtain the critical value by first computing the *degrees of freedom (df)*. For a test of significance between two independent means, the *df* are equal to $N_1 + N_2 - 2$. In this case, N_1 and N_2 are the number of subjects in the plain and the cereal plus groups. Therefore, the *df* are $10 + 10 - 2 = 18$. Now we check a table of t-values (see appendix E) to obtain the critical value corresponding to the *df* (18) and the level of confidence desired in this case (for example, $p < .05$). The critical value in this case is 2.101. You can see that the computed t-value of 5.31 is greater than the critical value of 2.101, meaning that we can be quite confident the observed mean difference is due to something other than chance alone. We can therefore claim that the cereal with the food additive is significantly better tasting than the plain cereal.

Now consider the somewhat different data in Table 11–2, reproduced here as Table 12–2. A comparison of column one (plain cereal) with column three (cereal plus) yields the following values:

$$t = \frac{1.4}{.64} = 2.19$$

Again, this value is significant at the .05 level of confidence with 18 *df*. (However, a computed t-value of 2.552 would have been required for the finding to be significant at the .01 level, had this more stringent standard been desired.)

Calculation of Independent Groups t-test

The data in Table 12−1 will be used in the following calculations.

    Step 1: Arbitrarily label one group level 1 and the other group level 2. In this case, plain cereal will be level 1; cereal plus, level 2.

    Step 2: Determine the number of subjects in each group.

$N_1 = 10$ $N_2 = 10$

    Step 3: Calculate ΣX_1 and ΣX_2, the sums of subjects' scores for each group.

$\Sigma X_1 = 29$ $\Sigma X_2 = 63$

    Step 4: Calculate ΣX_1^2 and ΣX_2^2, the sums of the squared scores for each group.

$\Sigma X_1^2 = 99$ $\Sigma X_2^2 = 419$

    Step 5: Calculate $\bar{X}_1$ and $\bar{X}_2$, the means of the scores for each group.

$\bar{X}_1 = 2.9$ $\bar{X}_2 = 6.3$

Insert the values into the formula for t given in the text:

$$t = \frac{2.9 - 6.3}{\sqrt{\dfrac{99 - \dfrac{(29)^2}{10} + 419 - \dfrac{(63)^2}{10}}{10 + 10 - 2} \times (1/10 + 1/10)}}$$

$$t = \frac{- 3.4}{\sqrt{\dfrac{99 - 84.1 + 419 - 396.9}{18} \times 1/5}}$$

$$t = \frac{- 3.4}{\sqrt{37/18 \times 1/5}}$$

$$t = - 5.31$$

Table 12–2   Ratings of Cereal and Cereal Plus

	Plain Cereal	Plain Cereal*	Cereal Plus	Cereal Plus*
	1	2	4	4
	5	3	2	5
	3	3	3	4
	3	4	4	4
	4	3	6	3
	1	3	7	4
	2	3	3	5
	3	2	4	5
	4	3	4	5
	3	3	6	4
Mean	2.9	2.9	4.3	4.3
Standard deviation	1.22	0.54	1.51	0.64
Number of subjects	10	10	10	10

Comparison of columns two (plain cereal*) and four (cereal plus*) yields the following values:

$$t = \frac{1.4}{.28} = 5.00$$

In this case, the mean difference is significant beyond the .001 level of confidence. This illustrates a point made in chapter 11: Reduced within-groups variability (reflected in smaller standard deviations) can result in higher t-values even when the actual mean difference is unchanged. Consequently, reducing variability within each group of scores increases the chance of obtaining a significant difference.

Computation of r

You will remember that the Pearson correlation coefficient (r) was presented in chapter 11 as an example of a statistical technique that measures strength of relationship. Correlation coefficients are quantified indices of how well two variables "go together." Are higher scores on one variable associated with higher scores (positive correlation) or with lower scores (negative correlation) on the other variable? Whether positive or negative, the closer the correlation coefficient is to 1.0 (or −1.0), the higher the *degree* of relationship between the two variables.

The formula for the Pearson r is:

$$r = \frac{N\Sigma XY - (\Sigma X)(\Sigma Y)}{\sqrt{[N\Sigma X^2 - (\Sigma X)^2][N\Sigma Y^2 - (\Sigma Y)^2]}}$$

where

N = number of pairs of scores.
ΣXY = sum of the products of the paired scores.
ΣX = sum of scores on variable X.
ΣY = sum of scores on variable Y.
ΣX^2 = sum of squared scores on variable X.
ΣY^2 = sum of squared scores on variable Y.

Let us calculate r for the data shown in Figure 11−4e, reproduced here as Figure 12−1. These data yield the set of ordered pairs
(X and Y) shown in Table 12−3. Each dot on the graph represents an
ordered pair; for example, the dot in the lower left-hand corner represents a value of 1 for X and 0 for Y. These values correspond to the first
ordered pair in Table 12−3.
Entering the values into the formula yields:

$$r = \frac{15\,(165) - (45)\,(45)}{\sqrt{[15(165) - (45)^2]\,[15\,(175) - (45)^2]}}$$

$$= \frac{2475 - 2025}{\sqrt{[2475 - 2025]\,[2625 - 2025]}}$$

$$= \frac{450}{\sqrt{[450]\,[600]}} = \frac{450}{519.62}$$

$$= .87$$

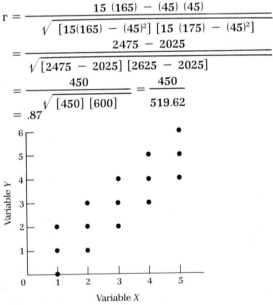

Figure 12−1 Scatter Plot of Relationship Between Two Variables

Table 12-3   Data from Figure 12-1

X	Y	XY	X^2	Y^2
1	0	0	1	0
1	1	1	1	1
1	2	2	1	4
2	1	2	4	1
2	2	4	4	4
2	3	6	4	9
3	2	6	9	4
3	3	9	9	9
3	4	12	9	16
4	3	12	16	9
4	4	16	16	16
4	5	20	16	25
5	4	20	25	16
5	5	25	25	25
5	6	30	25	36
$\Sigma X = 45$	$\Sigma Y = 45$	$\Sigma XY = 165$	$\Sigma X^2 = 165$	$\Sigma Y^2 = 175$

You may want to generate sets of ordered pairs from the data presented in the remaining parts of Figure 11—4 and compute the correlation coefficients for those data.

More Complex Statistical Techniques

Analysis of Variance

If I conducted a study to investigate the influence of an independent variable with two levels on a dependent variable, I might choose to analyze the results by means of a t-test. As explained in chapter 5, however, researchers often ask more sophisticated research questions, which, in turn, demand more complex designs. Chapter 5 considered investigations in which many levels of a particular independent variable would be considered simultaneously or in which multiple independent variables would be considered at one time (factorial designs). These more sophisticated designs often necessitate the use of statistical analyses more elaborate than the t-test. The analysis of variance (ANOVA) is an elaboration of the basic line of reasoning represented by the t-test. The analysis of variance yields F values rather than t values; but conceptually, these values have similar interpretations. The value of the analysis of variance is in its ability to handle the more sophisticated factorial designs.

Multivariate Analysis of Variance

Similarly, you will recall that in chapter 5 we considered instances in which multiple dependent measures were employed in a particular study. When considering differences between groups on multiple dependent measures, researchers can employ a statistical procedure called the multivariate analysis of variance (MANOVA). MANOVA considers whether groups are significantly different from one another when the data from all dependent measures are considered simultaneously.

Multiple Correlation

The multiple correlation is an elaboration of the Pearson correlation coefficient that is often used to handle more sophisticated correlational design questions. To this point, we have considered the correlation coefficient as a means of increasing the accuracy of predictions about values of one variable (the criterion) based on the score obtained on some other variable (the predictor). Most real-world applications involve the use of more than one predictor variable in making predictions. Multiple correlation is the procedure whereby we can measure the combined impact of several predictors on our estimate of a criterion.

An example of the use of multiple correlation is presented by the counseling psychology program at Notre Dame University, which considers various sources of information in an attempt to select Ph.D. students. Applicants are required to submit the results of their Graduate Records Examination (GRE), their college grade point average (GPA), and letters of recommendation (REC). From these data, the program hopes to predict which students will successfully complete the doctoral program (Ph.D.). Thus, Ph.D. is the criterion; and GRE, GPA, and REC are the predictors. None of these predictors is a perfect estimate of success in graduate school, but all have some predictive value. Some hypothetical correlations among these variables will demonstrate how multiple correlation can enable a researcher to predict more accurately.

Figure 12–2 provides graphic representations of possible pre-

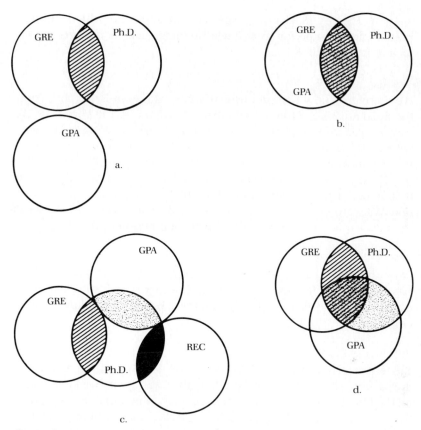

Figure 12-2 Possible Predictor-Criterion Relationships

dictor-criterion relationships. Consider Figure 12—2a for a moment. The overlap between GRE and Ph.D. is highlighted by diagonal lines. If the correlation between GRE and Ph.D. is .5, then the overlap between the two circles is equal to .25, which represents r^2. You can see that in Figure 12—2a, GPA is not correlated with either Ph.D. or GRE, as evidenced by the fact that GPA does not overlap with either variable. In this instance, then, adding GPA to the prediction adds nothing, since no area of Ph.D. is shared with GPA.

In Figure 12—2b, GRE and GPA totally overlap one another (that is, for GRE and GPA, r = 1.0); and so either can predict the criterion, Ph.D., equally well. Consequently, the addition of either of the predictors to the other to form a multiple correlation adds nothing to what the other could already predict.

193

In Figure 12–2c, we see an instance in which multiple predictors are superior to a single predictor. Let us assume the following relationships:

$$r_{GRE \cdot Ph.D.} = .5; \ r_{GPA \cdot Ph.D.} = .6; \ r_{REC \cdot Ph.D.} = .4$$

We therefore know that, in terms of the total size of Ph.D., the size of the lined area is .25; the dotted area, .36; and the shaded area, .16. We can also see from the figure that the areas of overlap of each predictor with Ph.D. do not overlap with one another. Therefore, the multiple prediction employing all three predictor variables is .77 (.25 + .36 + .16). If the predictors had been correlated, however, the multiple prediction could not have been obtained by this simple process of addition. We were only able to use that procedure in this case because all the predictors were uncorrelated with one another, or:

$$r_{GRE \cdot GPA} = r_{GRE \cdot REC} = r_{GPA \cdot REC} = 0$$

The most realistic example, pictured in Figure 12–2d, has been saved for last. In this example, GPA and GRE are correlated with Ph.D. and are also correlated with one another. Assume the following relationships:

$$r_{GPA \cdot Ph.D.} = .6; \ r_{GRE \cdot Ph.D.} = .5$$

The amount of overlap of GPA with Ph.D. is .36, and the amount of overlap of GRE with Ph.D. is .25. If the overlap between the area marked by diagonal lines and the area marked by dots had been zero, then we could simply add .36 and .25, yielding a multiple prediction of .61. However, as can be seen in Figure 12–2d, the area that includes both dots and diagonal lines would be counted twice if we did that. The amount by which the multiple prediction (.61) should be reduced to adjust for this area of overlap is, of course, related to the correlation between GPA and GRE. As this correlation increases, the amount by which the total of the two areas must be reduced is increased also.

Nonparametric Tests

Earlier in the chapter, it was noted that certain conditions (conditions related to the level of measurement of the dependent variable, for example) must be met before certain statistical tests can be appropriately employed. Return to the very first example in this chapter.

Computation of Chi-Square

Suppose that, as suggested in the text, we had received only "yes-no" answers in our study of cereal taste. If we wished to analyze these data for statistically significant differences, we might use a chi-square analysis. Chi-square analysis follows these steps:

Step 1: Organize the data into a table showing the number of scores for each possible combination of the two variables.

Table of Observed Values

Did you like taste?	Plain Cereal	Cereal Plus
Yes	18	36
No	32	14

Step 2: Add the numbers in each row to obtain row sums.

Sum of "yes" responses = 18 + 36 = 54

Sum of "no" responses = 32 + 14 = 46

Step 3: Add the numbers in each column to obtain column sums.

Sum of subjects who tasted plain cereal = 18 + 32 = 50

Sum of subjects who tasted cereal plus = 36 + 14 = 50

Step 4: Obtain the grand sum in two ways: Add the row sums together, and add the column sums together. These two procedures must give the same value.

Grand sum (rows) = 54 + 46 = 100

Grand sum (columns) = 50 + 50 = 100

Step 5: We now need to make up a table of *expected values*. Expected values are the mathematical expression of the results we would obtain if the null hypothesis was true.

(continued)

To calculate the expected value for each category in the table, multiply the row sum times the column sum for that category. (For example, for the "plain/yes" category, multiply total "plain" responses by total "yes" responses.) Then divide that product by the grand sum.

Expected value for plain/yes $= \dfrac{54 \times 50}{100} = 27$

Expected value for plain/no $= \dfrac{46 \times 50}{100} = 23$

Expected value for plus/yes $= \dfrac{54 \times 50}{100} = 27$

Expected value for plus/no $= \dfrac{46 \times 50}{100} = 23$

Table of Expected Values

	Plain Cereal	Cereal Plus
Yes	27	27
No	23	23

(Did you like taste?)

We are now ready to calculate the chi-square value (χ^2) by employing the following formula:

$$\chi^2 = \Sigma \; \frac{(\text{Observed - Expected})^2}{\text{Expected}}$$

We use the formula in the following manner:

Step 6: For each category, subtract the expected value from the observed value. Square the answer. Then divide that squared value by the expected value for that category. Repeat this procedure for each category.

Plain/Yes $= \dfrac{(18 - 27)^2}{27} = 3.00$

Plain/No $= \dfrac{(32 - 23)^2}{23} = 3.52$

Plus/Yes $= \dfrac{(36 - 27)^2}{27} = 3.00$

Plus/No $= \dfrac{(14 - 23)^2}{23} = 3.52$

(continued)

Step 7: Sum all the values obtained in step 6 to arrive at the value for chi-square:

$$\chi^2 = 3.00 + 3.52 + 3.00 + 3.52 = 13.04$$

Step 8: Evaluate the chi-square value by looking up the critical chi-square value in appendix E and following the instructions given there. The number of degrees of freedom is equal to the number of rows minus 1 multiplied by the number of columns minus 1.

$df = (2\text{-}1) \times (2\text{-}1)$
$df = 1 \times 1 = 1$

The critical chi-square value with one degree of freedom is 3.8 at the .05 level, 6.6 at the .01 level. Our chi-square value of 13.04 is greater than either of these critical values, suggesting that our results are statistically significant.

There, we used the t-test method to analyze subjects' numerical ratings. This procedure allowed us to decide whether an additive significantly improved the taste of a cereal. If, for whatever reason, we had only been able to obtain "yes" or "no" answers for the dependent measure, we would not have been able to employ the t-test method of analysis, because the statistical assumptions underlying a t-test are not adequately met by such answers.

If a dependent measure is made up of nominal data—data that are not quantitative—the data must be analyzed with one of a class of statistical techniques known as *nonparametric tests*. All of the statistical methods considered thus far are *parametric statistics*—statistical methods that make rather strong assumptions about the nature of the data being analyzed. Nonparametric statistical methods do not require such stringent assumptions for their proper use. One commonly used nonparametric test is the chi-square analysis, which is described in the box entitled "Computation of Chi-Square."

It must be emphasized that when the data support the assumptions of parametric statistical techniques, these techniques should be employed to guard against an overly conservative test of the hypothesis of interest. Statistics texts explain these matters in great detail, and the interested reader is referred to the additional readings listed at the end of chapter 11 for very clear treatments of these topics.

197

Computers in Research

The last quarter century has witnessed a revolution in electronic data processing. These remarkable developments have exerted a profound influence on research in the social sciences. Computers enable researchers to routinely perform complex activities that were heretofore extremely difficult and time consuming. The new freedom thus provided enables researchers to probe questions earlier generations of social scientists were unable to consider.

Researchers have benefited from computer-related developments in three broad areas. The first area involves the use of increasingly more complex statistical techniques. The calculations for the univariate statistical techniques discussed earlier (such as the t-test and Pearson r) can be easily performed without the aid of a computer. However, as mentioned, a researcher who begins to ask increasingly more sophisticated research questions immediately develops the need for more complex statistical techniques to analyze the resulting data. With some of the newer statistical techniques, the computation time a human would need to perform an analysis can easily be over a million times longer than the computer requires. Many complex analyses currently in use might be virtually abandoned if researchers had to perform the calculations by hand.

The second area in which computers have greatly aided research efforts involves the ability to handle extremely large data sets. Even simple statistical techniques become computational nightmares if they are to be performed on large amounts of data. Remember, for example, the demonstration of the computation of r presented earlier in this chapter. Suppose I had to compute the correlation coefficient between height and weight for every person in the United States. Think of the amount of work involved in calculating $\Sigma XY, \Sigma X, \Sigma Y, \Sigma X^2$, and ΣY^2 for that data set, if it had to be done by hand! You can easily see that computers enable us to handle large data sets in much the same way as they enable us to use complex statistical procedures.

The third general area in which computers have enhanced research efforts is somewhat different from the first two. It involves the use of models and simulations in research endeavors. Simply stated, there are techniques that allow investigators to construct computer representations of processes in which they are interested.

For example, Pritchard, Maxwell, and Jordan (in press) were interested in whether age discrimination actually existed in the job promotions granted by a multinational oil corporation. How could

198

they determine if older workers received fewer promotions than would be expected in a fair system? At first glance, one might think that if older workers were promoted at the same average rate as younger workers, then the system would be fair. However, a little thought quickly reveals that younger workers generally occupy lower-ranking positions in the organization than do older workers. Workers at higher ranks are typically promoted less often than workers at lower ranks, because of the pyramidal structure of large organizations. This serves to complicate comparisons of younger and older workers.

Alternatively, one might look at younger versus older workers' average promotion rates within a particular job level or category (such as "clerk" or "vice-president"). But might there not be differences in average amount of ability for younger and older workers within any job category? For example, young workers are more likely to be "bright individuals on their way up," whereas older workers may already have been advanced to the limits of their abilities. On the other hand, older workers tend to bring more experience to their jobs, which might improve their performance; might they not be better candidates for promotion because of this background? The crucial point here is that it is extremely difficult to ascertain what "fair" promotion rates should be for younger and older employees.

To deal with this complex problem, Pritchard and associates generated a computer simulation of their corporation and determined what would represent "fair" promotion rates for younger and older workers at a particular job level, given differences in average ability, experience, and so forth. After determining what would represent fair promotion rates (in a hypothetical sense), the researchers were able to compare the actual rates of promotion of the two groups with these hypothetical rates to ascertain if older workers were indeed being discriminated against by the corporation.

Computer simulations of economic activity, voting behavior, attitude changes, and human reasoning are but a few examples of modeling in other domains of the social sciences. Without computers, modeling and simulation efforts would be severely curtailed. Undoubtedly, social science research will continue to be influenced by changes in computer technology in the future.

Additional Readings

Linton, M., & Gallo, P. S. *The practical statistician: Simplified handbook of statistics*. Monterey, Calif.: Brooks-Cole, 1975.

Bruning, J. L., & Kintz, B. L. *Computational handbook of statistics*. Glenview, Ill.: Scott, Foresman, 1968.

199

Evaluation Research

Chapter Preview

Chapter 13 begins by distinguishing between research primarily interested in testing theoretical propositions and research aimed at program evaluation. Evaluation research, which is viewed as an aid to decision making, can be of two types—process evaluation and impact evaluation. Comprehensive evaluation involves both of these components; here, the impact evaluation is typically expressed as a cost-benefit analysis. The chapter also considers a number of difficulties involved in evaluation research and discusses some related issues, such as the statistical versus the practical significance of research findings.

There is a tendency among members of a society to demand accountability for the results of interventions supported by the society. For example, the federal government operates a number of social service programs specifically intended to address certain pressing problems. The general public demands that the large amounts of money expended on these programs be justified by some demonstration that the money is having an impact on the problem and that the appropriate recipients of the services are profiting from them.

The designs and procedures discussed in the earlier chapters of this book are important considerations in evaluation of the impact of social service programs. In most instances, the essential question is something like this: "Can the results X, Y, and Z be attributed to this particular program, and are X, Y, and Z the only effects of the program?" All the problems of internal validity discussed earlier are important in the determination of whether the program was successful. The extent to which the results of the program might be replicated in other situations and settings and with other populations falls under the domain of external validity. Considerations of construct validity center around which constructs or variables actually were influenced by the program. Therefore, as you read this chapter you should be aware that evaluation research is not essentially different from any other form of research in the social sciences. Rather, it is an example of research that addresses a specific set of questions relevant to a certain segment of society.

You might wonder, then, why a special chapter is needed for evaluation research. While evaluation research is essentially similar to other kinds, it is different in some important ways from research as this book has described it so far. The discussions to date have thought of researchers as being interested in a particular *theoretical* question and then formulating an experiment or two to obtain data relevant to this question. The experimenter's freedom to structure the studies enabled him or her to design studies as free as possible from threats to internal, external, and construct validity. With evaluation research, however, the circumstances are somewhat different.

Typically, the researcher is asked to assess the effectiveness of some ongoing program or some program that is being planned to meet a particular set of needs. Because programs are almost always multifaceted, it is difficult (in some cases impossible) to specify what constructs are really involved in the study. Also, since the goals of the individuals or groups who commission the study are often more practical than theoretical, the theoretical significance of the study generally takes a more secondary role than in research performed primarily to increase theoretical understanding. This distinction between theoretically oriented research and research designed to answer practical questions is sometimes called the distinction between *basic* and *applied* research. Program evaluation research generally deals with applied issues.

Since evaluation often involves ongoing programs or programs being designed specifically for certain populations, the researcher typically has little control over procedures (such as the random assignment of subjects to conditions) that might be helpful in eliminating threats to internal validity. Therefore, program evaluators often are forced to deal with the problems inherent in using quasi-experimental designs. However, the evaluation of ongoing programs has a potential strength in that it deals with a real problem or program—that is, not a program whose major or sole purpose is to test theoretical research ideas. Numerous writers have warned that the behavior of humans in settings specially designed for research purposes, such as research laboratories, might present special problems of generalization not experienced with *in vivo* studies (studies in real-life situations). Since most evaluation research is *in vivo*, the relationships between program evaluation findings and other ongoing real-life phenomena are generally felt to be good.

The unique problems and difficulties encountered in program evaluation research typically involve the difficulties associated with reaching causal inferences in situations where most of the specifics of the experiment are not directly under the control of the experimenter and thus are potential contaminants. Therefore, a consideration of program evaluation will bring us closer to the area of quasi-experimental research, or incomplete research designs. If the primary purpose of evaluation research was to enhance our understanding of the relationships among theoretical constructs in the world, having to frequently employ quasi-experimental procedures would be a very serious problem. However, as Freeman and Rossi (1982) point out, the primary purpose of evaluation research is not theoretical understanding; rather, evaluation research is a political decision-making tool.

203

Evaluation: An Aid to Decision Making

We live in a world of scarce resources. We as a society must choose among many possible ways in which we might allocate those resources. Typically, politicians are the people most involved in decisions regarding which direction a nation will take, while business executives decide what course their organizations will follow. Program evaluation can be a tool that provides information to help these people make those difficult decisions.

To begin thinking about program evaluation in specific terms, consider an article that appeared in the business section of the December 13, 1981, *Chicago Tribune*. The article discussed the savings a technique called teleconferencing might offer over the traditional sales procedure, which involves businesspeople's visiting clients to make their sales presentations. (Briefly, teleconferencing here involves salespeople's making a sales presentation in one location while potential customers at several other locations view the presentation on television screens. Two-way communication allows the customers to ask questions, and the presenters to answer them immediately.)

The cost-effectiveness of teleconferencing was demonstrated in the article with the data presented in Table 13—1, which related to Allied Van Lines, Inc. The newspaper article pointed out that teleconferencing was a less expensive way for businesses to get their

Table 13—1 Traditional Sales Presentation Compared with Teleconference

	Traditional Presentation	Teleconference
People reached	650	1,301
Employee expense	$54,000	$13,000
Facilities	$44,000	$42,000
Production	$89,000	$37,000
Coaching	0	$15,000
Printing	$ 1,100	$ 300
Air freight	$ 1,300	$ 1,100
Gross cost	$189,400	$108,400
Revenue	$16,250	0
Net cost	$173,150	$108,400
Cost per person	$266.38	$83.38

Source: Allied Van Lines, Inc. Cited in *Chicago Tribune*, Dec. 13, 1981.

messages to their customers. Is this program evaluation? Yes, but it is only part of a thorough program evaluation.

Comprehensive Evaluation

The most thorough and complete type of program evaluation is called comprehensive evaluation. It includes the two basic types of evaluation: *process evaluation* and *impact (or outcome) evaluation*. Wherever possible, comprehensive evaluation also includes a *cost-benefit analysis* of the program. Let us consider these topics within the context of a comprehensive evaluation of the teleconferencing alternative to the traditional sales procedure.

Process Evaluation

Process evaluation deals with whether or not a program was implemented in the manner stated in its guidelines. That is, did the program reach the people for whom it was intended and was it implemented as it was designed to be? Process evaluation is necessary if researchers are to be certain that the program has received a fair test. For example, a health organization might be interested in the effectiveness of a particular antibiotic in reducing dysentery in a village with an impure water supply. The program might call for each person in the village to take two antibiotic pills each day. But if the program administrators do not actually make sure each person swallows the two pills after receiving them, a black market for the pills might develop. Suppose half the villagers never take the drug but rather sell their pills. If the pills are totally effective in preventing dysentery, the problem still will not be totally eliminated; the incidence of dysentery will be cut only by half (for example, from 30 percent to 15 percent). Thus, the organization will underestimate the effectiveness of the program, which would have been twice as effective if it had been properly implemented.

How might a process evaluation of the teleconferencing project provide us with further useful information? In order to develop a sense of the potential value of a comprehensive evaluation, let us conduct a hypothetical evaluation study on the effectiveness of teleconferencing. Suppose we are conducting a study for IBM, which is interested in selling a new kind of computer software to a number

205

of stock brokerage firms. We might randomly select two groups of brokerage houses; one will receive the old method of sales presentation, and the other will receive the teleconference presentation. As part of the process evaluation, we will follow the salespeople involved in the usual sales procedure on their trips. We will also go to several brokerage houses to attend the teleconference sessions on the scene. What we see will help us place the results of the intervention in a fuller context, as well as allow us to ascertain if a cost-accounting procedure such as the one in Table 13—1 represents a fair analysis of the value of both sales approaches.

A number of observations might be made. For example, a salesperson who visits a brokerage house might come into informal contact (through lunches, office talk, rides to and from the airport, and so on) with many more brokers than those who actually attend the formal sales conference. In that case, perhaps the accounting procedure in Table 13—1 underestimates the cost-effectiveness of the traditional procedure. Or perhaps brokerage houses will send employees of a lower (or higher) rank in the organization to teleconference meetings than to meetings where a representative is actually present. Finally, we might note differences in attentiveness, note-taking, number and quality of questions, and so on between the two types of sales presentations.

Again, process evaluation observations are important in determining if the results obtained represent a fair comparison of the particular programs researchers have in mind. Further, these observations provide the first level of information that can enable researchers to speculate on why each intervention achieved its level of effectiveness.

Impact Evaluation

The second part of a comprehensive evaluation is impact (or summative, or outcome) evaluation. In a real sense, this is the most important part of the evaluation, because it attempts to specify precisely the various benefits of the program of interest. You will note that Table 13—1 presents an analysis only of the relative costs of the two sales programs. If the two approaches produce different levels of benefits (or outcomes), then we might need to rethink the meaning of the cost differences. Impact evaluation has as its goal the determination of whether the program had the predicted and desired effect.

Implicit in this goal is the understanding that there are criteria by which the success or impact of the program can be measured.

Goals can be of many varieties. In our example, IBM might be interested in cognitive goals—how much knowledge about IBM's products clients absorbed in the sales meetings. It can be argued that cognitive goals are important, because customers are unlikely to buy products they don't understand. A simple test of the brokers' knowledge might determine if more is learned in a live or a teleconference presentation. Potential customers' feelings about the presentation or their feelings about IBM products or services might also be important determinants of whether they will choose to buy IBM's new software. If the two differing sales approaches produce different feelings in brokers, we might favor the approach that yields the better set of attitudes.

You might argue that either of these sets of goals (cognitive or attitudinal) is only important insofar as it helps to increase sales. If that is true, you might simply wish to measure sales of IBM's new software as your dependent variable. If the two sales approaches produced very different levels of sales immediately after the presentations, that would be considered extremely important outcome data. However, such differences should not be demanded as an indicator of success. Nor should a failure to immediately see such differences be taken as an indication that the two sales techniques are equally effective.

Wise business executives rarely decide to buy new equipment simply because a manufacturer makes a sales pitch. Numerous other factors must first be carefully considered—such factors as the condition of the firm's present equipment, the company's cash-flow position, the need to gain tax breaks through additional capital expenditures, and the amount of time required to train personnel to use new equipment versus the projected work-load demands for the near future. You can easily see that a decision to buy or not to buy made soon after the presentation might have little to do with the adequacy of the sales method.

But eventually the time may arrive when the various business indicators point toward making a purchase of computer software. What factors that might be related to the sales presentations will be important then? Perhaps potential customers' knowledge of the capabilities of IBM equipment will be important. Or perhaps various brokers' feelings about IBM products or services might be crucial. Or

207

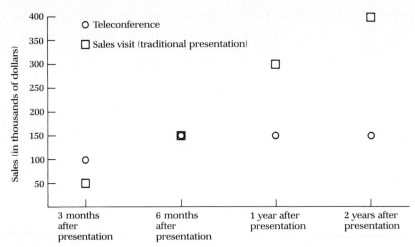

Figure 13–1 Hypothetical Data on Sales for the Two Sales Presentation Strategies

perhaps remembering the name of a sales representative with whom he or she had lunch might determine which company an executive will contact first. These examples demonstrate reasons why cognitive and attitudinal factors may be as important (or even more important) than immediate sales. Figure 13–1 presents hypothetical data that help make this point.

If we considered only sales three months following the presentation, we might conclude that the teleconference presentation produced outcomes superior to those of the "in-person" approach. However, a more long-term perspective demonstrates that, in this example, such a conclusion is misleading. How might we make sense of this crossover of sales at about six months after the presentation and the continued strong performance of the sales visit group several years later? If we collected data on outcome measures other than sales (such as attitudes toward the product and knowledge of the product), and if the sales visit resulted in better attitudes or greater knowledge, then hints as to the reasons for these trends might begin to emerge.

The crucial point here is that even though the "bottom line"—profits—can be readily identified and measured, we still would be short-sighted not to do a thorough assessment of the many consequences of our interventions. This is because obtaining a basic understanding of why one technique is more effective than another can set the stage for the development of even better strategies for the future. For example, further research might indicate that the optimum sales strategy involves an initial "in-person" contact followed by a less expensive yearly teleconference contact and update. You can see how an initial evaluation project can lead to subsequent research designed to fine-tune researchers' knowledge of how a program can be most effective.

It is important to note here that, while program evaluation is a powerful decision-facilitating tool, its appropriateness as a tool depends on the assumption that we can quantify the costs and benefits of our actions and programs. While the hypothetical example above assumed that we could do so, it did not demonstrate that we could. Cogent arguments have been made against the quantification of certain human endeavors, and many authors have decried the overquantification of things to which no quantitative value can, in principle, be assigned (see Schumacher, 1973).

Other Issues in Comprehensive Evaluation

Before we leave the topic of comprehensive evaluation, it should be noted that some program evaluators substitute the term *formative evaluation* for process evaluation. While these terms are generally synonyms for one another, formative evaluation sometimes includes activities specifically aimed at providing information that might alter and improve the program being evaluated. In order to obtain information that might aid in the fine-tuning of the program, formative evaluations often enlist *participant observers*.

Participant observation is a technique wherein individuals actually taking part, as consumers, in the program report their reactions to it. These reactions can often help evaluators identify problems that might diminish the impact and effectiveness of the program or obscure true program effects in the evaluation. Program administrators and evaluators can listen to the comments of participant observers as a last security check; the reactions of participants should reflect their experience of the program, and this experience should reflect what the program administrator and evaluator believe is to be evaluated. Chapter 14 will consider participant observation techniques further as a qualitative methodology.

While the program administrator and the program evaluator have similar sets of goals in the formative evaluation aspect of a comprehensive evaluation, the purposes of these individuals can differ in the outcome evaluation domain. Donald Campbell (1969) points out that conflicts inevitably arise between administrators, whose careers depend on conducting successful programs, and evaluators, whose careers require that they accurately evaluate other people's programs. Campbell notes that these conflicts can be reduced if administrators adopt the "experimental" attitude. That is, evaluators and administrators should experiment with the program and modify it to make it more effective. This goal is often facilitated by a *components analysis*, wherein various subparts (or components) of the total intervention package are studied individually to ascertain which are most effective.

If a component analysis demonstrates that one component, in itself, can produce the same effects as the total package, program administrators can consider offering only the effective component, possibly greatly reducing the cost of providing the service. However, in performing components analyses, researchers often find the whole to be greater than the sum of its parts. That is, sometimes a treatment package that contains components A, B, C, and D is very effective; but the components A and B and C and D are found to be totally ineffective when evaluated separately. It appears that the components must operate in concert to achieve their total effect in many cases.

Practical Importance versus Statistical Significance: The Cost-Benefit Analysis

Remember that chapter 11 made the distinction between differences that were statistically significant and differences that were large or important in an absolute sense. To find that a program significantly increases or decreases subjects' behavior on any dimension simply means to reasonably eliminate chance as the sole explanation for the differences between, for example, two group means. It is entirely possible that a program could reduce subjects' weight by 1 percent or increase their IQs by 1 percent and that these changes could be statistically significant. However, one must wonder about the practical importance of such differences.

In program evaluation, researchers are clearly more concerned with the practical significance of the programs they evaluate. The

210

formal tool they use to quantify the value of a program is the *cost-benefit*, or *cost-effectiveness, analysis*. Cost-benefit accounting involves determining all the costs (usually converted to dollar amounts) involved in providing the program. This cost is then weighed against the magnitude of all the benefits derived from the program. While it is helpful to express these benefits in dollar equivalents, it is not, strictly speaking, absolutely necessary to do so. Evaluators must be careful to consider *all* the costs and benefits of a program in estimating the cost-benefit breakdown.

Freeman and Rossi (1982) talk about the need to consider the indirect (and sometimes unintended) costs and benefits of programs in order to arrive at a total and fair picture of a program's impact. For example, suppose the Internal Revenue Service was considering establishing an agency to monitor taxpayers' returns, find taxpayers who are cheating, and require that they pay their taxes. The direct costs (for salaries, facilities, supplies, and so on) are obvious. The direct benefits are also obvious—taxes would be collected that would otherwise have gone unpaid. However, if the IRS staffed this center with qualified individuals who had previously been unemployed, the savings in unemployment compensation for these employees might be considered a second-order effect to be added to the total benefit analysis. Finally, these new IRS employees would themselves pay taxes; this might be considered a third-order benefit of the program.

Additional Readings

Anderson, S. B., & Ball, S. *The profession and practice of program evaluation.* San Francisco: Jossey-Bass, 1979.

Rossi, P. H., Freeman, H. E., & Wright, S. R. *Evaluation: A systematic approach.* Beverly Hills, Calif.: Sage, 1982.

14

Qualitative Methodology

Chapter Preview

The research methods presented thus far focus on an explanation of phenomena by the scientist, who is not a participant in the activity being studied. This chapter presents some qualitative research techniques designed to capture the subjects' interpretation of what is occurring. The chapter considers reality reconstruction methods such as interviewing techniques, participant observations, personal accounts, life histories, content analysis, and others. Students are encouraged to consider qualitative methods as appropriate measures for some theoretical questions and points of view and as helpful supplements to more traditional quantitative perspectives and methods.

Most of the methods covered thus far have dealt with the more quantitative approaches to understanding human beings. However, in each of the various social sciences there is a tradition that attempts to understand the phenomenon of interest from the actor's point of view. That is, why does the subject think he or she is doing whatever it is he or she is doing? We are especially indebted to a group called the *symbolic interactionists* in sociology—and, to a lesser degree, to some cultural anthropologists—for the understanding of the qualitative methodologies sketched in this chapter. By using these methods we come to know what is taking place from the perspective of a participant in the action.

Remember that in all the approaches studied thus far it was the researcher who decided what the experiment meant. If the researcher claimed that a particular operational definition measured frustration and another operational definition measured aggression, then we had to assume that whatever empirical relationships were observed told us something about frustration and aggression. The experiment was an experiment on frustration and aggression—by definition of the researcher. But were frustration and aggression relevant to what was going on for the subjects in the study?

An apocryphal example offered to me by my clinical practicum supervisor might prove instructive on this point. A clinician was asked to perform an assessment of an overly aggressive two-year-old boy. The psychologist decided to observe the child playing by himself in the family's back yard. The clinician had been observing the child's behavior for a few moments when the child saw a worm, which he picked up and studied intently. The child then ripped the worm in half and placed the two pieces back in the grass. The psychologist was busily scribbling notes to himself about the meaning of this episode when he heard the child mutter, "There! Now there's two of you. Now you won't be so lonely."

The point to be remembered here is that the *meaning* of behavior is not transparent. This realization should always keep the more quantitatively oriented social scientist appropriately humble about interpreting his or her findings. Some sociologists even assert that the goal of sociological research should be to gain access to the "member's point of view." For a scientist so inclined, very little presented thus far in this book would represent part of an adequate research methodology. This chapter will consider various techniques developed to make using the participant's perspective a viable research strategy. The techniques involve *reality reconstruction*—ways of understanding an event by coming to know how the persons involved in the event viewed their actions.

Interviewing

Schwartz and Jacobs (1979) have made the following statement about the general purposes of interviewing:

When interviewing is used to reconstruct the reality of a social group, individual respondents are treated as sources of "general" information. That is, they are asked to speak on behalf of people other than themselves and to give information about social processes and cultural conventions that transcend their own personal lives. In an interview setting, the respondent is called upon to assume the identity of a member of his group in formulating replies—to "become" a woman, an old person, a prison inmate. Either the researcher asks directly about general issues or he interprets individuals' responses in such a way as to throw light on general attitudes, situations and patterns. (p. 38)

Interviews can take one of two basic forms: structured or unstructured. In *structured interviews*, we assume that the interviewer already knows a lot about the phenomenon to be investigated. The portion of a structured interview presented in the box entitled "Now a Little Bit About Religion" illustrates that the researcher already knows quite a bit about what information it is important to obtain.

Now a Little Bit About Religion

45. Before now, have you ever been an active member of any church or religious group other than the one you were brought up in?

   No_____ Yes_____ Describe them _____

   _____

46. How do you feel about Christ? (Interviewer watch for love and emotion vs. disbelief and rejection.)

(continued)

---

47. Have you ever gone through a ceremony in which you accepted Christ as your savior?

    No_____ Yes_____
48. Have you a reading knowledge of Eastern religions besides the writings of Baba?

    No_____ Yes_____ Describe_____
    _____
    _____

49. Have you ever practiced Yoga?

    No_____ Yes_____
50. Have you ever undertaken macrobiotic or other diets?

    No_____ Yes_____ Describe, and why?_____
    _____
    _____

51. Have you ever experienced any of the following: (COMMENTS)
    (a) Spirit visitations   Yes _____ No _____
    (b) Unexplained
        unconsciousness   Yes _____ No _____
    (c) Visions   Yes _____ No _____
    (d) Experiences through
        mediums   Yes _____ No _____
    (e) ESP   Yes _____ No _____
    (f) Premonitions   Yes _____ No _____
    (g) Sudden insights   Yes _____ No _____
    (h) Any other?   _____
52. Have you ever sought insight or religious experience by any means other than the use of drugs?

    No_____ Yes_____ Describe _____

Source: Schwartz & Jacobs (1979), pp. 39–40.

You might notice that with slightly more structured response categories, the structured interview would look very similar to the self-report questionnaire considered a quantitative approach throughout this book. However, the structured qualitative interview leaves the subject greater freedom in choosing responses. While the resulting richness of responses can offer more interesting and provocative data, it has obvious drawbacks: The interpretation of the data (especially with statistical analysis) is not as straightforward as with more quantitative questionnaires.

Moving still farther into the qualitative domain, we find the *unstructured interview*. The following assumptions underlie unstructured interviews: the relevant dimensions to be covered will emerge in the course of the interview; the subject knows what issues are important as well as or better than the interviewer; and a lack of structure will lead to greater richness in data. In cases where these assumptions appear reasonable, more unstructured approaches might be indicated.

One might suspect that little interpersonal skill is required to administer a highly structured, objective questionnaire. A good deal more sensitivity is required to conduct an appropriate unstructured interview. In unstructured interviews, it is crucial that the interviewer be able to make the subject feel comfortable and be able to encourage the subject to explore relevant material and topics. Finally, it is not at all clear how the data from unstructured interviews should be collected, reduced, and analyzed—if indeed they should be reduced and analyzed at all. Note-taking by interviewers or raters or mechanical preservation (audiotaping or videotaping) for later careful scrutiny are suggested possibilities. Obviously, the aims of the researcher and the topic under investigation dictate how the data are to be collected, reduced, analyzed, and reported.

The Hite Report on female sexuality (Hite, 1976) is an example of a questionnaire approach. The famous Kinsey Report on the sexual behavior of the human male (Kinsey & Pommeroy, 1948) used a structured interview format. Studs Terkel's book *Working* (1972), which deals with people's jobs and their feelings about them, was researched through use of unstructured interviews. Reading these studies gives a sense of the type of data obtained with each method and shows the richness and also the looseness of data obtained through less structured approaches.

Participant Observation

With participant observation, the researcher goes one step beyond interviewing participants in some social activity; he or she actually becomes involved in the phenomenon. That is, the researcher

217

becomes a participant and then makes his or her observations as one who was involved in the activities under investigation.

For example, David Rosenhan's classic work "On Being Sane in Insane Places" (1973) chronicles his experiences as an inmate in mental hospitals. Rosenhan, a psychiatrist, and some of his colleagues were admitted to various institutions and made some telling observations about being inmates. One of the more interesting insights was that the clinical staff almost never caught on that the participant observers weren't insane—but the other inmates did. Anthropologists frequently visit other cultures and gain insight into the natives' lives by living with them *as* natives (see Glaser & Strauss, 1967). Finally, sociologists sometimes study nontypical groups, such as religious cults, by joining such a group and participating in the group's activities (for example, Robbins, Anthony, & Curtis, 1973).

While the researcher gains access to rich experiences by becoming a participating member of a group or society, this benefit must always be weighed against a possible loss of impartial detachment or scientific objectivity. (Anthropologists have long anguished over the pros and cons of researchers "going native.") The researcher's attitudes are not the only problem. Social scientists can participate in a group at various levels. What other group members think of the scientist and the role he or she adopts becomes an important issue in how the researcher will be treated and just how much inside information he or she will receive. The box entitled "Forms of Participation" presents Schwartz and Jacobs' (1979) analysis of the issue.

Forms of Participation

| | | How the researcher participates in the setting: | |
		By making observations	By normal, natural participation
Who others think the researcher is:	A scientist	1	2
	A bona fide member	3	4

(continued)

1. The investigator is known to others as a social scientist and confines his activities while among them to gathering information and observing.
2. The social scientist makes his identity as such known to all from the outset. However, he adopts the role of a bona fide member, such as a patient in a hospital or an employee in a factory. Others know him to be playing at being a member for purposes of getting an inside point of view.
3. The researcher conceals his identity but adopts a social role which is naturally defined by the group as someone who gathers information about other people. For example, he becomes a ship's recreation director, a town gossip, or a plant psychologist.
4. Unknown to others as a social scientist, the researcher adopts some role such as a factory worker and simply lives the life of that worker while letting nature take its course. He learns by being a factory worker, without any explicit attempt to observe or gather information about others.

Boxes 1 and 2 show two ways to be a known observer, while boxes 3 and 4 show two ways to be an unknown observer. With four kinds of social roles instead of two, new ways to plan for and assess old issues, such as detachment and involvement, emerge. The reader can figure out these elaborations for himself, as well as invent new variables and even more complicated roles to select from.

All of this should suffice to emphasize that the selection of who you are (to yourself and others) and where you are in a social world is worthy of being treated as a very delicate matter. Careful attention to this issue can perhaps bring more of a payoff in this kind of research than almost any other consideration.

Source: Schwartz & Jacobs (1979), p. 57.

Personal Accounts

If you want to know something about people's lives, why not just ask them? It seems strange that what serves in nonscientific contexts as a typical approach to gaining knowledge about the world needs to be justified as a scientific technique. If people did not respond to questions in a reasonably truthful manner most of the time, most of us would have stopped asking questions long ago. Then why not simply ask actors to reconstruct their experiences, and then consider whether that account is valid?

Of course, none of us would naively believe everything a person might offer as an account of his or her actions. Then how are we to tell the truths from the untruths? Let us again consider Schwartz and Jacobs' (1979) comments:

> Analyzing personal accounts is often the best way (perhaps the only way) to gain access to such phenomena. This strategy confronts the researcher with many of the same problems as do interviewing techniques, especially if the personal accounts are presented orally and in face-to-face interaction. He must rely upon the internal consistency and "integrity" of the account, the extent of the "rapport" he feels exists between himself and the one offering the account, the possible ulterior motives of the account giver, and why he might wish to engage in deception.
>
> Having decided on the extent of the account giver's good faith with respect to some part or all of the account, the researcher may seek to analyze not only where the account giver "is coming from" but also how he got there. In short, he seeks to establish the process whereby the personal circumstances recounted in the account were interpreted by the respondent, so as to produce the actions related in the account. Here particular attention is paid to the temporal sequences of events, the social contexts in which they occurred, their interpretation by the individual, and how all this led him to believe and behave as he did. An underlying assumption of this strategy is that an analysis of the individual's personal circumstances is necessary to reconstruct the reality of a social scene as it existed for him at some point in time. (pp. 61–62)

Personal accounts as a research method most often take the form of face-to-face interactions between the researcher and the subject. However, written accounts—such as autobiographies, diaries, letters, and suicide notes—can also appropriately be used.

Through personal accounts of experiences, the researcher can learn what factors—both internal and external—a person felt were important in determining why he or she acted in certain ways. Further, the researcher can begin to gain insight into how such characteristics as personally held (or believed) roles and rules can shape behavior: Rules, such as "One should always be honest," can have a profound impact on how a person behaves. Similarly, roles, such as "I am a

university professor," can strongly influence what people will allow
themselves to do. Access to these important considerations for understanding and explaining behavior is often only gained through personal
accounts. Garfinkel (1967) and Harŕe & Second (1972) demonstrate the
importance of personal accounts in the social sciences.

Life Histories

There are many types of life histories. Medical histories, psychi-
atric and psychological profiles, work histories of employees, and FBI
dossiers contain summary-like histories of different types. In each
case, the slice of a person's life considered relates to the unique purposes of the information gatherer. According to Schwartz and Jacobs
(1979), in order to be useful data, sociological life histories should
have as many of the following characteristics as possible:

1. The account ought to be autobiographical and, if possible, corrobo-
   rated by another in order to ensure against distortions in memory,
   selective perceptions, and the like.
2. The account ought to cover as much of the life of the individual as
   possible, as opposed to only a brief and discrete segment (or segments) of time.
3. The life history should be as detailed as possible, not only in the
   number of events included, but also with respect to how the individual felt about these events at the time of their occurrence.
4. Particular attention ought to be paid to the dates of the events so
   that not only the occurrences and how they were experienced but
   also their sequential ordering can be reconstructed.

As you learned in chapter 9, "Single-Subject Research," with personal accounts the researcher also must always wonder about the generality of the phenomenon being investigated. What group or population does this individual represent? One approach (called the
nomothetic approach) searches for empirical generalizations or behavioral regularities. From this perspective, the case-study life history is
usually unsatisfactory, since the researcher never knows just how idio-
syncratic and therefore nonrepresentative a particular example is.

On the other hand, *idiographic* social scientists stress the legiti-
macy—and, indeed, the value—of studying the individual. These
researchers are not really interested in the frequency of occurrence of

a phenomenon. Adherents of this approach tend to have as their primary goal understanding the phenomenon rather than quantifying it, classifying it, and predicting its occurrence in the future.

However, these two orientations might be used to complement one another. In studying a series of individual life histories and searching for the patterns within each one, researchers may come to understand patterns of phenomena that can be generalized across many individuals.

Unobtrusive Qualitative Measures

Chapter 2 mentioned a few unobtrusive measures; this final section will add to that list. The primary distinction between the methods presented thus far in this chapter and the remaining methods is this: The preceding techniques involved interfering with the natural flow of events to study the phenomenon or having an individual reconstruct a past event or series of events. The following techniques are intended to examine the residue of the natural process without exerting an impact on the process.

Content Analysis

Content analysis is an attempt to ascertain the meanings in a body of discourse in some systematic and quantifiable way. It involves performing quantitative analyses on novels, newspaper reports, television shows, advertising campaigns, political speeches, or the like. For example, a researcher might count the number of times particular words are used in a novel; analyze the roles played by members of various groups, such as women and racial minorities, in a television series; or consider the change over time from one stance (for example, pro-abortion) to another (anti-abortion) in a politician's speeches. Content analysis is usually employed to serve political or economic ends or to illuminate stereotypes of various sorts.

Analysis of Personal Documents

Autobiographies, letters, diaries, research journals, and so on—even when written for other purposes—can still serve as data for research. Researchers should take care, however, to understand the author's purposes in writing the document before attempting to employ it as data.

222

Nonverbal Communication

Scientists can learn a good deal about others by simply observing and noting the nonverbal communications they use. Clinicians, for example, are trained in the assessment of body language; and every good teacher knows when his or her class does not understand what is being presented, even when students do not verbally express their lack of understanding.

Audio-Visual Techniques

Various mechanical forms of data collection have been used to enhance the understanding of certain phenomena. For example, labor negotiation sessions might be videotaped and later analyzed in any of a variety of ways. Points seen as particularly important can be thoroughly analyzed; perhaps participants can take part in the analysis by reconstructing what they were thinking during the session. Another interesting use of audio-visual materials involves the researcher's giving the subjects a camera or tape-recorder, training them in the use of the instrument, and having them go home and compose an audio-visual essay on, for example, "a family argument" or "an average day."

The point of these brief sketches of qualitative methods is to broaden your understanding of how social scientists might appropriately approach research problems that seem intractable to traditional quantitative research strategies. This point highlights the need to understand the differences among the social sciences as to what level of theoretical explanations each seeks and what types of analysis each deems satisfactory. Appendix D presents some of these basic distinctions among the social sciences.

Additional Readings

Schwartz, H., & Jacobs, J. *Qualitative sociology: A method to the madness.* New York: Free Press, 1979.

Garfinkel, H. *Studies in ethnomethodology.* Englewood Cliffs, N.J.: Prentice-Hall, 1967.

Harre, R., & Secord, P. F. *The explanation of social behavior.* London: Basil Blackwell, 1972.

15

Ethical Principles
in Research

Chapter Preview

Chapter 15 presents the Research Code of Ethics of the American
Psychological Association as an example of the guidelines
professional groups give to their members. The problem of
deception in research is offered as a case study to illuminate
some of the important ethical considerations to be weighed by
researchers. The issues of cost-benefit analysis of research,
informed consent, and debriefing procedures are also touched on.

Ethical Guidelines

In any study, the researcher has the obligation to make a careful examination of the study's ethical appropriateness. Each of the social sciences has developed its own set of ethical guidelines, which serves as a guiding plan for researchers in that domain. The guidelines developed by the several disciplines are remarkably similar in spirit and content. The American Psychological Association's guidelines for research with human participants and animals are presented in the accompanying box as an example of a code of ethics. It is the obligation of every member of the American Psychological Association to adhere to these principles in his or her research endeavors. Failure to conduct research in accord with the guidelines can lead to censure or even expulsion from the association.

American Psychological Association Guidelines

Research with Human Participants

The decision to undertake research rests upon a considered judgment by the individual psychologist about how best to contribute to psychological science and human welfare. Having made the decision to conduct research, the psychologist considers alternative directions in which research energies and resources might be invested. On the basis of this consideration, the psychologist carries out the investigation with respect and concern for the dignity and welfare of the people who participate and with cognizance of federal and state regulations and professional standards governing the conduct of research with human participants.

a. In planning a study, the investigator has the responsibility to make a careful evaluation of its ethical acceptability. To the extent that the weighing of scientific and human values suggests a compromise of any principle, the investigator incurs a correspondingly serious obligation to seek ethical advice and to observe stringent safeguards to protect the rights of human participants.

b. Considering whether a participant in a planned study will be a "subject at risk" [such as in the Milgram study] or a "sub-

(continued)

---

ject at minimal risk," [such as in the McFall and Twentyman study] according to recognized standards, is of primary ethical concern to the investigator.

c. The investigator always retains the responsibility for ensuring ethical practice in research. The investigator is also responsible for the ethical treatment of research participants by collaborators, assistants, students, and employees, all of whom, however, incur similar obligations.

d. Except in minimal-risk research, the investigator establishes a clear and fair agreement with research participants, prior to their participation, that clarifies the obligations and responsibilities of each. The investigator has the obligation to honor all promises and commitments included in that agreement. The investigator informs the participants of all aspects of the research that might reasonably be expected to influence willingness to participate and explains all other aspects of the research about which the participants inquire. Failure to make full disclosure prior to obtaining informed consent requires additional safeguards to protect the welfare and dignity of the research participants. Research with children or with participants who have impairments that would limit understanding and/or communication requires special safeguarding procedures.

e. Methodological requirements of a study may make the use of concealment or deception necessary. Before conducting such a study, the investigator has a special responsibility to (i) determine whether the use of such techniques is justified by the study's prospective scientific, educational, or applied value; (ii) determine whether alternative procedures are available that do not use concealment or deception; and (iii) ensure that the participants are provided with sufficient explanation as soon as possible.

f. The investigator respects the individual's freedom to decline to participate in or to withdraw from the research at any time. The obligation to protect this freedom requires careful thought and consideration when the investigator is in a position of authority or influence over the participant. Such positions of authority include, but are not limited to, situations in which

(continued)

American Psychological Association Guidelines continued

research participation is required as part of employment or in which the participant is a student, client, or employee of the investigator.

g. The investigator protects the participant from physical and mental discomfort, harm, and danger that may arise from research procedures. If risks of such consequences exist, the investigator informs the participant of that fact. Research procedures likely to cause serious or lasting harm to a participant are not used unless the failure to use these procedures might expose the participant to risk of greater harm, or unless the research has great potential benefit and fully informed and voluntary consent is obtained from each participant. The participant should be informed of procedures for contacting the investigator within a reasonable time period following participation should stress, potential harm, or related questions or concerns arise.

h. After the data are collected, the investigator provides the participant with information about the nature of the study and attempts to remove any misconceptions that may have arisen. Where scientific or human values justify delaying or withholding this information, the investigator incurs a special responsibility to monitor the research and to ensure that there are no damaging consequences for the participant.

i. Where research procedures result in undesirable consequences for the individual participant, the investigator has the responsibility to detect and remove or correct these consequences, including long-term effects.

j. Information obtained about a research participant during the course of an investigation is confidential unless otherwise agreed upon in advance. When the possibility exists that others may obtain access to such information, this possibility, together with the plans for protecting confidentiality, is explained to the participant as part of the procedure for obtaining informed consent.

(continued)

Care and Use of Animals

An investigator of animal behavior strives to advance understanding of basic behavioral principles and/or to contribute to the improvement of human health and welfare. In seeking these ends, the investigator ensures the welfare of animals and treats them humanely. Laws and regulations notwithstanding, an animal's immediate protection depends upon the scientist's own conscience.

a. The acquisition, care, use, and disposal of all animals are in compliance with current federal, state or provincial, and local laws and regulations.

b. A psychologist trained in research methods and experienced in the care of laboratory animals closely supervises all procedures involving animals and is responsible for ensuring appropriate consideration of their comfort, health, and humane treatment.

c. Psychologists ensure that all individuals using animals under their supervision have received explicit instruction in experimental methods and in the care, maintenance, and handling of the species being used. Responsibilities and activities of individuals participating in a research project are consistent with their respective competencies.

d. Psychologists make every effort to minimize discomfort, illness, and pain of animals. A procedure subjecting animals to pain, stress, or privation is used only when an alternative procedure is unavailable and the goal is justified by its prospective scientific, educational, or applied value. Surgical procedures are performed under appropriate anesthesia; techniques to avoid infection and minimize pain are followed during and after surgery.

e. When it is appropriate that the animal's life be terminated, it is done rapidly and painlessly.

Source: American Psychological Association (1973). Material in brackets added by this author.

As you can see, the APA code of ethics offers a set of principles meant to serve as general guideposts to which researchers can easily refer when they are confronted with the need to make research decisions that have ethical implications. Bearing APA's explicit code in mind, and maintaining the spirit as well as the letter of the guidelines, each researcher makes whatever judgments are necessary in the course of the study.

However, institutions are becoming increasingly involved in helping investigators make these ethical research decisions. Virtually every institution in which research is routinely conducted (schools, hospitals, social work agencies, mental health agencies, and the like) has an in-house committee to review the ethical appropriateness of research performed in that institution. Often these committees for the protection of subjects' rights will disagree (for ethical reasons) with the research decisions individual investigators have made and require the investigators to follow a different course of action before allowing the research to continue. Further, granting agencies, such as the National Science Foundation and the National Institutes of Health, require assurance of the ethical appropriateness of all investigations before they will consider funding any project. Finally, professional journals have begun refusing to publish the results of certain studies because the editors felt that subjects' rights had been breached.

While the majority of social scientists applaud the increased attention given to subjects' rights, there are some responsible researchers who believe that it represents an overreaction. Typically, these critics contend that the benefit to society of a particular line of research justifies the minor cost to research participants. An example of this type of controversy will be elaborated on in the next section, which discusses the use of deception in psychological experiments.

An Example of an Ethical Dilemma: Deception in Research

The use of deception in psychological research is a good example of a problem with no clear solution. In most instances, unethical practices in research are obvious and are deplored by virtually all individuals who analyze the situation. However, the problem of deception is different. After hearing the arguments for and against the use of deception, sensitive, ethical scholars continue to disagree regarding the appropriateness of the technique. Since deception continues to be an important and controversial problem for psychological researchers, it can serve as an example of the important issues to be considered in making ethical research decisions.

In the early 1960s, Stanley Milgram conducted a series of studies on obedience to authority. In those studies, he employed deception to examine the lengths to which his subjects would go when told by an authority figure to give electric shocks to another research subject. The studies provoked enormous controversy. To understand the ethical principles involved, we must examine the general approach Milgram (1974) employed.

Newspaper ads solicited volunteers to take part in experiments on learning and memory (the experiments, in reality, did not deal with learning and memory). Upon arriving at the site of the experiment, a subject would meet another individual, who was introduced as another person who had answered the newspaper ad. This second "subject" was really a member of the research team following a prepared script (research team members who pass themselves off as subjects in order to help execute a deception are referred to as *confederates* of the experimenter). A rigged drawing was then conducted; the real subject would "draw" the role of "teacher" while the confederate would become the "learner" in what was supposed to be a learning experiment. The "teacher" was informed that he would administer punishment to the "learner" whenever the learner failed in a memory task.

The scientist who was supervising this "learning experiment" would attach electrodes to the "learner" and place the "teacher" in front of the control panel of a machine. A lever on the panel, when depressed, supposedly would deliver a shock to the "learner." The shock level began at 15 volts and increased by 15-volt increments (15, 30, 45, and so on) to a final value of 450 volts. These shock settings were labelled "slight shock," "moderate shock," and so on, up to "danger: severe shock" for values above 400 volts.

The "learner" was to learn some simple word pairs; and each time he or she missed a word pair when tested, the "teacher" was to deliver a shock—first 15 volts, then 30 volts, then 45 volts, and so on. When the shock level reached 120 volts, the learner would begin to yell that he or she wanted out of the experiment. The scientist would then instruct the "teacher" not only to continue administering increasing amounts of shock but also to ignore the "learner's" cries for help.

The deception in this study, as you probably guessed, was that the "learner" never received any shocks at all; but the elaborate bogus feedback system—which included cries of pain, calls for help, and the like—led the "teacher" to believe that he really was delivering electrical shocks to the "learner". As mentioned, the dependent variable in Milgram's studies did not concern learning or memory but rather concerned how much shock subjects would administer when ordered by an authority figure (the experimenter) to do so. In some studies, over half the subjects continued to deliver shocks up to the maximum level of 450 volts.

The Milgram studies generated enormous controversy. Why? It was not simply because they employed deception. Many other psychological studies employed deception, and no protest resulted from those investigations. Why did the Milgram work touch a nerve?

Two very different possible explanations should be mentioned. The first is that the research might have threatened us by suggesting some negative characteristics all of us might share. Perhaps we are all more compliant to the will of authority figures than we would like to admit. In that case, the public outcry might be understood as a form of societal denial. If this was true, and if it was the only reason for criticizing the study, the controversy would not be important for research in general. Scientists should weather this type of criticism and should not allow it to influence their work. However, the second type of criticism has much more serious implications for research in the social sciences.

This second critique deals with the scientist's right to produce psychological stress (and possibly even harm) in research subjects. To his credit, Milgram was quite candid about subjects' reactions to the experiment. Obviously, many people were upset about being pressured to perform an action they did not wish to perform. The thrust of this second critique is that no experimenter should create a situation in which a subject might experience psychological discomfort—discomfort that might even lead to emotional or psychological damage. Because this second critique obviously has some degree of validity, several of the ethical principles presented earlier were developed in part in response to the problems that Milgram's studies highlighted.

232

Additional Ethical Principles

Some additional ethical principles can also be considered in the context of deception in research. They involve cost-benefit analyses, informed consent, and debriefing.

Before any study is carried out, it should be subjected to a *cost-benefit analysis*. Chapter 13 discussed cost-benefit analyses in terms of dollar costs. Here, we balance the costs to subjects in terms of emotional or psychological discomfort against the potential benefits to science that might result from the study. This concept helps explain why deception, in and of itself, is not the problem. Rather, the crucial issue involves the possible detrimental impacts of deception on the subjects, weighed against the potential benefits of the study to society.

Remember the McFall and Twentyman telephone experiment described in chapter 2, in which a confederate asked to borrow a subject's class notes. You can see that the sort of deception this study used might be considered acceptable, while a Milgram-type deception might be deemed inappropriate. The important difference is that the one type of deception is relatively benign, whereas the other is potentially quite harmful. But the cost-benefit decision is more complex still, since the potential benefits to science must be carefully considered and factored into the decision on whether the investigation should be conducted.

The second principle to be considered for any study involves *informed consent*. In general, subjects should understand in advance everything that will be required of them in a study. In the overwhelming majority of studies in the social sciences, securing prior informed consent from subjects is not a problem and will not jeopardize the results. However, you can see that when a study will involve deception, complete disclosure of all procedures that will be used will make the deceptive procedures useless. This is obvious in such cases as the Milgram obedience studies.

The prevailing view is that, whenever possible, prior informed consent should be obtained from subjects. Whenever deception is to be involved, either a nonspecific or an open-ended consent should be obtained; and a prior cost-benefit assessment of the study by some appropriate review committee should have indicated clearly the relative value of the project. Finally, the researcher should have made a case for why one of the proposed alternatives to deception is not appropriate. These alternatives include role-playing (Mixon, 1972), simulation studies (Zimbardo, 1973), and honest experiments (Rubin, 1973). Interested students are encouraged to read the articles that describe these alternatives, as well as Kelman's (1967) general critique of deception, and to determine the potential scientific strengths and liabilities of deception and its alternatives.

Whenever deception is involved, the issue of *debriefing* assumes paramount importance. Researchers should debrief all subjects at the end of a study. The debriefing should include the rationale for conducting the study; an explanation of all research procedures employed; the opportunity for subjects to ask questions about the study; and either a description of the results obtained from the study or a promise that results will be made available to subjects as soon as they have been determined.

Debriefing is intended primarily to make the experience of being a research subject as rewarding and interesting as possible. However, numerous researchers have used the debriefing session as a method of obtaining additional anecdotal information, which often enhances the researcher's ability to understand and interpret the meaning of the data. The unintended consequences of debriefing are often beneficial to both the researcher and the subjects. For example, the free give-and-take of a debriefing discussion often counteracts subjects' feelings of resentment against the rigid and impersonal procedures studies sometimes must employ (see Argyris, 1968).

In general, pressures both from within the various disciplines in the social sciences and from society in general have forced social scientists to be more cognizant of the ethical implications of their research activities. While some researchers bemoan the fact that their freedom to pursue knowledge is inhibited somewhat because of recent developments (Gergen, 1973), researchers generally agree that the changes make sense and are appropriate to counter certain excesses. And finally, concern about ethical difficulties has forced social scientists to search for more ethically satisfactory solutions to several research problems. Some of these solutions (such as greater use of debriefing procedures) have even produced unexpected benefits.

Additional Readings

American Psychological Association, *ad hoc* Committee on Ethical Standards in Psychological Research. *Ethical principles in the conduct of research with human participants*. Washington, D.C.: American Psychological Association, 1973.

Milgram, S. *Obedience to authority*. New York: Harper & Row, 1974.

16

On Studying Humans

Chapter Preview

Throughout this book, it has continually been emphasized that by employing appropriate research methodology and proper experimental controls, we can come to a more precise and accurate understanding of the relationships among variables in the world. It has been implied that many of the distortions and misperceptions associated with commonsense ways of knowing can be avoided by use of experimental designs with their appropriate methodological controls. But sometimes, the value of research methods in the search for a proper understanding of human beings is overemphasized. This chapter highlights some human characteristics that suggest our current arsenal of research methods is not yet adequate for the task of fully understanding humans. The final section deals with a general strategy of how we might reduce the gap between current methods and a more fully adequate research methodology of the future.

This chapter is the most difficult to write, because there is so little agreement among social scientists on the topics covered and also because it probes the boundaries between the social sciences and disciplines such as philosophy of science and ethics. It is also different from the preceding chapters, because rather than simply describing research methods and commenting on their strengths and liabilities, it attempts to look toward the future and to set forth some ambitions for our cluster of sciences.

This might be a good place to note that throughout the book, the various ways in which the social sciences differ from one another have been glossed over. These differences were downplayed to emphasize that the logic underlying basic research methods cuts across the boundaries between disciplines. It seems likely that the various social sciences could profit from greater interaction and from attempts by each discipline to adapt the others' preferred research techniques to fit its own needs. However, some fundamental differences do exist among the disciplines, and a few of them are highlighted in appendix D.

Just as the social sciences have been discussed in a general way, the process of experimentation has also been broadly described. Chapter 1 traced some outlines of what it means to be a science. You will remember that scientific efforts have several general characteristics: they deal with observables; they control extraneous variables; they deal with phenomena that are repeatable; and so on. Chapters 2 through 12 described how social scientists have implemented methods and procedures in their research efforts that make the logic of their conclusions more compelling. Remember, the hallmark of scientific efforts lies in the disciplined logic that underlies the research, not simply the use of scientific techniques and instruments.

However, many voices—both from within the various social sciences and from other disciplines—have raised serious doubts concerning the wisdom of modeling social sciences after the more established sciences. Various writers offer varying sets of reasons why research in the social sciences should be considered different from research in other areas. This chapter will attempt to explicate three of these objections, to give you a feeling for some reasons why the scientific study of humans might need to be vastly different from other scientific approaches to gaining knowledge. Then, the chapter will offer a specific recommendation on how research methodology, as practiced, might be improved.

238

On the Reactive Nature of Humans

The philosopher of science Stephen Toulmin tells us that the present view of science in the social sciences is influenced by the classical notion of *rational objectivity*. That is, the scientist is seen as one who studies a system in nature without intervening in the operations of the system. The notion of rational objectivity in science requires a lack of reciprocal interaction between observer and object. A scientist can observe nature, but nature cannot reflect on being observed. The classical sciences, as exemplified by Newtonian physics, made substantial progress in part because their objects of study never knew they were being studied. Therefore, scientists could assume that these objects would continue to behave as usual; no perverseness could lead them to react to being observed. While the demands of rational objectivity seemed to be reasonably appropriate in many areas of the natural sciences, they never made sense for some areas of the social sciences.

For example, suppose I am interested in determining the temperature at which sodium and chlorine will combine to form salt molecules. I can be reasonably confident that the sodium and chlorine molecules do not "know" they are taking part in an experiment and therefore that they do not "care" how the investigation turns out. It makes no sense to think that sodium atoms will be concerned that the study will conclude they combine to form salt at too low a temperature; the sodium will not hold out for a higher temperature to avoid being thought of as "easy." Our current view of the behavior of chemicals sees them as passive respondents to invariant natural laws. That these laws could be modified by the willful intervention of the chemicals themselves seems unlikely. But how similar is the behavior of chemicals to human behavior?

In the classical view of science, the scientist could observe nature, but nature could not reflect on being observed. If that were true of human subjects, it would not be necessary to untangle their behavior—to try to determine what behavior would naturally have occurred if the subjects had not been under study and what behavior was a reactive effect of being studied. But, of course, humans do react; and because human beings acting as research subjects seem to be so uniquely unsuited to the demands of rational objectivity, many social scientists are persuaded that there can never be an adequate scientific study of human beings. However, efforts have been made to deal with the contaminating influences of reactivity in studies involving humans.

Two somewhat different approaches have been frequently employed. One approach involves the use of unobtrusive measures. Webb and associates (1981) speak of three broad types of unobtrusive measures: physical traces, archives, and unobtrusive observation. Physical traces—the durable remains of earlier events—can serve as evidence of the events' occurrence. For example, the amount of wear in the carpet in front of certain pictures in a museum might provide an indirect measure of the relative popularity of the pictures. It is extremely unlikely that museum patrons would purposely wear thin the rug in front of certain pictures because they knew (or suspected) that some social scientist would view that as an indication of the popularity of the pictures. In this sense, we can have confidence that such physical traces reduce the reactivity problems associated with collecting data from human subjects. It should be noted that Webb and his colleagues also point out that unobtrusive measures may be more subject to a different set of threats to validity than other, more reactive measures. However—since, as in the museum example, individuals who provide the data for an unobtrusive measure never even know they are involved in a study—the demands of rational objectivity are satisfied in studies of this sort. As will be pointed out in the next section ("On Studying Active Agents"), however, there are many important areas of social science research in which unobtrusive measures are either extremely difficult or impossible to obtain.

A second general approach to dealing with reactivity problems in research involves letting subjects know they are participating in an experiment but keeping them naive—or even deceiving them—regarding the actual purposes or hypotheses of the study. The logic underlying these practices involves the belief that if subjects knew exactly what area the experimental hypotheses involved, they would show more reactivity in that area. While keeping subjects naive lessens the threat of conscious distortion and possibly of unconscious distortion, it can also have negative consequences.

Chris Argyris (1968) demonstrated that employing control procedures, such as keeping subjects naive or deceiving them, can have important negative consequences. Apparently, people experience unintended negative reactions to being placed in the subordinate position of being a subject in a research situation. Argyris identified six unintended, and potentially contaminating, reactions, such as psychological withdrawal from the experiment and covert hostility toward the experimenter or the experiment. Ironically, the control procedures employed to reduce reactivity might actually produce *more* reactivity, because they also produce unintended consequences.

As noted earlier, it seems that problems involved in implementing control procedures are far greater in the social sciences than in the natural sciences, because chemicals (or plants, or stars, or numbers, or gravity) do not "care about" what a researcher sees when he or she studies them. Philosophers of science have pointed out that astronomers can claim with reasonable assurance that "It does not hurt the moon that I look at it!" (*Hurt* in this instance means, "change the behavior of.") We cannot have the same confidence that looking at humans will not alter their behavior.

On Studying Active Agents

In scientists' earlier efforts to understand the laws of nature, there was considerable disagreement about what type of explanation would be adequate to understand the actions of physical systems. For example, it might have been said that the speed at which an apple fell reflected the jubilation it felt about approaching its proper place. However, explanations of this sort were found to be lacking, because they anthropomorphized (attributed the qualities and capacities of a human being to an inanimate object). As already emphasized, the laws of gravity and other phenomena in the physical sciences could be precisely understood without consideration of what the objects of study felt, thought, or desired. Indeed, in most instances there was good reason to believe the objects didn't think, feel, or desire in the first place. But note that even when a thinking being is falling, his or her speed is still a function of the laws of gravity, not what he or she thinks or desires. For example, if I fell out of an airplane, my speed would be determined by physical forces, not by whether I wanted to hit the ground quickly (if, for example, I were trying to kill myself) or wanted to stop my hasty descent (if, for example, I had accidently

241

fallen out of the airplane). In this instance, gravity provides a totally adequate explanation of why I am falling at a certain speed but tells nothing of why I began to fall.

The point to be made here is that historically *certain types* of explanations became appropriate to serve as "scientific explanations." Invariant physical forces became preferred modes of explanation. In the natural sciences, as mentioned, the role of the scientist was to stand outside the system in operation and to come to understand the functioning of the system through observing it. The scientist, as a detached and distant onlooker, was the one who decided "what really caused what" in an experiment. This "third-person explanation" became preferred to the "first-person account" of one actually involved in the action under investigation.

Many social scientists saw the production of these third-person accounts of phenomena as the way their disciplines would make scientific contributions to an understanding of human behavior. And indeed, this approach has often proven effective and has produced many valuable insights into human action. But for several types of phenomena, sole reliance on the third-person perspective became inadequate to describe the actions of the system. Perhaps one of the first instances of this problem came from the work of sociologists who looked at the influence of social norms (rules of conduct generally agreed on by society) on human behavior.

Researchers found that a societal norm is often not enough to explain behavior. It became obvious that it was necessary to understand the societal norm *as seen by the individual* in order to adequately understand the individual's behavior. Understanding the individual's perception of the societal norm often involved obtaining a first-person account. In another domain, anthropologists have long known that their accounts of cultural events were drastically different from those offered by members of the culture who were enlisted to be participant observers. (Anthropologists now have come to a reasonably good accommodation of the discrepancies between third- and first-person accounts. Both are important elements for a total understanding of human action.)

Finally, a philosopher, Rom Harré, and a psychologist, Paul Secord (1972)—borrowing heavily from the works of the sociologists Garfinkel (1967) and Goffman (1959)—have outlined the importance of the "roles and rules" each of us adopts to an understanding of our social behavior. Each of us has an understanding of the role of a student, although it is slightly different for each of us. Your behavior in class is largely a reflection of how you believe students are supposed to act in class. Likewise, we believe certain rules of conduct are proper; and these rules guide our behavior. For example, my rule that a guest should not damage a host's property keeps me from deliberately spilling coffee on my host's rug. Our belief in certain social roles and rules and our determination that certain roles and rules are appropriate in certain situations affect how we act. But learning about people's personal roles and rules often involves accepting first-person accounts.

In summary, certain undeniable characteristics of humans, such as consciousness and purposeful cognitive thought, appear to influence human action. To the extent that these data (such as roles and rules) are only accessible through first-person accounts, we may have to accept such accounts as part of the evidence we will consider in obtaining an appropriate understanding of human action.

If you reflect on the topics covered in the first fifteen chapters of this book, you may realize that current research methods are really not well designed for the task of understanding the following: the meanings of experimental situations for subjects; subjects' interpretations of the reasons behind their behaviors; and the roles, rules, hunches, hypotheses, and so on that may guide subjects' actions. It is likely that the present state of affairs exists, in part, because social scientists have tried to copy the logic, techniques, and methods of the natural sciences in their effort to study human behavior in a scientific manner. As emphasized, this practice may not always be appropriate; and so social scientists may need to develop new and different research methods capable of taking into account the unique aspects of humans that combine to produce human behavior. In short, we need to learn how to study humans as *active agents*—people who not only respond to the physical and social world in which they find themselves but also act upon that world. In this view, plans, goals, purposes, rules, roles, intentions, and so on are important elements of research.

Quite possibly, substantial changes in the methodologies of all the social sciences will be made in the near future and will emphasize the following: qualitative methods in addition to quantitative methods (see Schwartz & Jacobs, 1979); the importance of roles, rules, and meanings in human action (see Harré & Secord, 1972); and treatment of research subjects as active, informed coinvestigators rather than as naive or deceived objects of investigation (Jourard, 1967). Advances on these fronts could lead to the formation of methodologies capable of providing a more balanced and complete account of the many influences involved in human behavior.

On the Role of Values in Research

Stephanie Shields (1975) reviewed much of the research conducted over the past century on differences between men and women and made some telling observations about how the findings reflect the beliefs, biases, and values of their periods. Rather than correcting or explaining current biases, the research more often was used to document and support them. Current beliefs and assumptions appear to be important determinants of what scientists choose to research, what findings they expect to obtain, what results they actually do obtain, and how they interpret those findings.

Rather than being an effective means of correcting biases, then, all too often research findings appear to be caused (or slanted) by biases. Consequently, two researchers with two entirely different perspectives on a problem might conduct two sets of studies that provide entirely different sets of results and, consequently, totally different answers to the research question. As an example, Figure 16−1 presents a diagram of the many ways in which sex bias can enter the process of psychological research. Several sections of this text (most recently chapter 10, under "Experimenter Expectancy Effects") have discussed how researchers can employ procedures that reduce the influence of biases of this sort. But even with the best controls conscientiously employed, assumptions and biases exert a powerful influence on findings. Therefore, it is possible to view the findings of research investigations as demonstrating not what must invariably occur in the world but what *may* occur when human beings are considered from a particular perspective.

Sigmond Koch (1981) has said that implicit in much of the research in the social sciences are several models of humans that present impoverished and distorted views of humans' best qualities.

244

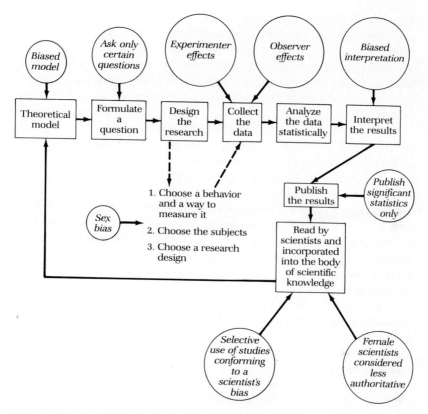

Figure 16–1 The Process of Psychological Research and Ways in Which Sex Bias May Enter

Source: Hyde and Rosenberg (1980), p. 8.

He points out that it is dehumanizing to think of people as if they were only reinforcement maximizers or information processors. The crux of Koch's critique is this: If these limited models of humans are basic to researchers' understanding of the meaning of their findings, then the researchers will gradually accumulate scientific evidence that appears to support their belief that these models do adequately capture the essence of humans. And when these results are conveyed to the nonscientific community, people might come to believe that they actually *are* (or worse, that they *must be*) what the research suggests. In viewing themselves in this manner, people might actually become more like the model because they expect that they will act in accord with the scientific evidence. Can you see that, by viewing people solely as, for example, reinforcement maximizers, scientists might actually unwittingly contribute to a self-fulfilling prophecy wherein humans actually become more like a dehumanized model of themselves?

By contrast, consider what might occur if we viewed research in the social sciences as giving knowledge of human *possibilities* rather than certainties. For a moment, view research findings as what *might be* true for people rather than what *is* true or what *must be* true. This view of research evidence takes into account the limiting constraints of the scientist's model. What are those constraints? The first consists of the assumptions, biases, and theoretical perspectives of the scientist. We considered this phenomenon above: The assumptions scientists hold when they approach a topic of inquiry are important determinants of what answers they will obtain to their questions.

The second limitation involves the currently accepted set of research tools (both research designs and statistical analyses)—the means by which scientists answer their questions. Scientists are always limited by what tools are currently available, documented, and accepted for general practice. As new tools are developed and refined, previously unanswerable questions become testable. Further, applying new tools to old questions often leads to answers different from those arrived at with an older set of research tools.

The third constraint relates to the human element of science. No one wishes to make a bad mistake in public; and science is in the public domain. It is safe to conduct research within the constraints of currently accepted assumptions, using the tried-and-true set of research tools. Unfortunately, few researchers interpret their findings with the humility called for by evidence constrained by so many factors. Even fewer researchers strive to develop new assumptions or create innovative tools to probe research questions from new perspectives. Koch makes us aware that human beings are complex, multifaceted beings. The challenge to research methodologists in the social sciences is to develop an array of research tools that will allow us to appreciate and understand humans in all their complexity.

On Improving Methodology Through Research on Research Methods

As you may already have concluded, research methodologies do not always provide a clear and undistorted view of the world. It is simply not true to assert that experimental methodology gives the researcher a set of clear glasses through which the world may be glimpsed as it truly exists. The current view of what constitutes appropriate research methodology is likely to change as researchers learn more and more about the strengths and limitations inherent in each methodology.

Perhaps a fictitious example offered by the astronomer Eddington will shed light on what kind of shortcomings research methods can have. Eddington tells of a scientist who wished to catalog the fish in the sea (the research question). He took a net of two-inch mesh and cast it into the sea repeatedly (a research method). After carefully cataloging his findings, he concluded that there were no fish in the sea smaller than two inches. In this example, the scientist's trust in the adequacy of his research method was misplaced and led him to draw an inaccurate conclusion. Here is an example of scientific methodology yielding misleading findings.

What if the researcher had doubted the adequacy of the netting procedure? Could he have performed a study to test the procedure? What would the results have demonstrated? If he had performed a study specifically designed to test the adequacy of the netting procedure compared with that of some specific alternative procedure, the misinterpretation might have been recognized. For example, our researcher might have considered an alternative research method such as damming a small inlet of the sea, draining the water, and examining the bodies of the fish left behind. When fish smaller than two inches were found, the limitations of the netting procedure would become apparent. But likely the largest fish obtained through the damming procedure would be substantially smaller than the largest fish obtained through the netting approach; that would present another problem. Research that tests the adequacy of research methods does not prove which technique is better; it simply provides evidence relating to the potential strengths and limitations of each approach. From this information, researchers can determine which of the two approaches is the method of choice, or whether both should be used.

Inherent in this example is a recommendation that we consider the currently accepted body of research practices as a body of scientific knowledge about how to go about seeking scientific knowledge. Rather than viewing current research practices as perfect, we might subdivide them into a collection of assumptions that we have come to implicitly trust in our search for scientific knowledge. But our trust in these assumptions need not remain implicit. Rather, we can systematically test each assumption by making the currently accepted research practice (such as netting) one level of an independent variable in a study, while some alternative practice (such as damming) serves as another level of the independent variable. The dependent variable consists of some index of the validity or adequacy of the data obtained from each approach. If the currently accepted practice prevails, we can use it in our subsequent studies with more explicit and justifiable confidence in its adequacy. However, if the alternative approach proves superior, it can be incorporated into future research; thus, our methodological practices will have been upgraded. Howard (1982) provides examples of several areas in which this approach has yielded improved research techniques.

You might have noticed that in conducting research on research, we seem to have come full circle. It was argued that the scientific approach, while not perfect nor the only way to gain knowledge, represents a good way to gain knowledge. The current body of accepted research practices can be thought of as a body of knowledge about how humans can go about securing valid knowledge. If we truly believe that scientific methodologies yield valid knowledge, it is inevitable that we will use the scientific method to test the adequacy of (and even improve on) currently accepted research practices. Finally, it is to be hoped that the development of more appropriate methodologies will, in turn, improve the fruits of the research efforts of all social scientists.

Additional Readings

Harré, R., & Secord, P. F. *The explanation of social behavior*. Oxford: Basil Blackwell, 1972.

Winch, P. *The idea of a social science and its relation to philosophy*. London: Routledge & Keegan Paul, 1958.

Appendix A

Conducting an Experiment

This appendix will outline the major aspects of designing, conducting, and analyzing a research project. The intention is to show you the variety of decisions and judgments that must be made by a researcher conducting an investigation in the social sciences and to show you when, in the progress of a research project, these various decisions are made.

The point of entry into the research process is the particular thought or idea a researcher wishes to investigate. The stimulus for the undertaking might have come from a theoretical set of predictions that have yet to be tested empirically; from the results of previous research investigations that appear to be especially promising or unsettling; from a specific problem encountered by applied social scientists, which the researcher chooses to investigate in a more formal research setting; as well as from a variety of other potential sources of ideas for empirical studies. The purposes of the researcher are almost too varied to consider here. Suffice it to say that they might involve any or all of the following:

1. To demonstrate an empirical relationship the researcher intuitively believes to be true.
2. To begin to understand a process that is currently poorly understood.
3. To learn more about a particular phenomenon of theoretical or practical interest.
4. To satisfy the researcher's (or his or her colleagues') curiosity about the operations defining a particular phenomenon.
5. To satisfy the researcher's need to publish and thereby gain stature in the scientific community.

The question a researcher decides to pursue can have theoretical or practical significance. Questions of the theoretical sort include the following: Does frustration lead to aggression? Is a single large block of practice on a particular test more effective in enhancing learning than practice spaced over a long period of time? What is the relationship between level of fear arousal and amount of behavior change attributable to that level of fear? Questions of a more practical nature, and of immediate significance because of practical problems, might include the following: Which therapeutic approach appears to produce the most important behavioral gains in subjects who fear flying? Can an assessment of job qualifications be developed to enable a company to determine the amount of strength, agility, and endurance required for workers on offshore oil rigs? Related to that question, are women who meet these minimal requirements hired for such jobs more or less readily than men? Do children who watch television programs that portray aggression and violence tend to exhibit more aggression than those who do not?

As you may have noticed, these interests and questions have been stated on something of a theoretical level. At this point, once the question is clear, the researcher can survey the existing literature to ascertain what relevant studies have been conducted on the topic and whether the question might be answered by the existing literature. If not—if further research is needed to probe the relationships in general or to probe them in the specific instance with which the researcher is concerned—then the researcher begins a dual process.

The first step is to ascertain if appropriate operational definitions of the constructs of interest exist (see chapter 2 for the issues involved with operational definitions). For example, a researcher can look through the literature on human factors to ascertain what measures of strength, endurance, and agility have been used in prior research. Or, in another example, a researcher can look for the ways other investigators have artificially induced frustration in order to probe its relationship with aggression, as well as for what standard measures of aggression have been used in prior research. The determination of whether adequate and appropriate indices of the variables of interest are available is a very important step. It is important because some theoretical questions are unanswerable owing to the lack of reasonable operational definitions for the variables involved in the study.

At this time, the researcher should also begin to consider the possibility that, to be feasible, the study needs a particular setting and population of subjects. Are real-life populations and settings available that would allow the investigator to have some degree of confidence in the study's external validity? (See chapter 7.) In the particular setting chosen, does the researcher have the ability to manipulate variables so that he or she can conduct a true experimental study rather than a passive observational study? (See chapter 3.) Finally—and this is of greater interest for studies with theoretical rather than practical motivation—the investigator must consider whether the variables as manipulated and measured in the study do indeed bear a high degree of similarity to the constructs he or she is interested in investigating. (See the discussion of construct validity in chapter 7.)

At this point, the investigator should formalize the design of the study. Is it a simple passive observational design? Is it a simple true experiment with one independent variable? Is it a complex experimental design with multiple independent variables and multiple levels of each independent variable? (See chapter 5 for a description of complex experimental designs.) Is it a complex correlational study such as a regression analysis or a time-lagged correlation analysis?

Next, the researcher must think very clearly and specifically regarding his or her ability to sample particular populations, to randomly assign subjects along various dimensions, to control irrelevant or contaminating variables that might counterfeit a true effect, and so forth. After a researcher has laid out the basic design and obtained the sample of subjects, his or her interest is turned to determining the measures to be employed in the study.

By this point, the researcher should have reviewed all prior decisions in light of the ethical and professional issues they might raise. Is the researcher infringing on the human rights of the subjects in the study? Is there any potential for physical or psychological harm to the subjects? If the study is being conducted under the auspices of an agency, might it violate the agency's charter and guidelines? Until all ethical considerations have been clarified and resolved, the experimenter should not begin working with subjects.

Another issue to be considered here is whether the study can be made to look plausible to the subjects. Will the study make sense from the perspective of the individuals who will be participating in it? Are subjects likely to be confused by the study or to feel hostile regarding their participation in it? Are they likely to translate this hostility into attempts to mislead the investigator or to sabotage the experiment? Additionally, can subjects' participation in the study be made a worthwhile, learning experience for them? These topics are covered in more detail in chapters 10 and 15. Finally, every investigator must ask himself or herself the question, "Are the potential benefits to my discipline's human clientele and the increase in understanding that are likely to result from this study large enough to justify the investment of time, energy, and effort on the part of the many individuals involved in the experiment?"

At this point, the experiment may be conducted, and the data gathered. The analysis of the data is usually conducted by the investigator. (See chapters 11 and 12, on statistics.) In analyzing the data, the researcher must give careful attention to deciding whether the results are reasonably reliable and valid, as well as whether they are worthwhile. If the researcher believes the data are sufficiently important that theoretical decisions and practical conclusions might be based on them, he or she begins the long and often painful task of commu-

A4

nicating the results to the appropriate audiences. This is typically done through project reports given to the agencies that have commissioned the investigation. If the results are sufficiently interesting and useful to the scientific community, they are generally written in the form of a research article and published in one of the many research journals in the social sciences. The format of project descriptions and reports varies from agency to agency. However, the basic format of the research report is standard and can be described in general terms.

Typically, a research article includes five major parts. The *abstract*, which precedes the article, is a very brief summary of the theoretical questions probed, the population on which the study was conducted, and the results obtained. The *introduction* is designed to acquaint readers with the lines of reasoning germane to the study and to set the scene for the study in terms of previous research or applied problems. In the *methods* section, the subjects, instruments, interventions, methods, and procedures of the study are described in sufficient detail that any other investigator could perform a replication of the study. The *results* section summarizes the data obtained and describes any statistics employed to analyze the data. The general rule of thumb here is to present, when space allows, all information other investigators would find of interest. In the final section, the *discussion*, the investigator is called upon to interpret the findings not only in light of any potential threats or biases but also in terms of the relationship of the findings to the existing research literature. Implications for future research and for practice among professionals in relevant disciplines also are often delineated and explained.

This appendix should have provided a general idea of the order of activities to be followed in conducting a research study. It should also have acquainted potential readers of research studies with the broad outlines of what is found in a research report. However, the description of a report was not sufficiently detailed to be useful as a guide for report writing. Appendix B discusses the writing of a research report in sufficient detail to enable students to translate the findings of their research investigations into finished reports.

Appendix B

Writing the Research Report

by Paul R. Solomon
Williams College

     Everyone knows what science is. After all, since we were in second or third grade, people charged with teaching us this subject have said basically the same thing: Start with a theory; devise a hypothesis to test the theory; conduct an experiment to test the hypothesis; and, on the basis of the results of the experiment, evaluate and modify the theory. What most of our teachers left out, however, is that once we have concluded our experiment, we have the responsibility to report our results.

Science is indeed a public venture. All researchers rely on the results of previous experiments; and for the most part, the way they find out about these experiments is by reading research reports in journals. Thus, one of the most important aspects of science is reporting the results of research. Since we have all had some experience in writing, this sounds rather straightforward. Scientific writing, however, is unique. It has its own rules, styles, and conventions; and before you attempt to report the results of an experiment, you must become familiar with these guidelines.

If you have had occasion to read scientific papers in their original form, you have probably noticed two things: (a) it is not easy to comprehend all the author is trying to convey after the first (and often even after more than one) reading, and (b) all journal articles appear in a similar format. Although it is probably not immediately apparent, point b is intended to help alleviate point a.

Journal articles are complicated. To compound this problem by presenting each one in a different format would probably make the articles unintelligible, especially to the beginning student. To prevent this, members of the scientific community have agreed on a set of conventions for reporting the results of experiments. In fact, as early as 1928, the editors of psychological and anthropological journals gathered to formulate guidelines for scientific writing. The result was a seven-page article outlining the standards and conventions to be used by all authors contributing to these journals. Since that time, these relatively informal guidelines have been revised six times; and the current version, published by the American Psychological Association (APA), provides authors with 208 pages of rules, regulations, and suggestions for report writing. While the APA manual is well used by the scientific writer, it is often difficult for the beginning writer to understand. The intent of this manual is to present the basic guidelines, rules, and conventions of scientific writing in a form that can be easily understood by the beginning scientific writer.

Research Report Writing

The purpose of this section is to acquaint you with the general structure of the report. To accomplish this, I have summarized both what should be included in each section of the report and how this information should be presented. To help you get started, I have also included a sample paper (which is entirely fictional). I recommend that as you finish each part of this section, you read the corresponding section in the sample report.

It might be useful to think about an experiment (and an experimental report) in terms of a question and an answer. The initial part of the report—the introduction—states the question as well as the reason for asking it. The methods section specifies the subjects, apparatus, and procedures used to answer the question. The answer to the question is presented in the results section, and the discussion section tells how "good" the answer was.

Title Page

The first page of the report serves as the title page. It is not numbered 1 in the upper right-hand corner and should contain: (1) the title, (2) the author's name, and (3) the author's institutional affiliation. This information is centered on the page.

The importance of the title should not be overlooked; after all, it determines if anyone will read the rest of the paper. The title should clearly indicate what the paper is about. Although it is not easy to further specify what makes a good title, several rules of thumb apply: (1) Keep the title as short as possible without sacrificing accuracy; twelve to fifteen words is generally the maximum. (2) Avoid beginning the title with words such as "a study of" or "an experiment on"; this is implied. (3) Also avoid beginning with a phrase such as "the effects of," as in "The Effects of Weekly Meetings with Undergraduate Teaching Assistants on General Psychology Exam Grades."

Abstract

The abstract is a brief summary description of the (a) problem, (b) methods, (c) results, and (d) conclusions. The purpose of the abstract is to give a short account of the experiment so readers can determine if it is relevant to what they are interested in (and thus if they should read the rest of the article).

In general, follow these guidelines in preparing the abstract.

1. The abstract page is numbered 1 in the upper right-hand corner.
2. Keep the abstract short; 100 to 150 words is typical.

B3

3. The first sentence should be a statement of the problem being investigated or the purpose of the experiment.
4. The next two or three sentences should discuss methodology; they might include a description of the subject population (number, type, age, sex, weight, or in general whatever is relevant to the experiment); a statement about the task and/or apparatus; and, where appropriate, an indication of the procedure or design.
5. Next comes a statement of the results. This is a general statement and should not include the results of statistical tests.
6. The last sentence or two should give the reader some indication of the context in which the results were discussed (for example, what theory the results support).

Introduction

The main body of the experimental report begins on page 2 with the introduction. Since, by convention, the introduction begins a report, it is not necessary to label it as such. However, the title is repeated at the top of the introduction's first page.

Three Basic Considerations

When writing the introduction, consider three basic points:

1. What is the point of the experiment; what is the problem I am trying to solve?
2. How is the experiment I have performed related to other research that has been done in the area?
3. How will the methods and design I am using help solve the problem?

It is important to cover each of these points. If you have difficulty in covering any of them, you might question why you did the experiment in the first place. (These are often good questions to ask before performing a study.)

General Format

When writing the introduction, you might proceed in the following manner. First, give a few general statements about the particular problem you are trying to solve. For example, in my report I might write a statement or two about how students seem to learn more in small classes than in large lectures and how methods should be developed to facilitate large-lecture learning. Next, go on to discuss the work other people have done in this area. This is called the literature survey and requires your having read the previous literature (how you go about finding experiments in a particular area will be discussed in the section "The Literature Survey"). This survey might include a discussion not only of the experiments but also of the theories in a particular area. You should then discuss how your work is related to other research and, more importantly, how it is different. That is, how will your methods and procedures yield information that other research has not provided? This section is of particular importance, because it represents the rationale and the logic behind your experiment.

The last paragraph of your introduction should present the hypothesis you have tested.

Length

The length of the introduction is primarily determined by how much literature you survey (how many experiments and theories you discuss). The literature survey need not be exhaustive, but it should be representative. With the exception of a few general references at the beginning of the introduction, the studies you cite should be directly related to your investigation. An analogy to a fast-tapering funnel seems appropriate. The beginning considers studies of broad interest, but the survey quickly gets down to highly relevant experiments.

Literature Citations

When writing the literature survey, keep one very important point in mind: If you make a statement you must document it; that is, you must cite the study (or studies) that supports your point. In scientific writing, neither footnotes nor quotations are appropriate.[1] Instead, the documentation is provided right in the text. If I wanted to state that previous research showed that students who participated

---

[1]In certain situations, it may be appropriate to use quotations—for example, if you want to indicate that a particular word or phrase has been copied *verbatim* from an article. But they should be used sparingly.

in small discussion groups got higher exam grades, I could use one or more of the following conventions.

1. Citing one author.
   Marx (1953) showed that students who participated in small discussion groups got higher exam grades than those who were taught in large lecture sections.
   One investigator reported . . . (Marx, 1953).
   In 1953, Marx showed . . .

As you can see, there is more than one way to make the same statement. To avoid monotony (for both you and the reader) try to intermix various styles.

2. Citing two authors.
   Laurel and Hardy (1972) reported . . .
   One experiment reported . . . (Laurel & Hardy, 1972).
   In 1972, Laurel and Hardy reported . . .

3. Citing more than two authors.
   Moe, Larry, and Curley (1958) indicated . . . (for the first citation)
   Moe et al. (1958) indicated . . . (for all subsequent citations)

The first time a study by more than two authors is presented, it is proper to acknowledge all authors. (How would you like to spend a year or two working on an experiment, publish it as the second or third author, and then see yourself cited as "et al."?) On all subsequent occasions, the first author's name followed by et al. (and others) is sufficient.

4. Citing more than one study.
   Often you will make a statement that is supported by more than one study. In that case, the citation might be:
   A number of researchers showed . . . (Laurel & Hardy, 1972; Marx, 1972; Moe, Larry, & Curley, 1958).

When you cite more than one reference, alphabetize them according to the first author and separate the references by a semicolon. Again, to avoid tedium, vary the form. For example, you might begin with "Researchers have shown" or "Studies have demonstrated" or "There are data to suggest" or "Recent studies indicate."

B6

5. Citing studies you have not read.

You will probably encounter the situation in which you read a summary of an experiment in a book and Iant to cite it. You should attempt to obtain the original study (summaries in books can be inaccurate); but if you cannot do that, use the following convention. If in a book by Mutt (1975) you have come across a study by Jeff (1972) that you wish to cite, write:

One study indicated . . . (Jeff, 1972; see Mutt, 1975).

6. Citing specific parts of books.

If you would like to cite a particular page, figure, or table in a book, do so as follows:

Chaplin (1972, p. 72); Chaplin (1972, pp. 10 – 20); Chaplin (1972, Chapt. 5); Chaplin (1972, Fig. 1); Chaplin (1972, Table 4).

7. Using exemplary citations.

In many instances, you might find literally dozens of studies with essentially the same findings. When this occurs, you may (and should) only want to cite a few exemplary references. Do so as follows:

Numerous studies indicated . . . (e.g., Laurel & Hardy, 1965; Marx, 1971).

The abbreviation "e.g." means "for example" and indicates to the reader that you are only giving some of the references.

A Note on Style

Literature surveys can become quite monotonous to read. This is usually due to the style in which they are presented. To avoid this, try to intermix styles of research citation as often as possible. In addition, try to avoid making the survey choppy. One way to do this is to indicate to the reader how studies are related.

Instead of this:

Marx (1972) suggested that students who learn under the Keller method do well in science courses. Moe, Larry, and Curley (1960) reported that the Keller Plan raises exam grades in science courses. Several investigators found no relationship between learning under the Keller Plan and grades (Allen, 1975; Chaplin et al., 1963; Mutt, 1972, Chapt. 5).

B7

Try this:

Marx (1972) suggested that students who learn under the Keller Plan do well in science courses. Similarly, Moe, Larry, and Curley (1966) reported that the Keller Plan raises exam grades in science courses. In contrast, several investigators found no relationship between learning under the Keller Plan and grades (Allen, 1975; Chaplin et al., 1963; Mutt, 1972, Chapt. 5).

Inserting a few connecting words between studies not only eliminates choppiness but also helps guide the reader through the experiments.

Although you should try to use a variety of words, such as *showed, indicated, suggested, reported,* or *provided evidence for*, avoid words that imply certainty, such as *proved* or *disproved*.

Methods

The methods section consists of four subsections: (1) subjects, (2) apparatus, (3) procedure, and (4) design (sometimes combined with procedure). The "golden rule" of this section is to be clear.

Subjects

The first step is to tell the reader about the people or animals that participated in the experiment.

1. List participants in the study (for example, "The subjects were 10 males and 15 females," or "The subjects were 25 albino rats").
2. Give the major demographic characteristics of the subjects, including age, sex, and any other information that may be relevant. For example, if the study involved college students, you might tell how many were freshmen, sophomores, and so on.
3. Indicate how the subjects were selected. Were they randomly selected, did they volunteer, did they participate as part of the requirements for a course?
4. If a subject did not complete the study, indicate that and give the reason why (for example, "One subject did not complete the experiment because she became ill").
5. If animals rather than people were used in the experiment, give the animals' age, sex, weight, strain, and maintenance conditions (for example, "The animals were housed in pairs and food and water were available ad lib," or "The animals were individually housed and deprived of food for 23 hours each day").

B8

Apparatus

Apparatus used in this context is a very general term. Broadly defined, it means whatever machines, equipment, devices, or materials you used to conduct the study.

1. When standard equipment is used, it is sufficient to give the name, model number, and manufacturer of the equipment—for example, "Three Lafayette (Model #85205) operant chambers were used," or "The Stanford-Binet (Form C) intelligence test was used."
2. When custom-made equipment is used, a more complete description is necessary. If you constructed your own operant chamber (you may be more familiar with the term *Skinner Box*) it is necessary to give the dimensions and the materials used. Often, a diagram will help.
3. It is not necessary to specify common equipment, such as pencil or paper. The statement "A number 2H yellow wooden pencil measuring 4 1/2 inches and having a medium sharp point and moderately worn eraser was used to record responses" is a bit too detailed.
4. Be sure to tell what each piece of equipment was used for; don't simply list them.

Procedure

The purpose of the procedure subsection is to explain, in detail, how the data were collected. The descripton of procedure should be written so that a person unfamiliar with your experiment could read it and then replicate the experiment. In fact, one excellent test of the clarity of this subsection is to give it to someone unfamiliar with your study. Upon completion, the reader should be able to tell you exactly what you have done. If you're thinking that the procedure subsection is like a set of directions, you're on the right track.

When writing about your procedure, you should attempt to answer two basic questions:

1. How was the independent variable administered (that is, what did you do)?
2. How was the dependent variable recorded (that is, how did you record what the subject did)?

The Administration of the Independent Variable. If the subjects were people, describe how they were treated. In most instances, this entails a description of the instructions given to each group (it may be appropriate to give a verbatim account of the directions) as well as a description of the task each subject was required to complete. If animals were used, just describe the task they completed (if you gave your animal instructions be sure not to admit it). If the task is a common one, it is usually sufficient to name it. For example, "Rats were trained to bar press by the method of successive approximations," or "Rats were put on a VI-6 sec schedule of reinforcement." If the task is novel, it is necessary to describe exactly what you did. Again, write this as a set of directions, but in the past tense.

The Recording of the Dependent Variable. This is simply a description of how the data were collected. If the data of interest were the number of bar presses a rat made in a ten-minute period, indicate whether you sat and counted them or whether it was done automatically. If you were measuring the number of times that two three-year-olds touched each other while playing, indicate whether you observed them directly and counted or recorded their actions on videotape and counted while watching the tape. If you counted more than one behavior simultaneously—for example, the number of times the children touched and the number of times they spoke—be sure to specify this.

Design

The design subsection may appear before or after the procedure subsection. Separate design subsections are generally not found in published articles. Rather, the material is distributed among the other parts of the methods section. But for the new writer, it is important to use a design subsection to explicitly state certain information.

1. Give an indication of the type of design you used—a randomized two-group design, a randomized three-group design, a two-matched-group design, a within-subjects design, a correlational design, or the like.
2. Tell how many subjects were assigned to each group and how assignment was done (randomly or in some other way).
3. Give the name of each of the groups. If you have not already done so, this is a good time to introduce any abbreviations you used for the group names (a later section will discuss abbreviating names).
4. Discuss any control procedures you used (such as randomization or counterbalancing).

B10

5. State what the independent and dependent variables were and how the dependent variable was operationally defined.

A Caution

One trap beginning students often fall into when writing a methods section is to give too much detail. It is not necessary to indicate that the door to the cage was opened, the rat lifted out of the cage, the door closed, and the rat placed in the right arm of the maze. The shorter statement that the rat was removed from its home cage and placed in the right arm of the maze would suffice.

It is difficult to give precise rules as to how much detail is enough. But you should fare well if you use common sense and this rule of thumb: Could someone else do this experiment just as you did it with nothing but the methods section?

What If It's Not an Experiment

While it is true that most research takes the form of experiments, your own research interests may require that you collect information by doing a systematic observation. Systematic observations usually take one of two forms: naturalistic observation or correlational studies.

In the naturalistic observation, the researcher simply observes the behavior of an organism. The primary rules to follow are to attempt to observe the subject in natural surrounding (although some observations are made in modified surroundings or artificial environments) and to be unobtrusive while collecting data (that is, try not to let your presence affect the behavior of the organism). Thus, the methodology of the naturalistic observation is quite different from an experiment, in which the researcher directly manipulates one factor (the independent variable) and observes the effects of this manipulation on a second factor (the dependent variable). Consequently, it is not appropriate to discuss how the independent variable was administered or how the dependent variable was recorded.

Rather, the methods section should be devoted to describing the behavior or behaviors you observed and how you recorded the frequency, length, magnitude, and so on of each behavior. If you were interested in finding out whether third-graders got out of their seats more during a science lesson or a history lesson, you might observe a third-grade class during each of these lessons. The procedure section, then, would indicate factors such as how many of each type of lesson you observed and the times the lessons were taught, as well as any other information you consider critical to the behavior you observed (Was a particular lesson taught just before gym? Did snow start to fall in the middle of one lesson?). After you have specified the conditions under which the data were collected, you must state how you observed the behavior of interest. Did you observe just one child, a group of ten children (if so, the subjects section should indicate how they were selected), or the entire class? Did you observe the behavior for the entire lesson, or sample parts of the time period (say, one minute out of every three)? What characteristics of the behavior did you observe? Just the number of times a child got out of his or her seat, or, in addition, the length of time spent out of seat? Perhaps you recorded what the children did when they left their seats. The point is, as in an experiment, you must provide enough information so that someone totally unfamiliar with your observation could replicate it after reading the methods section.

A second type of systematic observation is the correlational study. Here, as in the case of a naturalistic observation, the researcher does not manipulate anything (there is no independent variable). Instead, the researcher selects subjects who have the particular attribute he or she is interested in studying. For example, if you were interested in knowing whether people with blue eyes or brown eyes had higher IQs, you would select blue-eyed and brown-eyed people and give them an IQ test. As in the case of an experiment, the procedure subsection would describe how the IQ test was administered and how it was scored. How the subjects were selected would be included in the subjects section, and the IQ test used would be described in the apparatus section. Again, be sure to provide enough detail for someone to replicate your study.

The introduction and the descriptions of subjects and apparatus will take about the same form whether you are reporting an experiment or a systematic observation. The methods section has the same general purpose—to detail how you went about conducting your study—although in a systematic observation it is not appropriate to talk about independent and dependent variables. The description of design is different for a systematic observation, since different types of control procedures are used; but its general purpose remains the same. The results and discussion sections will remain basically the same in terms of the information presented in each. One point to remember, however, is that you cannot speak of cause and effect relationships in a systematic observation, as you can in an experiment; you can only point out the relationships among variables or behaviors.

Results

Text

Now that you have explained why and how you did your experiment, it's time to get to the most important parts of the report—the results of the study (in the results section) and your interpretation of the results (in the discussion section, which comes next).

As is the case with all other aspects of the report, the results portion should be written in paragraph form. It is not sufficient to simply tabulate or list the data, although you might (and often should) do this in tables and figures to supplement the written material.

The results section should present the data you collected, the statistical methods used to analyze the data, and the results of the statistical analysis. The following guidelines apply when writing this section.

1. Present the data in summarized form. In most cases, it is inappropriate to present raw data (the scores for each subject). Rather, a summary of the data from each group, usually the mean, should be presented.
2. Before presenting the results of a statistical analysis, tell the reader why it was conducted (for example, "A t-test was performed to determine if one group mean differed significantly from another").
3. When reporting statistical analyses, use this format:

   $t(56) = 2.76, p < .05$

   Here, t refers to the statistical test used, 56 the degrees of freedom (df), 2.76 the value of t, and .05 the probability of a type I error (the significance level). The carat ($<$) means less than; that is, the probability of a type I error is less than 5 in 100, and thus the difference between the two groups is significant at the .05 level. (If the probability of type I error had proved to be more than 5 in 100, you would have written $p > .05$.)

Figures and Tables

Figures and tables often add clarity to a report. They are used to present the data in summary form so the reader can get an overview

B13

of the results simply by glancing at them. They are also used to clarify data that are extremely complex and cumbersome in written form. A table should be capable of standing by itself; that is, it should have a title that clearly describes the data it contains. All parts of the table should be clearly labeled. Figures, too, should be clearly labeled and capable of standing alone.

Integrating Figures and Tables into the Text. Each figure or table must be referred to in the text. For example, in the results section, you might state "Figure 1 depicts ..." or "Table 6 shows ..." (note that when *figure* and *table* appear with a number they are capitalized, because they are names). At the end of the paragraph in which you refer to the figure or table, write:

Insert Figure 1 (or Table 6) about here.

This tells the reader where the figure or table should go. The actual figure or table is placed at the end of the report. Each is placed on a separate page (see the sample paper).

One final point: Keep in mind that the purpose of a figure or table is not to present raw data. If you would like to present (or your professor would like you to present) raw data, you may do so in an appendix.

Some Cautions

Save the Discussion for the Discussion Section. Don't discuss the importance or implications of your results in the results section. If you do, you won't have anything to write in the discussion section.

Present Only Significant Results. Be careful not to talk about the differences between groups if they are not significant. Even though the means of two groups differ, if the difference is not significant you really can't discuss it. (This topic will come up again, in relation to the discussion section.)

Don't Confuse Nonsignificant with Insignificant. Make the distinction between nonsignificant and insignificant. *Nonsignificant* is a statistical term ("A t-test indicated the difference between the means

B14

to be nonsignificant"), whereas *insignificant* represents a value judgment on your part. There are no insignificant results (though they may be nonsignificant), only insignificant experiments.

Accurately Report Data. Don't carry mean values to more decimal places than the original data. For example, if you are measuring reaction time in tenths of a second (as in 10.6 seconds), you shouldn't report that Group A had a mean reaction time of 10.7632 seconds.

Discussion

As you have seen, the results section of the research report simply presents the data. No attempt is made to interpret the data nor to discuss their implications; yet, interpretation is often the most critical aspect of the report. The purpose of the discussion, then, is fourfold— (1) to interpret the results of the statistical analysis presented in the results section, (2) to discuss the implications of these results, (3) to compare the results with those of previous experimenters, and (4) to make suggestions for future research.

Interpretation of Statistical Analysis

The most straightforward way to begin the discussion section is to state whether or not your results support the initial hypothesis (remember, results do not prove or disprove anything—these words are taboo). If the data clearly do or do not support the hypothesis, then a simple statement to this effect will usually suffice. For the beginning researcher, however, this is not often the case. In many instances, you will find that it is difficult to interpret the data because of a flaw in the study. The professional experimenter would do the experiment over, making the necessary modification. As a student, you do not have this luxury; rather, it is your job to discuss the flaws and explain how they might be corrected in subsequent studies. For example, you might have had some difficulty in controlling a particular variable (extreme noise in the hallway during part of the experiment); or perhaps you had apparatus problems (remember Murphy's Law as it pertains to apparatus: If something can go wrong, it will). Problems such as these do not necessarily void the entire experiment, but it is your responsibility to report them and to give the reader some idea of how disruptive they were. Keep in mind that even the

B15

best experiment can be improved, and it is hardly an admission of defeat to recognize and report a flaw. On the contrary, it is usually the sign of a careful and perceptive researcher.

Implications of Results and Comparison with Past Research

If you are in the fortunate position of having "clean" data (for example, statistically significant results and no confounding variables), the next step after making a statement about whether your data support the initial hypothesis is to discuss the implications of the data. One way to accomplish this is to discuss your data in terms of existing theories (thus the combination of these two aspects of the discussion section). Which theories do the data support? Which do they militate against? Keep in mind that one experiment does not make or break a theory; but it is important to place your experiment in theoretical perspective. This part of the report is also the place to compare your results with those of earlier studies. Are your results consistent with those of other researchers? If not, why not? Did you use a procedural modification that would account for the difference?

On a rare occasion, the researcher is in a position to propose a new theory on the basis of one experiment or a series of experiments. The discussion section is the place to do this. In general, one experiment is not sufficient to support a new theory; however, on the basis of your data, you might be in a position to suggest a modification in an existing theory.

Suggestions for Future Research

Knowing what to do is not nearly as important as knowing what to do next. One important aspect of the discussion section, then, is to suggest what experiment (or experiments) might be done next. The proposal should not go into any great detail. A short statement introduced by "Future research might examine . . ." or "Subsequent studies might investigate . . ." is sufficient.

Some Cautions

Explaining Away Nonsignificant Results. If you conduct an experiment well and it turns out that the independent variable (what you did) had no effect—that is, that the results are nonsignificant—you have a negative result. This does not necessarily mean that the results

B16

are insignificant or unimportant. Often, negative results provide information as useful as that supplied by positive findings. As mentioned earlier, negative results should be handled in much the same way as positive results: Write about them in terms of how they affect the initial hypothesis, how they fit in with existing theories (or suggest a new theory), how they relate to previous research, and how they might be used to suggest new research. Be careful not to fall into the trap of explaining away negative results—that is, making excuses for them. Don't be tempted to attribute negative results solely to faulty apparatus or poor design. While such things may sometimes be responsible, often you must simply face the fact that the experiment did not work (that is, the independent variable did not make a difference).

Discussing Nonsignificant Results. Do not discuss nonsignificant results as if they were statistically significant. For example, if the mean of Group 1 was 78.0 and the mean of Group 2 was 86.2, it might be tempting to discuss the importance of this difference despite the fact that the difference was not statistically significant. Don't do it. If the difference between the means is not statistically significant, you must assume that the means are not different at all (that is, the difference was due to chance). One way to think about nonsignificance is that it means if you ran the experiment again, the difference between the two groups might be zero or perhaps even the reverse of the original difference. In other words, you cannot rely on the results. One hedge used by some researchers in this situation is to state that although the differences are nonsignificant, they move in the right direction. This means the group that was supposed to do better (or worse) did, albeit not significantly so. This technique is appropriate in some situations—for example, when a small sample was used and the results approached statistical significance—but use it with caution.

References

All material cited in the research report must be included in the reference section. All references are included in the same list in alphabetical order by the last name of the first author. If you cite works with no author, alphabetize by the first significant word (not *The* or *A*) in the title.

Arrange each reference in the following order:

1. Author's last name, initial of first name, middle initial.
2. Year of publication (in parentheses).
3. Title of paper, chapter, or book.
4. Publication data:
   For a journal: *Journal name, volume number*, pages. (Note the journal name and volume number are underlined.)
   For a book: City of publication: Publisher.

Only the first word of the title of a journal article is capitalized. For a book, only the first word in the title is capitalized, and the entire title is underlined. Note the punctuation used: Periods follow the major subsections (author, year, title, and publication data). Commas separate the units of each subsection—for example, *American Psychologist, 28*, 312−317.

An example of each of the major reference types can be found at the end of the sample paper.

Mechanics of the Report

In some instances, writing the report is the easiest part of the task (especially as you become more and more proficient at it). Once you have gathered the materials, you must put them in a standardized form. As you might have anticipated, there are guidelines to abide by.

Typing

Reports should be typewritten. Not only does this give the report a "finished" appearance and make it easier to read, but several studies have shown that typewritten materials receive higher grades than the same materials in handwritten form.

Double-space the entire manuscript, with no exceptions. A margin of about 1 to 1 1/2 inches on all sides is acceptable. Paragraphs should be indented 5 spaces.

B18

Assembling the Report

The manuscript should be assembled as follows:

1. *Title, author, and affiliation* (separate, unnumbered page).
2. *Abstract* (separate page). The abstract is always written as one paragraph. The word *Abstract* is centered at the top of the page, which is numbered page 1.
3. *Introduction* (separate page). The introduction is not labeled.
4. *Methods*. Skip two lines (one double space) after the last line of the introduction and center the word *Methods*.
    Subjects
    Apparatus
    Design
    Procedure
   Each of these subheadings is capitalized, underlined, and typed at the left margin.
5. *Results*. Skip two lines after the methods section and center and underline the word *Results*.
6. *Discussion*. Skip two lines after the results section and center and underline the word *Discussion*.
7. *References* (separate page). Center the word *References* on the top of a new page.
8. *Tables*. Each table should appear on a separate page. Remember that each table should be labeled (for example, "Table 1," centered), should have a title, and should be referred to in the text.
9. *Figures*. The same rules apply to figures as to tables.
10. *Numbering of pages*. The page on which the abstract appears is numbered 1 in the upper right-hand corner, and all subsequent pages (including tables, figures, and references) are numbered consecutively. Do not identify any of the subsections with either letters or numbers.

In summary, the manuscript is assembled as follows:

New page
Title
(Centered on a separate, unnumbered page)

New page
Abstract
(Centered on a separate page, numbered page 1)

New page
Introduction
(Not labeled, on a separate page)
2 spaces
Methods
(Centered)
2 spaces

Subjects (underlined and not indented)
Indent and begin text two lines down.
2 spaces

Apparatus
Indent and begin text two lines down.
2 spaces

Design
Indent and begin text two lines down.
2 spaces

Procedure
Indent and begin text two lines down.
2 spaces
Results
(centered)
2 spaces
Discussion
(centered)

New Page
References
(Centered, on a separate page)

New Page
Table 1*
(Centered, on a separate page)

New Page
Figure 1
(Centered, on a separate page)

*Note there is a separate page for each figure or table.

Abbreviations, Numbers, and Metrication

Abbreviations

There are two types of abbreviations—those that are commonly used and those that are not. The former include abbreviations at least as familiar as the words they stand for—IQ, for example—and the latter comprise abbreviations unique to a particular research report. How do you tell the difference? Familiar abbreviations appear as word entries (are not labeled abbreviations) in the dictionary. If you use one of these abbreviations, you need not explain what it means; simply use it as you would any other word. If you use a nonfamiliar abbreviation, you must tell the reader what it means. For example, if you are conducting an experiment on reaction time, you will often find yourself writing the words *reaction time*; consequently, you may wish to abbreviate this term. You may do so by specifying the abbreviation in parentheses immediately after the first appearance of the words *reaction time*—for example, "The study sought to measure reaction time (RT) in college students." Now, each time you wish to refer to reaction time, you need only write RT. You can, of course, mix the term and the abbreviation throughout the paper to avoid tedium.

Abbreviations are especially useful in referring to various experimental groups. Such abbreviations are usually introduced in the design subsection.

Try to make the abbreviations logically follow from the name; this makes the readers' task much easier. For example, if a group was taught by use of the large-lecture method, abbreviate this group's name as Group LL, not Group A or B. (Note the G in Group LL is capitalized, like the T in Table 1 or the F in Figure 3; Group LL is the name of something.)

Numbers

When numbers are used in the text, the numbers smaller than 10 are usually spelled out (one, two, and so on). For 10 and above, you may use digits, except when the number begins a sentence (something to be avoided). Numbers below 10 can also be written as digits if they represent ages (5 years old), times or dates (5:30 P.M., May 7), ratios (7:1), numbers grouped in a sentence for comparison (7 dogs, 3 cats, 1 aardvark), percents (7-percent solution), exact sums of money (5 dollars), page numbers (page 2), or units of measurement or time (1 week, 10 trials per day, 6 ounces of milk, 3 hours per day). As the exceptions here seem to outnumber the rules, in most instances you will find some justification for using digits.

B21

Metrication

It appears that it is time for everyone to "give up an inch" and use the metric system. Scientists, however, have a head start, and measurements in research reports should be in metric units.

A good conversion table will help (see the suggested readings at the end of this appendix), but briefly:

1 inch = 2.54 cm
1 ounce = 28.35 g
1 pound = .45 Kg

Note that there are no periods after g, Kg, and cm. These abbreviations are always acceptable without explanation.

Stylistic Considerations

General Writing Style

Scientific writing should be clear and concise. A good rule of thumb is to delete any words or phrases that are not absolutely necessary to the clarity of the report.

Beginning writers have a tendency to attempt to use "flowery" language in research reports. Although onomatopoeia, simile, and alliteration are fine in short stories, they are not appropriate for scientific writing. If you want to make a point, state it as succinctly and clearly as possible. As Charles Darwin is reported to have said: "I think too much pains cannot be taken in making style transparently clear and throwing eloquence to the dogs."

Grammar and Spelling

Students often have the impression that papers written in the sciences need not adhere to the rules of spelling and grammar. Scientific papers may not specifically be judged on these points; but misspelled words, misplaced commas, and misused semicolons detract from the paper. They indicate careless authors and, by inference, careless researchers. Once the reader has made this inference, it will be difficult for him or her to fairly evaluate your paper, no matter how good the content.

A good dictionary is necessary and a good medical dictionary is often helpful. Several are listed in the suggested readings section. If you are uncomfortable with the basic rules of grammar, try *The Elements of Style* (see suggested readings list) for a painless review.

Finally, proofread, and then get someone else to proofread, and then proofread again. If you have invested the time to conduct a study, analyze the data, and write and type the report, it is a shame to let typographical errors detract from the final product. One technique that is very helpful is to read the paper backwards. This forces you to read every word and helps you detect many errors.

Voice and Tense

Voice

To give an air of objectivity, researchers have traditionally written their reports in the impersonal form—for example:

> "The experimenter observed" instead of "I observed."
> "The reader may note" instead of "You may note."

Recently, however, journal editors have relaxed these guidelines, and many journals now print reports that use personal pronouns. For the most part, we use personal pronouns to avoid the passive voice—for example:

> "I (or we) trained the rats" instead of "The rats were trained."
> "I (or we) performed a t-test" instead of "A t-test was performed."

Indeed, you should generally try to avoid the passive voice whenever possible:

> "Several experiments showed" instead of "It was shown."

As a general rule of thumb, then, you may choose to use personal pronouns to avoid using the passive voice. However, many researchers still prefer to use the impersonal voice in their reports and to avoid using personal pronouns.

Tense

Since the report is always written after the experiment has been completed, it should be written in the past tense. This especially applies to the methods and results sections. On occasion, it is appropriate to use the present tense in discussion, especially discussion of the implications of the data—for example, "In summary, the data from the present experiment suggest . . . ."

B23

One common error in the use of tense often occurs in the literature review. Be careful not to write "Moe (1974) suggests." All studies cited have already been completed; consequently, refer to them in the past tense—for example, "Moe (1974) suggested."

Nonsexist Writing

In June 1977, the American Psychological Association (APA) published guidelines for nonsexist journal writing (see the suggested readings). These guidelines were designed to make the writing less ambiguous and to eliminate derogatory or demeaning terms. Consider the following examples, taken from the APA guidelines.
Poor:

The client is actually the best judge of the value of his counseling.

This sentence is inaccurate, since it indicates all clients are men.
Better:

The client is currently the best judge of the value of the counseling.

Poor:

The average man.

This phrase is inappropriate unless it refers to males only.
Better:

The average person; people in general.

Poor:

Men and girls.

Does this really mean men and girls, or should it be:

Men and women.

Sexist writing can occur in many other instances, and not all of them can be considered here (again, see the APA guidelines); but awareness of the issue is often sufficient to avoid the problem.

George Orwell on Style

Perhaps George Orwell summarized style in scientific writing best in "Politics and the English Language."

1. Never use a metaphor, simile, or other figure of speech which you're used to seeing in print.
2. Never use a long word where a short one will do.
3. If it is possible to cut a word out, always cut it out.
4. Never use the passive where you can use the active.
5. Never use a foreign phrase, a scientific word or jargon word if you can think of an everyday English equivalent.
6. Break any of these rules sooner than saying anything outright barbarous.

Write, Rewrite, and Rewrite Again!

Students often ask how many times they should rewrite their papers. My answer is I really don't know. We've all heard about the wonder who lives on the third floor. He or she gets straight A's, and is rumored to be able to sit down at the typewriter without written copy or even an outline and produce a letter-perfect report. If you have this talent, you certainly don't need anyone's advice. If you don't, you should take comfort in knowing that most researchers revise their manuscripts many times before submitting them for publication. Three, four, and even five drafts are not uncommon.

The number of drafts you can write will be constrained by the amount of time you have. But if the paper isn't perfect after two drafts, don't be discouraged; you're still a draft or two ahead of most of us.

Learning to Write

We are taught to read, to add, and to spell, but it seems no one ever teaches us to write. Writing is something we're supposed to pick up along the way. However, it is unlikely that we can have learned much about scientific writing in that way. This manual should give you some idea of how to begin writing scientific reports. Once you know the fundamentals, the best way to learn to write is to read. Read journal articles and, in addition to attending to the content, pay attention to how the author presents the information. The more you do this—and, of course, the more you write—the easier scientific writing will become.

B25

The Literature Survey

One of the most difficult parts of the research report is the literature survey. This is not so much because it is difficult to write, but rather because the information is difficult to gather. This section is intended to help you get started.

Conducting the literature survey involves two basic processes: (1) finding the information, and (2) determining what aspects of the information are relevant.

For the most part, the literature you cite will be in the form of journal articles. There are a number of ways to find the relevant journal articles; one of the following should get you started.

Psychological Abstracts

Psychological Abstracts is published monthly and contains abstracts of articles published in over 400 journals. If a psychological study has been performed, the abstract is here; the problem is finding it. To aid you in this task, a semiannual cumulated index is published in June and December. Each index has three basic parts: author index, subject index terms, and subject index. To find relevant articles in the abstracts, get the most recent semiannual cumulated index and turn to the section marked "Subject Index Terms." This tells you the topics under which the abstracts are listed. From this section, you select the terms most closely related to your topic. Next, look up the terms you've selected in the cumulative subject index. Appearing next to each of the terms you will find numbers. These are not page numbers; rather, they are abstract numbers that will enable you to locate abstracts dealing with your topic in the preceding six issues (remember, each cumulative index covers a six-month period). Note that I suggested you begin with the most recent cumulated index. This is because once you find relevant articles you can use their reference sections to locate earlier works.

In addition to using the subject index, you may also want to use the author index. As you progress in the literature survey, you will probably identify several researchers who are active in your particular area of interest. It is a good idea to check these researchers' names in the author index to see what related studies they have performed.

B26

Other Abstracts

Virtually every discipline has an abstract or index that serves the same purpose for that discipline that *Psychological Abstracts* serves for psychology. Although there are too many abstracts and indices to list here, among the more useful to psychologists are: *Biological Abstracts, BioResearch Index, Child Development Abstracts and Bibliography, Education Index, Indicus Medicus, Mental Retardation Abstracts, Perceptual Cognitive Development, Psychopharmacology Abstracts, Research in Education, Social Sciences and Humanities Index,* and *Sociological Abstracts*.

Review Articles

There are three main sources of review articles in psychology: *Psychological Review, Psychological Bulletin,* and *Annual Review of Psychology*. The first two are journals published bimonthly, and the third is an edited book published annually. If you are fortunate enough to find a review article on your topic, your literature survey becomes considerably easier. The reviews typically cite most of the work done in a particular area (sometimes hundreds of studies). In addition, they often summarize the results of studies. By reading these articles, you will not only gain insight and perspective into the work being done in a particular area, but you will also have access to the references of the papers being discussed.

Single Paper (Journal Articles)

Often, a single paper on a particular topic can serve the same function as a review article. This is especially true if the paper is recent. The introduction to the paper will give a literature review, and the reference section will tell you where to find the studies cited. In many instances, one of the best ways to begin a literature survey is to scan the table of contents in a journal that typically deals with the topic you are interested in. If you begin with the most recent issue and scan issues covering about a one-year period, you are likely to find relevant papers; and these up-to-date reports will cite much of the earlier literature.

B27

Scientific Citation Index

What if you find a review or journal article that thoroughly covers the area of interest but was published in 1972? If you rely on this article as the sole source of other references, you will necessarily exclude all papers published since 1972. Fortunately, *Scientific Citation Index* provides a way out of this dilemma. *Scientific Citation Index* lists all the papers published each year that cite a particular paper. Thus, by checking the index for each year since 1972, you can find out what papers cited the paper you are interested in. It is reasonable to assume that if a paper cites another paper, the two are related. Once you have a list of papers that cite your 1972 review paper, you can check them to see which ones are most pertinent.

Textbooks

One relatively painless and efficient way to begin a literature search is to consult the most recent and comprehensive textbooks in the area of interest. For example, if you were interested in the use of brain stimulation as a reinforcer, you might check a physiological psychology textbook. The advantage of doing this is that the text summarizes the most important studies. The disadvantage is that even in a textbook published today the studies covered are a year or two old. In addition, books are necessarily biased by the opinions of the author; consequently, not all the relevant literature in a particular area may be reviewed.

Does It Have to Be Dry?

Few students read journal articles to relax or be entertained. Who can blame them? Scientific writing can be dry, especially for the beginning student. After all, the primary role of the scientific report is to present information as clearly and as systematically as possible. It is intended to inform, not to entertain, the reader. Nevertheless, some authors, and even some entire journals, make science a bit more entertaining by introducing some humor into scientific reports. This is not an easy thing to do and perhaps should not even be attempted by the beginning writer. However, you should certainly know that it can be done, and more importantly, that it can be done without sacrificing the integrity of the report.

A number of journals have emerged to poke fun at the scientific community. In psychology, the most famous of these is the *Worm Runner's Digest*. The founder, J. V. McConnell, started the journal to describe his experiments (which involved the biochemistry of learning in planaria) to interested high-school students. In this journal, you might read an article on "Learned Helplessness in Pet Rocks (*Roccus pettus*)" or a piece on "The Worm World of Sports." Embedded in the *Worm Runner's Digest*, you will also find the *Journal of American Statisticulation* (the official journal of the "I Collecta Data Statisticulation Society"). The editor, Francis Sikalinowski, defines *statisticulation* as the art of lying with statistics while maintaining the appearance of objectivity and rationality. The journal has everything from advertisements ("Tired of being a *flat* worm? Become a real specimen. Send $2 to Mark Sweden Developers.") to contests ("Can you draw this curve?") to comic strips ("The Abnormal Curves") to articles ("Anita Bryant Blasts Homogeneous Grouping"). It claims to publish anything outlandish and ridiculous but nothing serious.

The grandfather of the humorous journals is the *Journal of Irreproducible Effects*. Among the many important results presented here are the discoveries of a new contraceptive—no-acetol, a compound active because it has *no* in every position—and a new antibiotic—bubamycin. In addition, the journal has reported some fundamental laws of human behavior, including Murphy's Law (if anything can go wrong it will) and Old and Kohn's Law (the efficiency of a committee meeting is inversely proportional to the number of participants).

Humor is not limited to specialized journals. Some is nicely intermixed with serious scientific reporting. In a chapter on learning in pigeons, for example, Eliot Hearst confessed that the content of the chapter was based more on speculation than on empirical fact. While admitting that this caused him some pain, he stated: ". . . but I suppose that years of watching pigeons stick their necks out has inspired me to do the same." George Miller, in his now-famous article "The Magical Number Seven Plus or Minus Two," wrote: "My problem is that I have been persecuted by an integer. For seven years this number has followed me around, has intruded in my most private data, and has assaulted me from the pages of my most public journals." One article that appeared in the well-respected and usually staid *Journal of the Experimental Analysis of Behavior* was entitled "Failure to Combat Writer's Block Through the Use of Operant Techniques." The page was blank.

There is also some generally undetected humor hidden in scientific writing. A recent paper, the publication draft of a doctoral dissertation, poked fun at the difficult job market by indicating in a footnote that correspondence concerning the manuscript might be sent to the author in care of Hogie's Submarine Shop, Madison, Wisconsin. In yet another article, on drug effects, the author spoke of a newly discovered drug—3-blindmyacin.

Again, this type of humor is not easy to attain; and even when it is done well, some may not like it. But it does demonstrate that scientific writing need not be dull.

A Sample Paper

Weekly Meetings with Undergraduate Teaching
Assistants Improve General Psychology Exam
Grades

Paul R. Solomon
Department of Psychology
Williams College
Williamstown, MA 01267

Abstract

An experiment was performed to determine if small, weekly meetings with undergraduate teaching assistants would improve the test performance of students in a large lecture course in introductory psychology. Students in an introductory psychology course were randomly assigned to either 1 of 10 small discussion groups (10 students per group) or to a group that received no additional instruction (100 students). The results of the experiment indicated that students who met weekly in small discussion groups did significantly better on the final exam than students who received no additional instruction. The results were discussed in terms of optimum group size for learning and the use of undergraduate teaching assistants to facilitate test performance.

Weekly Meetings with Undergraduate Teaching Assistants Improve General Psychology Exam Grades

A number of studies indicate that students who attend small classes learn more than students who are presented with the same material in large lectures (e.g., Laurel & Hardy, 1975; Moe, Larry, & Curley, 1969). These data suggest that optimal learning occurs in classes with fewer than 30 students. Since limiting class size to 30 is often impossible, however, it becomes important to investigate methods that may improve learning in large lecture classes.

Early research by Marx and his coworkers (Marx, 1955, 1957; Marx, Harpo, & Chico, 1961) indicated that the grades of students in a large lecture course (400 students) in chemistry improved if the students met in groups of 10 to 15 for an hour a week with a graduate teaching assistant. Similarly, Mutt and Jeff (1972) found a significant improvement in the grades of sociology students following small (10 students or less) biweekly group discussions with a graduate student. Results consistent with these findings have also been reported for history (Abbott & Costello, 1973), anthropology, (Dangerfield, 1974), and psychology (Allen, 1975).

In contrast to these studies, several recent investigations examined the effects of larger weekly meetings (30 to 40 students) with graduate assistants and found no effect on exam performance (Marx, 1974; Moe, Larry, & Curley, 1976).

Although previous research suggests that small meetings with graduate assistants improves test scores in large lectures, there currently are no data to indicate whether test scores would also improve if undergraduate students were used to lead the small group meetings. The purpose of the present investigation was to determine if weekly meetings of 10 students with a senior psychology major would raise their test scores in a large lecture course in introductory psychology.

Methods

Subjects

The subjects were 200 undergraduate students enrolled in the introductory psychology course during the fall semester. There were 105 males and 185 females, ranging in age from 17 to 36. Four subjects dropped the course at the midpoint, and their data were deleted from the study.

Apparatus

All students were assigned the same text: Krech, D., Crutchfield, S., & Levison, N. Elements of psychology (3rd ed.). New York: Alfred A. Knopf, 1974. Course performance was judged on the basis of a final exam that consisted of 200 multiple-choice questions. The questions were selected randomly from the test-item file for the textbook with the restriction that there be 10 questions on each of the 20 chapters in the text. All exams were graded by computer.

Procedure

During the first meeting of the large lecture class, students were told that the psychology department was giving senior majors credit for teaching small discussion sections in introductory psychology. Students were also told that half of them would be required to attend weekly meetings with an undergraduate teaching assistant (TA).

The 100 students who attended the small group meetings were randomly selected and assigned to 1 of 10 small discussion groups (10 students per group). Each discussion group met for one 50–minute session per week. Although the exact material the TAs were to cover was not discussed before each meeting, the TAs were asked to discuss material from that week's lectures. To ensure that each student would attend the small discussion section, attendance at the meetings was made mandatory.

The teaching assistants were selected on the basis of performance in psychology courses during their sophomore and junior years. The selection criteria were that each TA be a senior and have at least a B+ average in his or her psychology courses. The TAs were required to attend each large lecture meeting as well as a weekly meeting with the instructor. Each TA received 3 credits.

As an evaluation of their performance in the large lecture course, all students were given a 200–item multiple–choice test during final exam week. Students were allowed two hours to complete the exam.

Design

A randomized two–group design was used in this experiment. Subjects were randomly assigned to one of two groups: a group that attended both the lecture and the small discussion sessions (Group SD) and a group that attended only the large lecture (Group LL).

The independent variable in this experiment was whether or not students attended the small discussion group, and the dependent variable was the amount of material they learned. The amount of learning was operationally defined as the score on a 200-item multiple-choice test. Higher scores indicated better performance.

Results

The mean number of items the students in Group SD correctly answered on the 200-item multiple-choice test was 174.5, and the mean for the students in Group LL was 153.3. A t-test was conducted on the means of the two groups to determine if the difference between them was significant. The results of the analysis indicated that Group SD did significantly better on the exam than Group LL: $t(193) = 2.83$, $p < .05$.

Figure 1 shows the mean test score for the 10 small discussion sections. The figure suggests that all sections did about the same, with the exception of Group SD-5, which had a higher mean score (190). An anlysis of variance confirmed this observation by indicating a significant difference between the groups: $F(986) = 6.72$, $p < .05$. Individual comparisons indicated that only Group SD-5 was significantly better than the other groups.

Insert Figure 1 about here.

Discussion

The results of the experiment support the idea that small weekly discussion groups improve test scores of students in large lecture courses. In this respect, they are consistent with the findings of a number of earlier studies (Abbott &

Costello, 1973; Allen, 1975; Dangerfield, 1974;
Marx, 1955, 1957; Marx et al., 1961). In
addition, the results extend the findings of
these studies by indicating that undergraduate as
well as graduate assistants can be used to run the
discussion groups. In the present study, students
who met with an undergraduate TA scored, on the
average, 10.5 percent better than controls. In an
earlier experiment (Allen, 1975), which
investigated the effects of meeting with graduate
TAs on students' test scores in a large lecture
course in introductory psychology, the students
who met with TAs scored an average 9.5 percent
better than controls. Although the two TA types
should be compared in the same experiment, these
data suggest that undergraduate and graduate TAs
facilitate test scores to about the same degree.

Whereas the data from this and other
experiments indicate that small group meetings
improve test scores, no studies address the
question of what is the optimum group size. There
are, however, some data in the present experiment
to suggest that smaller groups may do better.
Figure 1 indicates that Group 5 did better than
the other 9 SD groups. It is interesting to note
that of the 5 students who dropped the course at
the midpoint, 4 were in Group SD-5. Thus, the
higher test scores in Group 5 relative to the
other SD groups may be related to group size. This
would be consistent with other work that has
found the amount of learning inversely related to
class size (Chaplin, 1971; see Marx, 1973). It is
also possible that the 4 students who dropped
were poor students and this inflated the scores
of Group SD-5. Future studies might
systematically examine the effect of the size of
small discussion groups on their members' test
scores in large lecture classes.

The results of this experiment suggest that institutions with no graduate programs can still gain the benefit of using weekly discussion groups in large lecture courses by having undergraduate teaching assistants conduct them.

References

If this were a real reference section, it would contain entries for <u>all</u> studies mentioned in the paper. This section, however, is only intended to give examples of the various types of references.

A. <u>Journal papers</u>.
Abbott, B., & Costello, L. (1968). Improving test scores in a large history lecture. <u>Historian</u>, <u>22</u>, 519–531.
Allen, W. (1973). Meetings with graduate teaching assistants facilitate performance in large lectures. <u>Teaching of Psychology</u>, <u>3</u>, 114–121.

B. <u>Books</u>.
Marx, G. (1973). <u>Methods in education</u>. New York: McGraw–Hill.

C. <u>Chapters in edited books</u>.
Laurel, S., & Hardy, O. (1973). The effects of class size on test performance. In A. B. Jones (Ed.), <u>Research on teaching</u>. Boston: Allyn and Bacon.

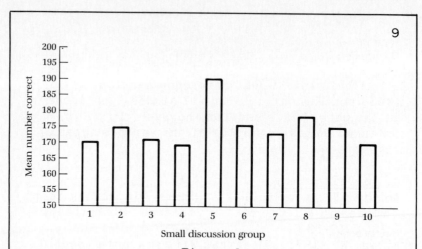

Figure 1
Mean Number of Items Correct (200 possible)
for Each of the Small Group Discussion Sections

Suggested Readings

Day, R.A. (1983) *How to write and publish a scientific paper* (2nd ed.). Philadelphia: ISI Press. A general guide to writing and publishing in the sciences. It includes sections on scientific papers, review papers, conference reports, theses, and oral presentations.

Dorland's Illustrated Medical Dictionary (24th ed.). Philadelphia: W.B. Saunders & Co. A dictionary of medical terms.

Ebbitt, W.R. & Ebbitt, D.R. (1978). *Writer's guide and index to English* (6th ed.). Glenview, Illinois: Scott, Foresman & Co. A general guide to usage, this book will be useful for all types of writing.

Guidelines for Nonsexist Language. (1977). *American Psychologist*, *32*, pp. 487–494. These guidelines are also reprinted in the current (3rd ed.) of the APA publication manual.

Maimon, P., Belcher, G.L., Heran, G.W., Nodine, B.F., & O'Connor, F.W. (1981). *Writing in the arts and sciences*. Boston: Little, Brown. A general guide to writing for students, it includes sections on library and laboratory research in the sciences and a section on preparing the research report.

National Bureau of Standards. (1979, December). Guidelines for the use of the modernized metric system. Dimensions/NBS, pp. 13–19. Provides tables for metric units and their equivalents as well as guidelines for metric writing.

Publication Manual of the American Psychological Association. (3rd ed.). (1983). Washington D.C.: American Psychological Association. This book forms the basis for this manual and can be consulted if additional information on any topic is needed.

Ross-Larson, B. (1979). *Edit yourself*. New York: Norton. Discusses techniques editors use to identify and correct common problems in writing.

Strunk, W. & White, E.B. (1979). *The elements of style* (3rd ed.). New York: McMillan. A concise and readable manual of style.

Van Leunen, M.C. (1978). *A handbook for scholars*. New York: Knopf. A general guide to references, format, and text preparation.

Webster's new collegiate dictionary (8th ed.). (1981). Springfield, MA: Merriam Webster.

Yarenko, R.M., Harari, H., Harrison, R.C., & Lynn, E. (1982). *Reference handbook of research and statistical methods in psychology*. New York: Harper & Row. A dictionary of psychological terms, statistical tables, metrication, and other useful information.

Appendix C

Rival Hypotheses

One skill you should develop in this course is the ability to critique research projects. You can develop it by practicing on examples from real life. In your studies, you will frequently come across summaries of research projects, their results, and interpretations of those results. In many cases, the conclusions drawn are not fully justified in light of the way the data were collected and analyzed. Alternative interpretations of the results are entirely possible. We call these alternative interpretations rival hypotheses.

This appendix presents a few examples of research results. In most of the projects, the researchers did not adequately rule out rival interpretations of their findings before stating their conclusions. See how many rival hypotheses you can pick out for each project described in the section entitled "Research Results," then check your ideas against the ones in the section entitled "Rival Hypotheses."[1]

Research Results

1. The Common Denominator

Over 100 years ago, the philosopher John Stuart Mill dealt with the issue of cause and effect. He attempted to set forth "canons of logic" by which cause-and-effect relationships could be determined. One of these canons was the "method of agreement." Briefly, Mill reasoned that if two or more occurrences of a phenomenon have only one circumstance in common, then that circumstance is the cause of the observed phenomenon. In our day-to-day lives, we come across numerous instances of the method of agreement being used to explain common events.

Recently, an election took place in a large metropolitan city located in the southeastern United States. One of the local newspapers was interested in why certain candidates won while others lost. After conducting a superficial investigation, the newspaper printed the following story:

What was the common denominator that decided the races for Knox County court house offices? It wasn't incumbency since school superintendent Mildred Doyle lost. It wasn't party since three Republicans and one Democrat won.

The answer is age. In all four races (sheriff, property assessor, law director and school superintendent) the younger candidate won.[2]

The article was entitled, "Age Was Big Factor in Knox Elections." The title and text of the article give the impression that age had a causal influence on the election outcome. After reading the article, elderly people might think twice before running for elected offices.

[1]The rest of this appendix was excerpted from Huck and Sandler, 1979. The research results and corresponding rival hypotheses numbered 1 to 5 here were numbered 1, 4, 8, 11, and 23 in the source.

[2]Copyright 1976 by the Knoxville News-Sentinel. Reprinted by permission.

Should they think twice, or is there some plausible rival hypothesis other than the common denominator proposed by the local newspaper?

2. Beer: Brand Differences in Image

Whenever we go to certain people's houses for dinner or an evening of bridge, we get the distinct impression that the magazines on the coffee table never have been and never will be read by the host and hostess. We are confident that you, too, know at least one person who puts intellectual-type magazines out on display, hoping to impress you and other guests who attend the formal get-together or simply drop by unexpectedly. The next time you are at the home of one of these people, you might like to drop off, surreptitiously, a copy of the research study described below. If the individuals read about this investigation, it probably won't cure them of their magazine put-on; instead, it will give them a tip on how they might extend their phony "impression-ism" into the kitchen!

This research endeavor had to do with beer, and the researcher was interested in whether the images of different brands of beer vary. By "image," the researcher meant the personality characteristics we might think of as being associated with or typical of the individuals who buy and consume any given brand of beer. Of course, surveys conducted by the marketing research departments of the various beer companies could probably provide us with fairly accurate descriptions of the people who actually buy each brand; in this particular study, however, the focus was on the *perceived notions* (which potentially might be in error) that people have of the types of consumers who purchase the different brands.

To investigate the hypothesis that different brands do have different images, an experiment was conducted at the University of South Carolina. The subjects in this investigation were 157 students enrolled in a business course, and their experimental task was both interesting and simple. On the first day of class, each student was given a sheet of paper containing a short list of grocery items preceded by these directions:

Read the shopping list below. Then try to project yourself into the situation as far as possible until you can more or less describe the student who purchased the groceries for a small informal party. Then write a brief description of his personality and character. Whenever possible try to indicate what influenced your judgment. This is a test to see how well you can size up an individual's personality on the basis of very little information.[3]

Six familiar items typically associated with student parties (for example, five pounds of hamburger, three packages of Sunbeam hamburger buns, and three large packages of potato chips) were identical on all the shopping lists. However, the lists differed with respect to the seventh item. One-third of the subjects received lists in which the seventh item was "2 cases Pabst Blue Ribbon beer," a brand of beer that might be thought to have a good image because of its consistent increases in yearly sales plus a high market share. Another third of the subjects received lists in which the seventh item was two cases of a different brand of beer (unnamed in the technical report), a brand that conceivably would have a bad image because of its decreasing sales and a lessening share of the market. The final third of the subjects received lists that did not contain any beer item at all, just the six items on the other lists. The three versions of the shopping list were randomly mixed (by means of a table of random numbers) and distributed among the 157 subjects, who were unaware, of course, that three versions were being used.

After the written descriptions of the hypothetical party planner had been collected, two judges evaluated each description and classified each sentence as being positive, negative, or neutral in effect. (If a sentence had both positive and negative components, judges were instructed to score it as neutral.) The two judges evaluated the 157 papers independently of one another, yet there was a 94 percent agreement between them on the scoring of the 539 sentences produced by the subject pool. To avoid any rater bias, the two judges scored each paper without knowing which of the three versions of the shopping list had been given to the author.

Upon subjecting the judges' evaluations to a formal statistics analysis, the researcher discovered that the descriptions from the Pabst group, when compared with each of the other two groups, contained a significantly greater proportion of positive statements and a significantly smaller number of negative statements. A separate statistical analysis focused on the 157 subjects and their net scores, defined as the numerical result obtained by subtracting each subject's

[3]Reprinted from the *Journal of Applied Psychology*, 1976, *56*, pp. 512–513. Courtesy of A. G. Woodside.

C4

number of negative sentences from the number of positive sentences. By means of these net scores, each subject could be classified as being positive, negative, or neutral in the description of the party planner. The results were that a significantly greater (smaller) percentage of the Pabst subjects were classified as positive (negative) than was the case in either of the other two groups. The non-Pabst beer group produced the smallest percentage of positive descriptions, even smaller than the no-beer control group.

The researcher interpreted his significant findings as support for the hypothesis that different beer brands carry different images. Clearly, this study's conclusions imply that a cause-and-effect relationship had been found to exist, with the causal variable being the brand of beer contained in the shopping list and the effect variable being the positive, neutral, or negative nature of the written description of the shopper's personality. In your opinion, were the differences obtained truly attributable to the seventh item on the shopping list? Or can you identify one or more plausible rival hypotheses that complicate and potentially invalidate the conclusions associated with this study?

3. Wilt Thou Take This Plant . . .

As any backyard gardener knows, newly planted vegetables or flowers need lots of sunshine and water to grow properly. Some nutritious plant food often helps, as does an occasional dusting for insects or disease. To help the plants grow quickly, the gardener must keep certain things away—such as rabbits, the lawnmower, and small children who think the rose or tomato is a red ball. Recently, gardeners have also been told to keep loud noises away from their growing plants.

In a large metropolitan city, the Sunday newspaper has a column in the spring and summer entitled "Your Lawn and Garden." One Sunday, the column dealt with fertilizer, planting seeds from magnolia trees, watering dogwoods, and noise. With respect to the last topic, the article went as follows:

A year or so ago we had much to say here pro and con about how plants appreciate a kind word now and then and that such treatment helps them to thrive. A researcher at Drexel University in Philadelphia says that while science still doesn't know if plants appreciate kindness, it has learned that they don't like to be yelled at. It has nothing to do with tender feelings. Apparently, loud noise increases the amount of water normally given off by the leaves, causing the plants to wilt and grow at a slower rate.

The researcher, Dr. Arthur Lord, a physics professor, and some of his students discovered this in two experiments with coleus plants. In the first experiment a student grew two coleus plants under the same greenhouse conditions, except that one plant was exposed to about 100 decibels of noise, approximately the same as a person would hear while standing on a busy subway platform. After 1 1/2 weeks of continuous exposure the sound-treated plant wilted.[4]

Let us assume that the phrase "same greenhouse conditions" means exactly the same everything—same amount of water, same amount of natural and artificial light, same type of soil, same amount of insect and disease repellent, and so on. Let us also assume that a coin was flipped to determine which of the two coleus plants would receive the noise treatment. Even if both of these assumptions are true, there is still a plausible rival hypothesis—other than noise—to explain the outcome. What is it?

4. Air Force Officer School and Dogmatism

According to a personality theorist named Milton Rokeach, dogmatism can be defined as "a relatively closed cognitive organization of beliefs about reality, organized around a central set of beliefs about absolute authority which, in turn, provides a framework for patterns of intolerance and qualified tolerance toward others."[5] In less formal terms, the person who is highly dogmatic tends to be closed-minded, inflexible, and often more concerned about the status of a communication source than about the substance of what's being communicated. We are confident that you know at least one person who fits this description.

Many people believe that the structure of the armed services and the inherent chain-of-command basis of communication attract highly dogmatic volunteers. Military commanders, of course, disagree; they claim that they have a need for officers who are open-minded, tolerant, and able to win the respect and loyal cooperation of the personnel they direct. Aside from this question as to the type of per-

[4]Copyright 1975 by the Knoxville News-Sentinel. Reprinted by permission.

[5]Milton Rokeach. "The nature and meaning of dogmatism." *Psychological Review*, 1954, *61*, p. 195.

son attracted to a military career, a researcher recently wondered whether a 14-week stint at officer training school would affect the participants' degree of dogmatism. Would this training program cause the junior officers to become more or less dogmatic, or would it have no effect on dogmatism? And would the influence of the 14-week program be the same for those participants who began with high levels of dogmatism as it was for those who began with low levels?

The subjects in this investigation came from a pool of 764 officers who completed the three-and-a-half-month Squadron Officer School (SOS) at Maxwell Air Force Base in Alabama. As the researcher saw it, there were several facets of the SOS program that might have made for a change in dogmatism. For example, each student was given extensive feedback from peers, the opportunity to discuss the personality characteristics of other trainees, a chance to deal with unstructured situations, and experience in planning military strategy in areas divorced from his field of expertise. These and other similar activities might, according to the researcher's hypothesis, cause the students' dogmatism levels to decrease over the 14-week time interval.

During the first and last weeks of training, all students in the SOS program were given a copy of the Rokeach Dogmatism Scale, Form E. (In this study, it was titled the Rokeach Opinion Scale.) This measuring instrument is made up of 40 statements, each of which is rated on a -3 to $+3$ scale so as to indicate the extent of one's disagreement or agreement. Two of the statements go as follows: "Most people just don't know what's good for them," and "A group which tolerates too much difference of opinion among its own members cannot exist for long." From among the SOS students who completed and returned the Rokeach Scale at both the pretest and posttest periods, 250 were randomly selected. Then, based upon an examination of the pretest scores, the 250 subjects were subdivided into five groups of 50 subjects each. In terms of the dogmatism continuum, these subgroups were described as high, above average, average, below average, and low.

The data were statistically analyzed in two ways. First, the pretest mean for all 250 subjects was compared to the overall posttest mean. Results indicated no significant difference. Next, a two-way analysis of variance was used to see whether the five subgroups were changing in a similar fashion between the beginning and end of the SOS program, or possibly not changing at all. The pre- and posttest means for the five subgroups turned out as follows:

C7

		Pretest	Posttest
Grouping	High	170.04	161.14
based on	Above average	151.02	145.42
pretest	Average	138.12	137.26
performance	Below average	126.12	128.78
	Low	108.24	117.32

The statistical analysis indicated a significant interaction between subgroups and pre-post trials. (Such an interaction simply means that the change from pretest to posttest is not the same for all subgroups.)

Based on the subgroup means presented in the preceding table and the significant statistical finding, the researcher stated that "Subjects high in dogmatism on the pretest tended to become less dogmatic by the last week of training while those scoring below the mean tended to become more dogmatic" (Gleason, p. 35). In a way, it looks as if the SOS training program causes the participants to become more homogeneous in terms of dogmatism. Before drawing such a conclusion, however, it might be worthwhile to stop and ask whether there are any plausible rival hypotheses to account for the statistically significant result.

5. Counseling Practicum

During their formal training in their master's program, prospective school counselors are exposed to research articles, theory, and role models. It is not unlikely that during this period, students develop an initial set of thoughts concerning ideal counselor characteristics. Near the end of the graduate program, however, students are often placed, through a practicum course, into a field setting so the counselor-trainees can put into practice the things that have been learned and, of course, learn some new things. As a result of this field-based experience, one might ask whether there is a change in the perception of the desirable characteristics associated with a competent counselor's role and responsibilities.

In an attempt to answer this question, a pair of researchers recently conducted a study at Northwestern Illinois State College. The subjects in this investigation were 36 graduate students in guidance and counseling, all of whom had completed 30 credit hours of required courses and were enrolled in the practicum experience. This eight-week experience involved four half-days a week in a public school, with supervision provided by local school personnel and the college faculty. Besides conducting individual and group counseling sessions, the practicum students also performed a variety of typical guidance activities.

At the beginning and end of the eight-week practicum experience, each of the 36 subjects was administered the Occupational Characteristics Index (OCI). This instrument provides 12 scores, each associated with a trait that workers might have to varying degrees (for example, organizational realist, leader, innovator). On each administration of the OCI, the practicum students were asked to indicate the ideal characteristics that they believed a counselor should possess. For each of the 12 traits, prepracticum and postpracticum means were computed and compared statistically.

The results of the data analysis indicated that the 36 practicum students, on the average, changed from pretest to posttest with respect to 11 of the 12 OCI scales. At the end of the practicum experience, the students believed that five of the traits were more important than they had thought prior to their eight-week field experience; however, for six other traits there was a feeling after the practicum that these traits were less important. Hence, there appeared to be substantial evidence that the practicum students had changed their perception of what an ideal counselor was like.

The researchers clearly attributed this change to the field-based practicum experience that had taken place during the eight weeks between the pretest and posttest. For example, near the end of the formal report of this study, the investigators state that "on-the-job experience did provide a statistically significant change in their perception of the ideal counselor characteristics" (Langley and Gehrman, p. 79). Do you agree with this interpretation of the data? Can we assume for certain that it was the counseling practicum that brought about the change? Or might there be one or more plausible rival hypotheses to account for the change in perception?

Rival Hypotheses

1. The Common Denominator

While the local newspaper states that age is the "common denominator," there are several rival hypotheses to account for why these four elections turned out the way they did. It is quite possible that the four winning candidates spent much more money for advertising in the local newspapers, on the radio, and on television. Or possibly each winner had a larger group of more energetic campaign workers. Perhaps the winners were more conservative in political ideology than the losers. Perhaps they were taller. The simple fact is that the four winners, as a group, probably had numerous things in common that separated them from the four unsuccessful candidates.

In order for Mill's method of agreement to work, the various occurrences of the phenomenon (here, winning any of the four elections) must have *one and only one* circumstance in common. If there is more than just one common denominator, then there is no logical way to claim that one of them was the causal agent that brought about the observed phenomenon. However, upon seeing a common denominator, people often jump to the conclusion that they have identified *the* cause, when in fact they have overlooked other commonalities that might also be the explanation. For this reason, G. C. Helmstadter has warned that Mill's canons of logic (including the method of agreement) "must not be applied automatically or carelessly. Without thoughtful attention to the requirements of each approach, inappropriate conclusions are all too easy to come by."[6]

2. Beer: Brand Differences in Image

As far as we can tell, there are *no* rival hypotheses associated with this research investigation. We can think of no plausible explanation to account for the significant differences among the three groups besides the study's manipulated independent variable—the seventh item on the shopping list.[7]

Because the conclusions from this study appear to be based upon a respectable research design and methodology, we feel that you are justified in passing it along to your acquaintances who put their untouched intellectual magazines out on the coffee table to impress their guests. Maybe they can start putting certain brands of

---

[6]G. C. Helmstadter. *Research concepts in human behavior.* (New York: Appleton-Century-Crofts, 1970), p. 95.

[7]Recall that we gave you a warning in the Foreword that some of our rival hypotheses would have no discernible design or logical problem. Be on guard for a few more of these sound studies. But in most of what you encounter as you read about additional research endeavors or other less formal types of alleged cause-and-effect relationships, there *will* be blatant or subtle rival hypotheses that we feel are plausible.

beer in their refrigerators to impress even further the people who come to visit.[8]

3. Wilt Thou Take This Plant . . .

The fact that one of the two coleus plants wilted after one and one-half weeks could have been caused by an initial difference between the quality or healthiness of the two plants. Even if the two plants had been grown under the same auditory conditions (either 100 decibels of noise or no noise), it is altogether possible that one of them would have wilted after a 10-day period. This is certainly the case in our vegetable and flower gardens each year, when we put in several new plants that all look similar at planting and that receive equal soil, sun, and water treatment; in spite of these similarities, some of the plants grow while others do not.

Randomization—flipping a coin, pulling names out of a hat, or using a table of random numbers—is an important characteristic of good experimental design. But if there are potential differences in the units of experimental material (in this experiment, the coleus plants), then randomization has a much better chance of equalizing the comparison groups prior to treatment application if the sample sizes are large. With small samples, randomly assigning the units of experimental material to the treatment and control conditions may not work very well. And when there is only one unit of material to be assigned to each of the comparison groups, randomization cannot achieve its desired goal at all. If the two coleus plants did, in fact, differ in healthiness, then the chances are even that the healthier plant would be assigned to the quiet growing condition. Had there been four plants, the chance that the two healthiest would end up being assigned to the quiet conditions would be only 1 out of 4. Had there been 20 plants, the chance that the ten healthiest would end up in the non-noise group would become 1 out of 1024. Within the context of any single experiment, randomization is much more likely to equalize the comparison groups on all variables except the manipulated treatment variable when the sample sizes are large.

Let us attempt to make our point about the coleus plant experiment by using an analogous hypothetical study about children and language development. Suppose we wanted to see whether first-born

[8]However, a few of our beer-drinking friends have really raised their eyebrows in surprise that Pabst was the "high-image beer." On our campuses, it evidently would not fare so well—in spite of the blue ribbon.

children begin to talk earlier (or later) than second-born children within the same family. Since the sex of a child is determined pretty much at random, we might think that sex, as an extraneous variable, is controlled in our comparison of first-born and second-born children. But what if the study involves only a single family that has just two children? And what if the first child is a boy and the second a girl (or vice versa)? Has the randomization of sex to the two "comparison groups" really equalized the two groups on sex, thereby permitting any observed difference to be attributed to order of birth?

4. Air Force Officer School and Dogmatism

Of the five subgroups involved in this study, the ones having higher pretest means ended up with means that were still above average, but not so far above average as they were at the start. On the other hand, the groups that began with lower pretest means finished the 14-week program with means that were still below average, but they weren't nearly so low as they had been to begin with. Although such an outcome tends to make it look as if the SOS program had a moderating effect on the subjects' dogmatism levels, the researcher felt that a plausible rival hypothesis might be the phenomenon of regression toward the mean. We agree.

Whenever a group of people is measured twice, the ones with extremely high (or low) scores on the first measurement will still tend to have high (or low) scores on the second measurement, but they will be less extreme than they were initially. In other words, extreme scorers (based on the first measurement) will "regress" toward the overall mean of the second set of measurements. This phenomenon will be observed no matter how close in time the two measurement periods are, even when the intervening activities have no influence at all on the measured characteristic. The only time regression will not exist is when the correlation between the two sets of measures is $+ 1.00$ (which isn't very often!). To the degree that this correlation moves from $+ 1.00$ toward zero, the amount of regression increases to the point, at $r = 0$, where the high and low scorers (based on the first measurement) tend to perform equally well on the second measurement.[9]

[9]This brief discussion of statistical regression may leave the impression that people only regress in one direction—from the first to the second measurement. In actuality, regression operates in both directions. Hence, high scorers on a posttest tend to regress toward the mean of the pretest.

C12

The observed correlation between the Rokeach pretest and post-test dogmatism scores for the 250 subjects in this particular study was + .71. Based on this correlation, the researcher made a prediction about how high each of the five subgroups would have scored on the posttest, assuming that the SOS training program had absolutely no impact on the participant's dogmatism levels and that any pre-post changes were caused entirely by the phenomenon of regression. These "estimated" posttest means for the five subgroups turned out to be almost identical to the actual posttest means (which are presented on page 20) with the biggest discrepancy being only 1.34 points. Given the amazingly close similarity between the actual and estimated posttest means, the researcher concluded that the "significant interaction is most likely due to regression to the mean" (Gleason, p. 38).

Before leaving this topic, let us attempt to make one final point about the regression phenomenon. This point concerns the fact that regression exists in terms of subgroup means, not in terms of individual scores. A subgroup of high scorers on the pretest will have, on the posttest, a subgroup mean that is less extreme, but some of the members of this subgroup, as individuals, will probably end up with posttest scores that are equal to (or even higher than) their pretest scores. Were this *not* the case, the dispersion among the posttest scores would have to be less than the dispersion among the pretest scores. But regression has no effect whatsoever on the variability of the scores in the full group at either measurement period, as evidenced by pretest and posttest standard deviations in the SOS study of 22.41 and 22.50, respectively.

5. Counseling Practicum

There are, in our judgment, two alternative explanations that might account for the changes that took place between the pretest and post-test responses to the OCI. One of these has to do with non-practicum experiences taking place during the eight-week duration of the study, while the other has to do with the phenomenon of testing.

The subjects of this study spent four half-days a week in a public school throughout the eight-week practicum. Unfortunately, we have no idea what these individuals were doing during the rest of the time. Were they taking a half-time load of graduate courses? Or working on their master's theses? Or working at a part-time job to support themselves and their families? Since we don't know what the 36 subjects

C13

were doing besides the practicum during the eight-week period, it seems quite possible that the significant changes on 11 of the 12 OCI scales were brought about by some activity *other than* the field-based practicum. Perhaps during the eight weeks many of the subjects read a book about counseling. And possibly it was this activity (or something like it, say a television program on school counselors) that served as the true cause of the observed pre-post changes.[10]

The second rival hypothesis associated with this study is related to the phenomenon of testing. Research has shown that people often perform differently on the second administration of a test from the way they did when it was initially administered, even if there is no training or feedback provided after the first testing. This phenomenon of doing better the second time has been found to operate on both achievement tests (where people appear to be smarter on the second test) and personality instruments (where they appear to be "more normal" the second time tested). And the phenomenon can exist even if two different versions (parallel forms) of the test are used at the two testings.

Because of the proven phenomenon of testing, we wonder whether the 36 subjects in this study might have changed from pre to post even if there had been nothing happening during the eight weeks to prompt a change—in other words, no practicum, no television shows, no courses, no work on the master's thesis, nothing. And the fact that significant changes were found on 11 of the 12 OCI scales (rather than just one or two) does not make this suggested rival hypothesis any less plausible. It is possible that a group of graduate students might show similar changes if tested on each side of an eight-week interval with nothing in between (or, more realistically, if tested on two consecutive days).

In summary, the results of this study would be more believable if a control group had been built into the investigation. If this had been done properly, the two suggested rival hypotheses discussed above could be ruled out entirely.

[10]Some authors use the term "history" to describe the possibility that some other activity, besides the presumed causal activity, that takes place *between* the pretest and posttest may actually be the true cause of observed changes.

C14

Appendix D

Differences Among the Social Sciences

Since I am a psychologist, I have given relatively greater emphasis in this book to problems and methods of importance in psychological research and less attention to research problems unique to other social sciences. While virtually every issue raised in this book is of some concern to all social scientists, scientists in each discipline are also concerned with a certain subset of research techniques that may not be important for colleagues in other disciplines. For example, whereas anthropologists are more concerned than psychologists with topics such as participant observation and the strengths and liabilities of archival data, they are less concerned with issues associated with true experimental designs. Similarly, while economists share anthropologists' concerns about the validity of archival data, they are not as interested in issues surrounding participant observation. To complete this triangle of comparisons, economists do not generally share psychologists' interest in true experimental approaches, but they do agree with the great emphasis psychologists place on statistics in their research. In this latter regard, economists and psychologists are different from anthropologists, who are less likely to employ statistical techniques. Several other important issues that separate the various social sciences merit attention in this appendix.

Differences in Problems Considered

Economics provides a good example of how a topic central to one discipline (the economic behavior of humans) represents a more peripheral interest to other social scientists, such as political scientists, sociologists, anthropologists, and so on. As economics focuses on economic behavior, political science focuses on political behavior. If one were to consider theology a social science, then it could become yet another example, since the religious or ethical lives of individuals and groups represent theology's central issue.

Some social sciences seem to range over a broad array of areas. Psychology, sociology, history, and anthropology are likely to consider religious, economic, political, emotional, familial, and a host of other issues as lying within their domain. Stated slightly differently, economists are likely to have economic outcomes as dependent (or criterion) measures. Similarly, political scientists are likely to have political behavior as their dependent variables. Conversely, one would be hard-pressed to specify one area of interest that characterizes other social scientists' dependent measures. For sociologists and psychologists, economic or political variables are as likely to be independent (predictor) variables as dependent (criterion) variables. Again, the argument becomes complete when we realize that variables concerned with, for example, emotionality might be either independent or dependent variables for psychologists and sociologists, while they are much more likely to be independent than dependent variables for economists and political scientists.

D2

Differences in Level of Analysis

If an economist and a psychologist were interested in how money is allocated to one type of purchase rather than another, the psychologist would likely be interested in the decision process as it is articulated in the mind of an individual (see the work of Kahneman and Tversky, 1974). The economist, on the other hand, would more likely be interested in studying distinct groups of people who had arrived at different patterns of resource allocation. In contrast, if different social classes were found to allocate resources in different ways, that finding would be of interest to both the economist and the sociologist. That is because the concept of social class represents a level of abstraction of particular interest to the sociologist.

There has been a recent realization on the part of all the social sciences that phenomena at any one level of abstraction are not in themselves capable of completely explaining complex human actions. This realization has led researchers to consider the interactions of factors at various levels of abstraction (levels represented by biology, individual psychology, reference groups, class, society, and so on) in coming to appreciate human action. Therefore, the differences in the levels of abstraction used by various social sciences are becoming even more blurred.

Differences in Preferred Type of Explanation

Psychologists and anthropologists are more likely to look for, and to find, a biological substrate for behaviors of interest than are sociologists, economists, theologians, historians, and political scientists. However, it is important to note that certain psychologists (such as social psychologists) and certain anthropologists (cultural anthropologists) are unlikely to search for a biological understanding in their studies. Again, types of preferred explanations are meant to characterize general tendencies in disciplines; there is no *a priori* reason for any social scientist to avoid invoking any type of explanation.

Another type of preference relates to the type of design typically employed in the various social sciences. Because their hands are often tied by the nature of the phenomena they study, anthropolo-

D3

gists and historians often use case studies. The designs most common to economics, sociology, and political science are observational or quasi-experimental. Psychologists often employ single-subject experiments and true experimental designs, since they can phrase their research questions in such ways that experimental evidence can be obtained. However, it must be noted that we are dealing with general tendencies—for example, psychology still profitably employs case studies (see for example Hill, Carter, & O'Farrell, 1983).

Conclusion

As you can see, while several gross distinctions can be made among the social sciences, I believe these disciplines are characterized more by their shared interests and research methods than by their differences. That belief prompted me to write a book of methods for the social sciences in general, rather than a book solely for research in psychology.

If overlap is the highlight of the social sciences, then in learning about one area you learn something about all the related disciplines. Perhaps our compartmentalization of approaches to understanding humans has led us to see differences among disciplines where differences are more apparent than real. True wisdom and understanding is, in my opinion, all of one fabric. Chapter 1 claimed that the efforts of the artist, author, and scientist are directed toward the same goal. Similarly, it seems apparent to me that the efforts of the various social sciences are directed toward one goal—an understanding of human action in all its complexity.

Appendix E

Statistical Tables

Table E-1 Random Numbers

10	09	73	25	33	76	52	01	35	86	34	67	35	48	76	80	95	90	91	17	39	29	27	49	45
37	54	20	48	05	64	89	47	42	96	24	80	52	40	37	20	63	61	04	02	00	82	29	16	65
08	42	26	89	53	19	64	50	93	03	23	20	90	25	60	15	95	33	47	64	35	08	03	36	06
99	01	90	25	29	09	37	67	07	15	38	31	13	11	65	88	67	67	43	97	04	43	62	76	59
12	80	79	99	70	80	15	73	61	47	64	03	23	66	53	98	95	11	68	77	12	17	17	68	33
66	06	57	47	17	34	07	27	68	50	36	69	73	61	70	65	81	33	98	85	11	19	92	91	70
31	06	01	08	05	45	57	18	24	06	35	30	34	26	14	86	79	90	74	39	23	40	30	97	32
85	26	97	76	02	02	05	16	56	92	68	66	57	48	18	73	05	38	52	47	18	62	38	85	79
63	57	33	21	35	05	32	54	70	48	90	55	35	75	48	28	46	82	87	09	83	49	12	56	24
73	79	64	57	53	03	52	96	47	78	35	80	83	42	82	60	93	52	03	44	35	27	38	84	35
98	52	01	77	67	14	90	56	86	07	22	10	94	05	58	60	97	09	34	33	50	50	07	39	98
11	80	50	54	31	39	80	82	77	32	50	72	56	82	48	29	40	52	42	01	52	77	56	78	51
83	45	29	96	34	06	28	89	80	83	13	74	67	00	78	18	47	54	06	10	68	71	17	78	17
88	68	54	02	00	86	50	75	84	01	36	76	66	79	51	90	36	47	64	93	29	60	91	10	62
99	59	46	73	48	87	51	76	49	69	91	82	60	89	28	93	78	56	13	68	23	47	83	41	13
65	48	11	76	74	17	46	85	09	50	58	04	77	69	74	73	03	95	71	86	40	21	81	65	44
80	12	43	56	35	17	72	70	80	15	45	31	82	23	74	21	11	57	82	53	14	38	55	37	63
74	35	09	98	17	77	40	27	72	14	43	23	60	02	10	45	52	16	42	37	96	28	60	26	55
69	91	62	68	03	66	25	22	91	48	36	93	68	72	03	76	62	11	39	90	94	40	05	64	18
09	89	32	05	05	14	22	56	85	14	46	42	75	67	88	96	29	77	88	22	54	38	21	45	98
91	49	91	45	23	68	47	92	76	86	46	16	28	35	54	94	75	08	99	23	37	08	92	00	48
80	33	69	45	98	26	94	03	68	58	70	29	73	41	35	53	14	03	33	40	42	05	08	23	41
44	10	48	19	49	85	15	74	79	54	32	97	92	65	75	57	60	04	08	81	22	22	20	64	13
12	55	07	37	42	11	10	00	20	40	12	86	07	46	97	96	64	48	94	39	28	70	72	58	15
63	60	64	93	29	16	50	53	44	84	40	21	95	25	63	43	65	17	70	82	07	20	73	17	90
61	19	69	04	46	26	45	74	77	74	51	92	43	37	29	65	39	45	95	93	42	58	26	05	27
15	47	44	52	66	95	27	07	99	53	59	36	78	38	48	82	39	61	01	18	33	21	15	94	66
94	55	72	85	73	67	89	75	43	87	54	62	24	44	31	91	19	04	25	92	92	92	74	59	73
42	48	11	62	13	97	34	40	87	21	16	86	84	87	67	03	07	11	20	59	25	70	14	66	70
23	52	37	83	17	73	20	88	98	37	68	93	59	14	16	26	25	22	96	63	05	52	28	25	62
04	49	35	24	94	75	24	63	38	24	45	86	25	10	25	61	96	27	93	35	65	33	71	24	72
00	54	99	76	54	64	05	18	81	59	96	11	96	38	96	54	69	28	23	91	23	28	72	95	29
35	96	31	53	07	26	89	80	93	54	33	35	13	54	62	77	97	45	00	24	90	10	33	93	33
59	80	80	83	91	45	42	72	68	42	83	60	94	97	00	13	02	12	48	92	78	56	52	01	06
46	05	88	52	36	01	39	09	22	86	77	28	14	40	77	93	91	08	36	47	70	61	74	29	41
32	17	90	05	97	87	37	92	52	41	05	56	70	70	07	86	74	31	71	57	85	39	41	18	38
69	23	46	14	06	20	11	74	52	04	15	95	66	00	00	18	74	39	24	23	97	11	89	63	38
19	56	54	14	30	01	75	87	53	79	40	41	92	15	85	66	67	43	68	06	84	96	28	52	07
45	15	51	49	38	19	47	60	72	46	43	66	79	45	43	59	04	79	00	33	20	82	66	95	41
94	86	43	19	94	36	16	81	08	51	34	88	88	15	53	01	54	03	54	56	05	01	45	11	76

Source: From tables of the Rand Corporation from *A Million Random Digits with 100,000 Normal Deviates* (New York: The Free Press, 1955) by permission of the Rand Corporation.

Table E-1   Randon Numbers (continued)

```
09 18 82 00 97   32 82 53 95 27   04 22 08 63 04   83 38 98 73 74   64 27 85 80 44
90 04 58 54 97   51 98 15 06 54   94 93 88 19 97   91 87 07 61 50   68 47 66 46 59
73 18 95 02 07   47 67 72 62 69   62 29 06 44 64   27 12 46 70 18   41 36 18 27 60
75 76 87 64 90   20 97 18 17 49   90 42 91 22 72   95 37 50 58 71   93 82 34 31 78
54 01 64 40 56   66 28 13 10 03   00 68 22 73 98   20 71 45 32 95   07 70 61 78 13

08 35 86 99 10   78 54 24 27 85   13 66 15 88 73   04 61 89 75 53   31 22 30 84 20
28 30 60 32 64   81 33 31 05 91   40 51 00 78 93   32 60 46 04 75   94 11 90 18 40
53 84 08 62 33   81 59 41 36 28   51 21 59 02 90   28 46 66 87 95   77 76 22 07 91
91 75 75 37 41   61 61 36 22 69   50 26 39 02 12   55 78 17 65 14   83 48 34 70 55
89 41 59 26 94   00 39 75 83 91   12 60 71 76 46   48 94 97 23 06   94 54 13 74 08

77 51 30 38 20   86 83 42 99 01   68 41 48 27 74   51 90 81 39 80   72 89 35 55 07
19 50 23 71 74   69 97 92 02 88   55 21 02 97 73   74 28 77 52 51   65 34 46 74 15
21 81 85 93 13   93 27 88 17 57   05 68 67 31 56   07 08 28 50 46   31 85 33 84 52
51 47 46 64 99   68 10 72 36 21   94 04 99 13 45   42 83 60 91 91   08 00 74 54 49
99 55 96 83 31   62 53 52 41 70   69 77 71 28 30   74 81 97 81 42   43 86 07 28 34

33 71 34 80 07   93 58 47 28 69   51 92 66 47 21   58 30 32 98 22   93 17 49 39 72
85 27 48 68 93   11 30 32 92 70   28 83 43 41 37   73 51 59 04 00   71 14 84 36 43
84 13 38 96 40   44 03 55 21 66   73 85 27 00 91   61 22 26 05 61   62 32 71 84 23
56 73 21 62 34   17 39 59 61 31   10 12 39 16 22   85 49 65 75 60   81 60 41 88 80
65 13 85 68 06   87 64 88 52 61   34 31 36 58 61   45 87 52 10 69   85 64 44 72 77

38 00 10 21 76   81 71 91 17 11   71 60 29 29 37   74 21 96 40 49   65 58 44 96 98
37 40 29 63 97   01 30 47 75 86   56 27 11 00 86   47 32 46 26 05   40 03 03 74 38
97 12 54 03 48   87 08 33 14 17   21 81 53 92 50   75 23 76 20 47   15 50 12 95 78
21 82 64 11 34   47 14 33 40 72   64 63 88 59 02   49 13 90 64 41   03 85 65 45 52
73 13 54 27 42   95 71 90 90 35   85 79 47 42 96   08 78 98 81 56   64 69 11 92 02

07 63 87 79 29   03 06 11 80 72   96 20 74 41 56   23 82 19 95 38   04 71 36 69 94
60 52 88 34 41   07 95 41 98 14   59 17 52 06 95   05 53 35 21 39   61 21 20 64 55
83 59 63 56 55   06 95 89 29 83   05 12 80 97 19   77 43 35 37 83   92 30 15 04 98
10 85 06 27 46   99 59 91 05 07   13 49 90 63 19   53 07 57 18 39   06 41 01 93 62
39 82 09 89 52   43 62 26 31 47   64 42 18 08 14   43 80 00 93 51   31 02 47 31 67

59 58 00 64 78   75 56 97 88 00   88 83 55 44 86   23 76 80 61 56   04 11 10 84 08
38 50 80 73 41   23 79 34 87 63   90 82 29 70 22   17 71 90 42 07   95 95 44 99 53
30 69 27 06 68   94 68 81 61 27   56 19 68 00 91   82 06 76 34 00   05 46 26 92 00
65 44 39 56 59   18 28 82 74 37   49 63 22 40 41   08 33 76 56 76   96 29 99 08 36
27 26 75 02 64   13 19 27 22 94   07 47 74 46 06   17 98 54 89 11   97 34 13 03 58

91 30 70 69 91   19 07 22 42 10   36 69 95 37 28   28 82 53 57 93   28 97 66 62 52
68 43 49 46 88   84 47 31 36 22   62 12 69 84 08   12 84 38 25 90   09 81 59 31 46
48 90 81 58 77   54 74 52 45 91   35 70 00 47 54   83 82 45 26 92   54 13 05 51 60
06 91 34 51 97   42 67 27 86 01   11 88 30 95 28   63 01 19 89 01   14 97 44 03 44
10 45 51 60 19   14 21 03 37 12   91 34 23 78 21   88 32 58 08 51   43 66 77 08 83

12 88 39 73 43   65 02 76 11 84   04 28 50 13 92   17 97 41 50 77   90 71 22 67 69
21 77 83 09 76   38 80 73 69 61   31 64 94 20 96   63 28 10 20 23   08 81 64 74 49
19 52 35 95 15   65 12 25 96 59   86 28 36 82 58   69 57 21 37 98   16 43 59 15 29
67 24 55 26 70   35 58 31 65 63   79 24 68 66 86   76 46 33 42 22   26 65 59 08 02
60 58 44 73 77   07 50 03 79 92   45 13 42 65 29   26 76 08 36 37   41 32 64 43 44
```

Table E-2 Critical Values of t

df	Level of significance for two-tail test	
	.05	.01
1	12.706	63.657
2	4.303	9.925
3	3.182	5.841
4	2.776	4.604
5	2.571	4.032
6	2.447	3.707
7	2.365	3.499
8	2.306	3.355
9	2.262	3.250
10	2.228	3.169
11	2.201	3.106
12	2.179	3.055
13	2.160	3.012
14	2.145	2.977
15	2.131	2.947
16	2.120	2.921
17	2.110	2.898
18	2.101	2.878
19	2.093	2.861
20	2.086	2.845
21	2.080	2.831
22	2.074	2.819
23	2.069	2.807
24	2.064	2.797
25	2.060	2.787
26	2.056	2.779
27	2.052	2.771
28	2.048	2.763
29	2.045	2.756
30	2.042	2.750
40	2.021	2.704
60	2.000	2.660
120	1.980	2.617
∞	1.960	2.576

Source: Table E-2 is abridged from Table III of Fisher and Yates: *Statistical Tables for Biological, Agricultural, and Medical Research.* Published by Longman Group Ltd., London, (previously published by Oliver and Boyd Ltd., Edinburgh), and by permission

Table E-3   Critical Values of Chi Square

df	.05	.01
1	3.84	6.64
2	5.99	9.21
3	7.82	11.34
4	9.49	13.28
5	11.07	15.09
6	12.59	16.81
7	14.07	18.48
8	15.51	20.09
9	16.92	21.67
10	18.31	23.21
11	19.68	24.72
12	21.03	26.22
13	22.36	27.69
14	23.68	29.14
15	25.00	30.58
16	26.30	32.00
17	27.59	33.41
18	28.87	34.80
19	30.14	36.19
20	31.41	37.57
21	32.67	38.93
22	33.92	40.29
23	35.17	41.64
24	36.42	42.98
25	37.65	44.31
26	38.88	45.64
27	40.11	46.96
28	41.34	48.28
29	42.56	49.59
30	43.77	50.89

Source: Table E-3 is abridged from Table IV of Fisher and Yates: *Statistical Tables for Biological, Agricultural, and Medical Research,* Published by Longman Group Ltd., London, (previously published by Oliver and Boyd Ltd., Edinburgh), and by permission

References

Anastasi, A. *Psychological testing*. New York: Macmillan, 1982.

Anderson, S. B., & Ball, S. *The profession and practice of program evaluation*. San Francisco: Jossey-Bass, 1979.

American Psychological Association, *ad hoc* Committee on Ethical Standards in Psychological Research. *Ethical principles in the conduct of research with human participants*. Washington, D.C.: American Psychological Association, 1973.

Argyris, C. Some unintended consequences of rigorous research. Psychological Bulletin, 1968, *70*, 185−197.

Aronson, E., Willerman, B., & Floyd, J. The effect of a pratfall on increasing interpersonal attractiveness. *Psychonomic Science*, 1966, *4*, 227−228.

Bronowski, J. *The ascent of man*. Boston: Little, Brown, 1973.

Bruning, J. L., & Kintz, B. L. *Computational handbook of statistics*. Chicago: Scott, Foresman, 1968.

Campbell, D. T. Reforms as experiments. *American Psychologist*, 1969, *24*, 409−429.

Campbell, D. T. *Qualitative knowing in action research*. Kurt Lewin Award Address, American Psychological Association Convention, New Orleans, 1974.

Campbell, D. T., & Fiske, D. W. Convergent and discriminant validation of the multimethod matrix. *Psychological Bulletin*, 1959, *56*, 81−105.

Campbell, D. T., & Ross, H. L. The Connecticut crackdown on speeding: Time series data in quasi-experimental analysis. *Law and Society Review*, 1968, *3*, 33−53.

Campbell, D. T., & Stanley, J. C. *Experimental and quasi-experimental designs for research*. Chicago: Rand-McNally, 1963.

Caporaso, J. A. *The structure and function of European integration*. Pacific Palisades, Calif.: Goodyear, 1974.

Christensen, L. B. *Experimental methodology* (2nd ed.). Boston: Allyn & Bacon, 1980.

Cook, T. D., & Campbell, D. T. *Quasi-experimentation: Design and analysis issues for field settings*. Chicago: Rand-McNally, 1979.

Cronbach, L. J. *Essentials of psychological testing*. New York: Harper & Row, 1960.

Cronbach, L. J. Test validation. In R. L. Thorndike (Ed.), *Educational measurement* (2nd ed.). Washington, D.C.: American Council on Education, 1971.

Eron, L. D., & Huesmann, L. R. Adolescent aggression and television. *Annals of the New York Academy of Sciences*, 1980, *347*, 319–331.

Freeman, H. E., & Rossi, P. H. *Evaluation: A systematic approach*. Beverly Hills, Calif.: Sage, 1982.

Garfinkel, H. *Studies in ethnomethodology*. Englewood Cliffs, N.J.: Prentice-Hall, 1967.

Gergen, K. J. Social psychology as history. *Journal of Personality and Social Psychology*, 1973, *26*, 309–320.

Glaser, B. G., & Strauss, A. L. *The discovery of grounded theory: Strategies for qualitative research*. Chicago: Aldine, 1967.

Glass, G. V., Wilson, V. L., & Gottman, J. M. *Design and analysis of time-series experiments*. Boulder: Colorado Associated University Press, 1975.

Gleason, E. M. Stability of dogmatism and relationship of dogmatism to performance in two Air Force officer schools. Unpublished doctoral dissertation, University of Tennessee, 1973.

Gleitman, H. *Psychology*. New York: W. W. Norton, 1981.

Goffman, E. *The presentation of self in everyday life*. New York: Anchor Books, 1959.

Goldstein, M., & Goldstein, I. F. *How we know: An exploration of the scientific process*. New York: Plenum Press, 1978.

Harré, R., & Secord, P. F. *The explanation of social behavior*. Oxford: Basil Blackwell, 1972.

Hersen, M., & Barlow, D. H. *Single case experimental designs: Strategies for studying behavioral change*. New York: Pergamon Press, 1976.

Hill, C. E., Carter, J. A., & O'Farrell, M. K. A case study of the process and outcome of time-limited therapy. *Journal of Counseling Psychology*, 1983, *30*, 3–18.

Hite, S. *The Hite report: A nationwide study of female sexuality*. New York: Dell, 1976.

Holmes, D. S. Effects of grades and disconfirmed grade expectancies on students' evaluations of their instructor. *Journal of Educational Psychology*, 1972, *63*, 130–133.

Howard, G. S. Improving methodology via research on research methods. *Journal of Counseling Psychology*, 1982, *29*, 318–326.

Howard, G. S. On studying humans. *The Counseling Psychologist*, 1983, *11*(3), 57–63.

Howard, G. S. A modest proposal for a revision of counseling research. *Journal of Counseling Psychology*, 1984, in press.

Howard, G. S., & Maxwell, S. E. The correlation between student satisfaction and grades: A case of mistaken causation. *Journal of Educational Psychology*, 1980, 72, 810−820.

Howard, G. S., & Maxwell, S. E. Do grades contaminate student ratings of instruction? *Research in Higher Education*, 1982, 16, 175−188.

Howard, G. S., Maxwell, S. E., Weiner, R. L., Boynton, K. S., & Rooney, W. M. Is a behavioral measure the best estimate of behavioral parameters? Perhaps not. *Applied Psychological Measurement*, 1980, 4, 293−311.

Howard, G. S., Ralph, K. M., Gulanick, N. A., Maxwell, S. E., Nance, D. W., & Gerber, S. L. Internal invalidity in pretest-posttest self-report evaluations and a re-evaluation of retrospective pretests. *Applied Psychological Measurement*, 1979, 3, 1−23.

Huck, S. W., Cormier, W. H., & Bounds, W. G. *Reading statistics and research*. New York: Harper & Row, 1974.

Huck, S. W., & Sandler, H. M. *Rival hypotheses: Alternative interpretations of data based conclusions*. New York: Harper & Row, 1979.

Huff, D. *How to lie with statistics*. New York: W. W. Norton, 1954.

Hyde, J. S., & Rosenberg, B. G. *Half the human experience: The psychology of women*. Lexington, Mass.: D. C. Heath, 1980.

Jourard, S. Experimenter-subject dialogue: A paradigm for a humanistic science of psychology. In J. F. T. Bugental (Ed.), *Challenges of humanistic psychology*. New York: McGraw-Hill, 1967.

Kahneman, D., & Tversky, A. Judgment under uncertainty: Heuristics and biases. *Science*, 1974, 185, 1124−1131.

Kelman, H. C. Human use of human subjects: The problem of deception in social psychological experiments. *Psychological Bulletin*, 1967, 67, 1−11.

Keppel, G. *Design and analysis: A researcher's handbook* (2nd ed.). Englewood Cliffs, N.J.: Prentice-Hall, 1982.

Kinsey, A. C., & Pommeroy, W. B. *Sexual behavior in the human male*. Philadelphia: W. B. Saunders, 1948.

Kirk, R. *Experimental design* (2nd ed.). Belmont, Calif.: Brooks-Cole, 1982.

Koch, S. Psychology and its human clientele: Beneficiaries or victims? In R. A. Kasschau & F. S. Kessel (Eds.), *Psychology and society: In search of symbiosis*. New York: John Wiley, 1981.

Langley, E. M., & Gehrman, J. L. Impact of practicum−field experience on perceptions of counselor characteristics. *Journal of the*

Student Personnel Association for Teacher Education, 1971, *9*, 76–80.

Linton, M., & Gallo, P. S. *The practical statistician: Simplified handbook of statistics*. Monterey, Calif.: Brooks-Cole, 1975.

McCain, G., & Segal, E. M. *The game of science*. Monterey, Calif.: Brooks-Cole, 1969.

McFall, R., & Twentyman, C. T. Four experiments on the relative contributions of rehearsal, modeling and coaching to assertion training. *Journal of Abnormal Psychology*, 1973, *81*, 299–318.

Mees, C. E. K. Scientific thought and social reconstruction. *Sigma Xi Quarterly*, 1934, *22*, 13–24.

Milgram, S. *Obedience to authority*. New York: Harper & Row, 1974.

Millham, J., & Jacobson, L. I. The need for approval. In H. London & J. Exner (Eds.), *Dimensions of personality*. New York: John Wiley, 1978.

Mixon, D. Studying feignable behavior. *Representative Research in Social Psychology*, 1976, *7*, 89–104.

Moore, D. S. *Statistics: Concepts and controversies*. San Francisco: W. H. Freeman, 1979.

Pritchard, R. D., Maxwell, S. E., & Jordan, W. C. Interpreting relationships between age and promotion in age discrimination cases. *Journal of Applied Psychology*, in press.

Robbins, T., et al. The limits of symbolic realism: Problems of empathic field observation in a sectarian context. *Journal for the Scientific Study of Religion*, 1973, *12*, 259–271.

Rogers, C. R. Some new challenges. *American Psychologist*, 1973, *28*, 379–387.

Rosenhan, D. On being sane in insane places. *Science*, 1973, *179*, 250–258.

Rosenthal, R. *Experimenter effects in behavioral research*. New York: Appleton-Century-Crofts, 1966.

Rossi, P. H., Freeman, H. F., & Wright, S. R. *Evaluation: A systematic approach*. Beverly Hills, Calif.: Sage, 1979.

Rubin, Z. *Liking and loving*. New York: Holt, Rinehart & Winston, 1973.

Schumacher, E. F. *Small is beautiful*. New York: Harper & Row, 1973.

Schwartz, H., & Jacobs, J. *Qualitative sociology: A method to the madness*. New York: Free Press, 1979.

Shields, S. A. Functionalism, Darwinism and the psychology of women: A study in social myth. *American Psychologist*, 1975, *30*, 739–754.

R4

Sidman, M. *Tactics of scientific research*. New York: Basic Books, 1960.

Slonim, M. J. *Sampling in a nutshell*. New York: Simon & Schuster, 1960.

Terkel, S. *Working*. New York: Avon Books, 1972.

Toulmin, S. Foresight and understanding: An inquiry into the aims of science. New York: Harper & Row, 1961.

Toulmin, S. *Foresight and understanding*. Princeton, N.J.: Princeton University Press, 1972.

Webb, E. J., Campbell, D. T., Schwartz, R. D., Sechrest, L., & Grove, J. B. *Nonreactive measures in the social sciences*. Boston: Houghton Mifflin, 1981.

Williams, W. H. *A sampler on sampling*. New York: John Wiley, 1978.

Winch, P. *The idea of a social science and its relation to philosophy*. London: Routledge & Keegan Paul, 1958.

Zimbardo, P. G. The mind is a formidable jailer: A Pirandellian prison. *New York Times*, April 8, 1973, p. 38.

Index

I1